KENTUCKY AND THE SECESSION CRISIS

KENTUCKY AND THE SECESSION CRISIS

A Documentary History

Edited by
Dwight T. Pitcaithley

THE UNIVERSITY OF TENNESSEE PRESS | KNOXVILLE

First Edition.

Library of Congress Cataloging-in-Publication Data
Names: Pitcaithley, Dwight T., editor, writer of introduction.
Title: Kentucky and the secession crisis : a documentary history / [compiled by] Dwight T. Pitcaithley.
Description: First edition. | Knoxville : The University of Tennessee Press, [2022] | Includes bibliographical references and index. |
Summary: "As division over the fate of slavery swept the US leading up to and following the 1860 election, border slave states like Kentucky found themselves literally caught in the middle. This collection showcases the discourse that followed the election and sheds light on the Bluegrass State's political thought processes as it considered joining its Deep South sister states in secession. The volume includes addresses by Governor Beriah Magoffin; Senator John J. Crittenden's December 1860 address proposing a constitutional solution to secession; speeches by various proponents and opponents of the Crittenden amendment; various constitutional amendments proposed by Kentuckians; and documents related to the second session of the Thirty-Sixth Congress, the Washington Peace Conference of 1861, and the Border Slave State Conference. With a lengthy introduction and questions for discussion, the work is both a valuable resource for historians and suitable for the classroom"—Provided by publisher.
Identifiers: LCCN 2022022450 (print) | LCCN 2022022451 (ebook) | ISBN 9781621907237 (hardcover) | ISBN 9781621907244 (kindle edition) | ISBN 9781621907251 (pdf)
Subjects: LCSH: Crittenden, John J. (John Jordan), 1787–1863. | Secession—Kentucky—History—19th century—Sources. | Kentucky—Politics and government—1861–1865—Sources. | Kentucky—History—Civil War, 1861–1865—Sources.
Classification: LCC F455 .K385 2022 (print) | LCC F455 (ebook) | DDC 976.9/03—dc23/eng/20220518
LC record available at https://lccn.loc.gov/2022022450
LC ebook record available at https://lccn.loc.gov/2022022451

FOR

Richard West Sellars

CONTENTS

INTRODUCTION

The slave South's secessionist response to Abraham Lincoln's election prompted an impassioned debate among the country's elected officials over the future of slavery and the constitutionality of secession. Deep South Democrats presumed that the incoming president was an abolitionist, that the Republican Party was founded on abolitionist principles, and that, following inauguration day, the new regime would begin its attack on the South's peculiar institution. The conversation among elected officials and appointed delegates revolved around the founding nature of the Constitution and its acknowledgment of slavery. Questions abounded. Did the Constitution protect slaves as property? Did Congress have the right to prohibit slavery in the western territories? Did states have an inherent right to secede from the Union? Did the federal government have the right to prevent states from seceding? Was the United States a country where freedom was national and slavery local, or a country where slavery was national and freedom local? Was slavery better protected under the United States Constitution or a new constitution formed by the Confederate States of America? And, most importantly, did political compromises exist that would prevent secession and civil war?

These and other questions defined the political landscape over Secession Winter, the period between Lincoln's election on November 6, 1860, and April 12–13, 1861, when Confederate guns bombarded the federal fort in Charleston Harbor. The answers to these questions varied depending on geography and political persuasion. Southern and northern Democrats held different opinions from northern Republicans. Party leaders in the Deep South, Upper South, Border South, and North clung to different interpretations of the Constitution and, hence, different ideas for solving the problem posed by the specter of secession.

Being part of the Border South (the four slave states that eventually cast their lot with the United States), Kentucky was less eager to jump on the secessionist's bandwagon, more reluctant to race into an unknown future, and more willing to pause and consider alternatives than her Deep South sister states. The Bluegrass State was well aware of its position bordering three non-slave-state neighbors across the Ohio River, and equally aware that secession would nullify the Fugitive Slave Act. Believing that its 225,483 slaves would be better protected by staying in the Union, Kentucky rejected secessionists' enticements to join a southern confederacy. The conversations and debates conducted in the aftermath of Lincoln's election (represented by the documents that follow this introduction) provide windows into the thinking of Kentucky's officials as they sorted through the constitutional crisis posed by the shadow of secession.

Arguably the most consequential in the nation's history, the election of 1860 concluded a turbulent decade that spiraled around the issue of the extension of slavery into the western territories. Following the acquisition of the Mexican Cession in 1848, the burning political question that ultimately led to the firing on Fort Sumter was whether Congress would allow or prohibit slavery in the new lands west of Texas. The Compromise of 1850 temporarily solved the problem by creating the New Mexico and Utah Territories and allowing the inhabitants there to decide the issue for themselves—a political decision termed "territorial" or "popular sovereignty." Congress admitted California as a non-slave state because its much larger, gold rush–inspired population did not want to compete with slave labor. For a time, but only for a short time, the territorial slave problem seemed settled.

Four years later, Congress divided the northern part of the Louisiana Purchase into the Kansas and Nebraska Territories and, overturning the thirty-four-year Missouri Compromise which prohibited slavery north of the 36°30' parallel, opened the possibility of introducing slavery there. Congress neither encouraged slavery in the new territories, nor discouraged it, but allowed the inhabitants to decide for themselves, as in the New Mexico/Utah model. The resulting violent clashes in Kansas that pitted pro-slave settlers against anti-slave settlers intensified due to numerous fraudulent elections exacerbated by the Buchanan administration's support for the minority pro-slave faction.[1] Finally, the Supreme Court's 1857 proslavery decision in the *Dred Scott* case attempted to resolve the agitation over slavery in the territories by declaring that Congress must protect slavery in a territory during the territorial period until the inhabitants, upon application for statehood, decided for or against the institution.

These events, plus the publication of *Uncle Tom's Cabin*, the beating of Massachusetts Senator Charles Sumner by South Carolina Representative

Preston Brooks over an antislavery speech made by the senator, and the ill-fated 1859 attack on the Harpers Ferry Arsenal by John Brown, set the stage for the 1860 election. The Democratic Party could not agree on the proper approach to slavery in the territories—overt protection by the federal government or territorial sovereignty—and split into northern and southern factions. Illinois Senator Stephen A. Douglas became the northern candidate on a platform that supported his idea of popular sovereignty. Kentuckian (and then vice president) John C. Breckinridge represented the southern branch advocating federal protection of slavery during the territorial period. Abraham Lincoln ran as the Republican Party's candidate on a platform that opposed any further extension of slavery into the western territories but, very importantly, supported the right of each state to decide for or against the institution of slavery. The Republican position purposely did not support the abolition of the slavery which it correctly believed was an issue determined constitutionally by state authority. Its core doctrine was that slavery should be contained within the fifteen states where it already existed. Eventually, Republicans presumed, as a result, human bondage would eventually die out. Tennessean John Bell rounded out the race as the Constitutional Union Party candidate who stood firmly on the Constitution as the final arbiter of the nation's troubles.[2]

Bell took all twelve of Kentucky's electoral votes and forty-five percent of the state's popular vote. Breckinridge followed with thirty-six percent, then Douglas with seventeen percent. While Lincoln overwhelmingly won in the Electoral College nationally, his birth state gave him only 1,364 votes (fewer than he received in Virginia) or just under one percent of the total number of Kentucky votes cast. The 1860 congressional election also revealed a strong sentiment in Kentucky for Union and against secession. As political lines hardened and political parties realigned, Kentucky elected twelve Unionists and three Democrats to Congress. The previous delegation (1859–1860) consisted of six Democrats, five Opposition Party members, and one American Party member. Nationally and significantly, however, the Democratic Party attained majorities in both the United States House and Senate.[3]

By the time the second session of the Thirty-Sixth Congress convened on December 3, 1860, seven states had begun the process of calling conventions to determine whether they would stay within or leave the Union. The future status of slavery in a country about to be administered by a presumed abolitionist became the focus of political conversation and debate.

President James Buchanan, a northerner with southern sympathies, opened the session with a speech that left no doubt about his assessment of the problem. The long "interference" of the northern people with the "question of slavery in the southern States has at length produced its natural effects." To Buchanan's mind, the threatened secession by numerous southern states was directly due to a decades-long agitation against the institution of slavery by the non-slave states. Buchanan considered secession to be unconstitutional, but, at the same time, did not believe he had any constitutional authority to prevent states from leaving. The solution to the white South's distress over Lincoln's election was not complicated. The northern states should simply leave the South alone and allow them to "manage their domestic institutions in their own way." Doubting that the people of the North would cease their assaults upon slavery, Buchanan offered another solution. Near the end of his address, he proposed that the Constitution be amended to protect the institution in three ways: ensuring that runaway slaves be returned to their owners, guaranteeing slavery in the territories until the territories apply for statehood "with or without slavery," and recognizing the "right of property in slaves in the States where it now exists or may hereafter exist."[4] With this proposed constitutional amendment, the president was the first to suggest solving the threat of secession by increasing protections for slavery at the federal level.

It is important to note that the regulation of slavery in the United States had always been the legal purview of the individual states and not the federal government. With the exception of the Fugitive Slave Law of 1850, state law defined and controlled slavery. After the American Revolution, as northern states began the process of emancipation, the general agreement throughout the country was that states could retain or abolish slavery. As a result, each state developed unique laws regulating the way slaves would be treated. The killing of a slave by an owner might be considered murder in one state while deemed manslaughter in another. Some states forced emancipated slaves to leave the state upon gaining their freedom, other states allowed them to stay.[5] Freedom was national, slavery was local until the latter years of the 1850s when the reverse notion of freedom and slavery began to develop. Southern white support for federal protections for the institution increased after 1857 when Supreme Court chief justice Roger B. Taney announced in his *Dred Scott* decision that "the right of property in a slave is distinctly and expressly affirmed in the Constitution." If Taney was correct, slavery would be protected throughout the country by the "due process" clause of the Fifth Amendment. This interpretation of the Constitution encouraged many Democrats, led by Buchanan, to make federal protection explicit.

Three days after Buchanan's address, Kentucky senator Lazarus Powell proposed that a committee of thirteen be established to study the "agitated and distracted condition of the country" and suggest legislation or constitutional amendments that would give "certain, prompt and full protection to the rights of property of the citizens of every State and Territory of the United States."[6] The Senate acted on Powell's proposal and established the Committee of Thirteen with him as its chair. The committee contained many of the luminaries of the Thirty-Sixth Congress: William Seward, Robert Toombs, Jefferson Davis, Stephen Douglas, and John J. Crittenden. Although they met throughout the month and proposed numerous constitutional amendments, the members were unable to agree on any one solution. On December 31, Senator Powell submitted the committee's proceedings with the announcement that "the committee have not been able to agree upon any general plan of adjustment."[7]

Among the six compromise amendments proposed by the Committee of Thirteen, the Crittenden "resolutions" became the best known over Secession Winter and the most widely referenced in textbooks today. Crittenden was seventy-four years old in December of 1860 when he introduced his amendment. A graduate of William and Mary College, he had served as attorney general of the United States under Presidents Harrison and Fillmore, been elected governor of Kentucky in 1848, and served in Congress on four different occasions beginning in 1817. The oldest member of the Senate during the Thirty-Sixth Congress, Crittenden was an adherent of the policies of Henry Clay whose Senate seat Crittenden filled following Clay's resignation in 1842.[8] While genuinely attempting to devise an acceptable political compromise, Crittenden embraced the awkward task of making the implausible appear plausible. In return for a prohibition on slavery north of the 36°30' parallel (an issue Republicans believed had been settled with the election of Lincoln) and a small adjustment to the 1850 Fugitive Slave Act, Crittenden's quid pro quo involved placing numerous permanent protections on the institution in the United States Constitution. Crittenden's lengthy introduction craftily makes this sleight of hand appear reasonable. Two weeks after the opening of the second session of the Thirty-Sixth Congress, Crittenden introduced his solution to the national controversy under the *Congressional Globe* heading "Compromise on the Slavery Question."

The problem, according to Crittenden, had to do with the rights of the slaveholding states in the territories and generally with the rights of the "citizens of the latter [slaveholding states] in their slaves." "Great dangers surround us," he intoned. The greatest danger, the greatest difficulty the country faced, regarded the subject of slavery in the western territories. On December 18, Crittenden proposed six articles as an amendment to the Constitution. Tackling the most pressing issue first, he suggested that the Missouri Compromise line of 36°30' latitude be revived and extended across the New Mexico Territory to the eastern line of California. Slavery would be prohibited in all territory "now held, or hereafter acquired" north of the line and allowed south of it during the territorial period. When a territory, north or south of the line, applied for statehood, it would be admitted with or without slavery "as the constitution of such new State may provide." Crittenden assumed that future states north of that line would reject slavery while those created from the territory south of it would be admitted as slave states. Articles two and three stated that Congress had no power to abolish slavery in either the District of Columbia or in federal installations located within slaveholding states. Crittenden's fourth article sought to discourage the freeing of slaves passing through a nonslaveholding state with their owners. Congress shall have no authority, it read, "to prohibit or hinder the transportation of slaves" from one state to another. Crittenden intended his fifth article to strengthen the fugitive slave provisions of the Constitution, and then capped his proposal with an article preventing Congress from interfering with slavery in the states where it already existed, and from amending, in any way, the previous five articles.[9] Like twenty-one other proposals to amend the Constitution offered over Secession Winter, Crittenden wanted to ensure that the "slavery question" would not be revisited in the future.

Of Crittenden's six proposals, it was the first dealing with new territories that garnered the strongest opposition from Republicans. While the article would have reinstated the Missouri Compromise line (with added protections for slavery south of 36°30'), Crittenden's "hereafter acquired" served as a red flag for antislavery northerners. It would have automatically protected the institution in any new territory acquired south of that line. Southern adventurers had already attempted to expand the slave empire into Central America and Cuba, and there remained lingering hopes that more of Mexico could be annexed. The prospect of acquiring Cuba heated up especially after United States ambassadors to England, France, and Spain signed the Ostend Manifesto in 1854 declaring that if Spain would not sell the island, then it ought to be taken by force. Crittenden included the provision in his compromise proposal to encourage southern states to remain in the Union. For Lincoln and his fellow Republicans, however, the "hereafter acquired" clause, in addition to being an affront to the territorial policy upon which Lincoln had been elected, would have announced to the world that the United States was a proslavery expansionist nation.[10]

Because Crittenden's six articles addressed all of the complaints raised by southern Democrats, his solution to the crisis became the one most discussed and debated throughout the country. By early January, almost every session of the House and Senate opened with the presentation of petitions and memorials sent to Congress from engaged citizens. Mass meetings in northern cities gathered signatures supporting compromise based on Crittenden's design. Democratic senator William Bigler, for example, introduced petitions from Philadelphia, Harrisburg, and Carlisle, Pennsylvania, all urging Congress to "adopt promptly the measures of adjustment suggested by the Senator from Kentucky." Other voices of support came from North Carolina, Virginia, Missouri, New Jersey, Minnesota, Massachusetts, and Maine. Other petitions implored Congress to stand by the Constitution as it was and not compromise with the "slave power" of the South. One petition from Philadelphia begged Congress not to entertain any amendment that would give new guarantees to the "present holders of slaves."[11]

Crittenden's proposed amendment was passionately debated in Congress, state legislatures, and secession conventions. While hardline Republicans and disunion Democrats were unwilling to consider compromise of any sort, the Border States provided several advocates for Crittenden's proposal. James H. Moss, for example, a delegate to Missouri's convention who voted against secession, argued that "the Crittenden resolutions stand without rival." They presented, he maintained, "a fair and equitable basis of settlement" and were "in the truest sense of the word, a compromise."[12] William E. Niblack, a Democratic representative from Indiana, believed them to be "more feasible and complete than any other" heretofore proposed.[13]

On the other hand, Republicans, still fuming over the repeal of the Kansas-Nebraska Act and Justice Taney's *Dred Scott* opinion, rejected any suggestion that slavery should be given a chance south of the 36°30' line in return for an absolute prohibition of the institution north of the line where nature had ordained slavery could not exist. In addition, they consistently argued that Lincoln had been fairly elected on a platform opposed to the extension of slavery into the western territories. Why, they asked, should they concede the very point upon which the election had turned and upon which they had won the White House? Massachusetts representative Daniel W. Gooch insisted it was no compromise to prohibit slavery to the north of 36°30' where "it can never go," a nod to the environment of the Great Plains and the failure to plant slavery in the Kansas Territory.[14] Ohio representative John Hutchins reminded his colleagues in the House of Representatives that the "verdict has been rendered fairly, without fraud, and without connivance, in favor of the principle that our Territories are forever to remain free." Conceding the issue, he continued, would "invite similar rebellion in relation to any interest that may feel disturbed by the result of an election."[15] In a more contentious vein, New York representative Luther C. Carter expressed disgust that Congress should be asked to "compromise with treason." "Can it be possible," he inquired of his House colleagues, "that we are now called upon by any of these gentlemen to change the Constitution in order to compromise with secession, which I conceive to be the greatest of felonies? *It is rebellion!*"[16]

On February 12, 1861, a frontal attack on Crittenden's amendment was launched by none other than Senator Charles Sumner from Massachusetts. Rising to the bait after Crittenden introduced petitions in support of his propositions signed by 22,313 citizens from the Bay State, Sumner rose "to say a few words on that petition," and to attack the amendment. The subsequent exchange between the two senators exemplified the political gulf that separated those who favored compromise from those who stood by the Constitution as written. Sumner objected to Crittenden's solution because it would "foist into the Constitution of the United States constitutional guarantees of slavery which the framers of that instrument never gave." Crittenden's reputation in Massachusetts was great, Sumner intoned, with the voters there willing "to adopt anything that bears his respectable name." Had the signers of the petition read fully and understood the import of the amendment, however, they would never have agreed to write protections for "property in man" into the Constitution.

Twenty-five years Sumner's senior, Crittenden, who identified with the

American Party during the Thirty-Sixth Congress, responded logically and methodically with a reasoning that challenged Sumner's adamant position. His proposal, he countered, would violate nothing "but some dogma that has been sometimes asserted by extreme members of the Republican party." Would you, he lectured, stand upon your platform and witness the dissolution of the nation, or sacrifice your platform "manufactured by a few politicians" and "preserve the Union of this country"?[17] While no proposed amendment shaped the national debate more than Crittenden's, the United States Senate rejected it by a vote of 20–19 on the morning of March 4.[18]

The House of Representatives was somewhat more successful than the Senate in finding common ground. It established the Committee of Thirty-Three on December 4 with one member from each state. The Speaker of the House appointed Ohio's Thomas Corwin (Republican) chair of the committee; Francis Marion Bristow (Opposition) from Todd County was Kentucky's representative. Over the course of the next thirty days, the committee agreed upon five resolutions designed to encourage the states to respect their "constitutional obligations" to each other, prevent the "lawless invasion" of other states, and generally maintain order and comity among the states. The committee also proposed a bill for admitting the territory of New Mexico into the Union and, most importantly, an awkwardly worded constitutional amendment designed to prevent federal interference with slavery within the states. As the House debated the amendment, Chairman Corwin withdrew it and presented in its place an alternative earlier proposed by Republican senator William H. Seward. In its final version, the Seward/Corwin amendment read: "No amendment shall be made to the Constitution which will authorize or give to Congress the power to abolish or interfere, within any State, with the domestic institutions thereof, including that of persons held to labor or service by the laws of said State." The full House approved the amendment on February 28 and the Senate on March 4; five states (including Kentucky) ratified it before the country turned from protecting slavery in the Constitution to abolishing it.[19]

As the national debate on the future of slavery played out in Congress, similar conversations took place in state secession conventions and state legislatures. Issues of slavery in the territories, fugitive slaves, transit of owners with their slaves, racial equality, and others dominated the deliberations of elected officials. In Kentucky, necessary decisions brought on by threats of southern secession became the responsibility of Governor Beriah Magoffin, the General Assembly, the state's congressional delegation, and its delegation to the Washington Peace Conference.

Ten days after Lincoln's victory, Governor Magoffin shared his thoughts on the election with the people of Kentucky via a letter to the editor of the *Kentucky Yeoman*. Magoffin, very much aware of his state's geographical position between Tennessee and Virginia to the south and east, and the non-slave states of Illinois, Indiana, and Ohio to the north and west, professed a "let's wait and see" approach to the threat of secession. Believing that slavery was, in the long term, menaced by the Republican Party, he also believed that Lincoln's election was "no cause for secession or rebellion." "We must wait for an overt act," by the new administration, Magoffin contended. The governor assumed that the institution of slavery was well protected by the Constitution, laws, and the courts. Kentucky would not back away, he asserted, from well-recognized southern rights regarding property in slaves. Magoffin, understanding that Democrats held majorities in both houses as a result of the 1860 congressional elections, argued that fears that Lincoln would attack slavery were misguided. "He [Lincoln] can do nothing," he insisted, "with the present House of Representatives and Senate, backed by the Supreme Court, to violate our rights."[20] As an alternative to secession, Magoffin believed a conference of the slaveholding states should determine the southern response to Lincoln's election. "[T]he voice of the South should be heard in potential, official, and united protest."[21] The South should act unitedly and not separately.

Like most white Kentuckians, Magoffin found himself torn between his support for the institution of slavery and his traditional loyalty to the Union. As with Texan Sam Houston and many other white southerners, he was both proslavery and pro-Union, believing that slavery was better protected by the United States Constitution than by any newly designed secessionist constitution. After all, the Fugitive Slave Act of 1850 enabled the return of Kentucky slaves who escaped across the Ohio River. Secession would negate the law and create a foreign country to the north of the Bluegrass State. Since Kentucky led the nation in fugitive slaves (119 in 1860), maintaining the 1850 act was advantageous to Kentucky's slave owners.[22] As historian Patrick Lewis has shown, the majority of white Kentuckians sided with the United States over the winter of 1860–1861 "for the *benefit* of slavery" rather than "*despite* slavery (emphasis added)."[23] Preserving the state's domestic institution was of utmost importance to this border state, as it was to the rest of the slave-owning South. Magoffin represented the majority of Kentucky's white population by rejecting secession as the solution to the perceived Republican threat to slavery.

Attempting to assume the role of the honest broker, Magoffin sent a letter to southern governors in early December "urging a conference" and offering six propositions in order to further "the maintenance of the institution of slavery." Two of the governor's suggestions dealt with the passage of (and changes to) laws that would better enforce the fugitive slave clause of the Constitution. Three of the other proposed solutions took the form of constitutional amendments designed to guarantee the return of fugitive slaves, divide the western territories between the "free and slave States," and assure the unimpeded navigation of the Mississippi River. Magoffin's final proposition most tellingly reflected the core of southern concerns. To the governors of the slave-owning states, he advocated amending the Constitution "so as to give the South the power, say in the United States Senate, to protect itself from unconstitutional and oppressive legislation upon the subject of slavery."[24]

On January 17, with the secession of South Carolina, Mississippi, Florida, and Alabama a reality, Magoffin addressed the opening session of Kentucky's General Assembly. "Our present unfortunate political complications" he attributed to the Republican Party and its singular "idea of hostility to the institution of African slavery."[25] Aware that additional Deep South states were on the brink of leaving the Union and that Virginia had issued an invitation to the states (north and south) for a convention in Washington, Magoffin expressed the hope that a gathering of border slave states be called to approve Senator Crittenden's amendment. The General Assembly declined to heed immediately Governor Magoffin's call for a border slave state convention, postponing that action for over two months. Perhaps the state's elected officials knew that plans for a national gathering were already underway in Virginia. Perhaps too many of Kentucky's public officials recalled that only a decade earlier the state had presented its memorial stone to the Washington Monument with the inscription: "Under the Auspices of Heaven, & the Precepts of Washington, Kentucky will be the last to Give up the Union."[26]

While Kentucky's General Assembly did not respond to Magoffin's proposal for a gathering of the states, Virginia's General Assembly eagerly endorsed the idea. On January 7, 1861, Governor John Letcher opened Virginia's Senate and House of Delegates in extra session with an address that reflected his conviction that the Old Dominion should not immediately follow South Carolina out of the Union, but rather act the role of mediator. "The cotton states seem to be looking to their own interests alone," he declared, "and why should we not look to ours?" Believing, as Magoffin did, that the people of the northern states were solely responsible for the "present state of exasperation existing between the two sections of the Union," but unwilling to join in the secession frenzy manifest in the Deep South states, Letcher proposed a "convention of all the states." Invoking Article V of the Constitution, he declared that the "present condition of public affairs" required that amending the Constitution, not secession, was the proper response to southern discontent.[27]

Like Governor Magoffin, Letcher proposed his own solution in the form of a constitutional amendment. Containing six articles, the governor's plan would greatly strengthen the fugitive slave clause of the Constitution, protect the interstate slave trade and slavery in the District of Columbia and the territories, and ensure the transportation of slaves by their owners through free states and territories. His sixth article would have prevented the federal government from appointing "persons who are hostile to their [southern] institutions" who would "sow seeds of strife and dissension between the slaveholding and nonslaveholding classes in the southern states."[28] Also like Magoffin, Letcher was quite comfortable recommending that protections for the institution of slavery be transferred from individual states to the federal constitution.

Twelve days later, Virginia's General Assembly issued an invitation to all the states to send delegates to the "City of Washington, . . . to consider, and if practicable, agree upon some suitable adjustment." Forsaking, however, Governor Letcher's proposed solution, Virginia announced that the "unhappy controversy which now divides the States" would best be resolved by adopting John J. Crittenden's resolutions as "presented to the Senate of the United States." The endorsement was not without conditions. The call suggested that Crittenden's amendment be "modified" so that slavery would specifically be protected in any present or future territory south of 36°30' latitude during the "continuance of the Territorial government," and that Crittenden's fourth article protect the rights of slave owners traveling "between and through" nonslaveholding states and territories. With these changes, however, the General Assembly announced that the Kentuckian's plan "would be accepted by the people of this commonwealth."[29]

The Washington Peace Conference convened at Willard's Hall (Hotel) on February 4. Twenty-one states sent 131 delegates with Tennessee appointing the largest number—twelve—and New Hampshire sending the smallest—three. Kentucky's General Assembly appointed as delegates to the conference William O. Butler (Carrollton), James B. Clay (Lexington), Joshua F. Bell (Danville), Charles S. Morehead (Louisville), James Guthrie (Louisville), and Charles A. Wickliffe (Bardstown).[30] With an average age of sixty-one, Kentucky's delegation arrived in Washington with impressive political credentials. Two had served as governor (Morehead and Wickliffe), Bell had served as Kentucky's secretary of state, Guthrie as United States secretary of the treasury under Franklin Pierce, Wickliffe as postmaster general under John Tyler, and William Butler had been Lewis Cass's vice-presidential running mate in 1848. Clay, son of Henry Clay, served as chargé d'affaires to Portugal under Zachary Taylor. Of the six, only Clay and Morehead supported the Confederacy once war commenced. Morehead later openly criticized the Lincoln administration and was arrested and imprisoned for disloyalty in September 1861. Upon his parole in January of the next year, he fled to Canada, Europe, and then Mexico before returning to the United States after the war. A former Whig who became a Democrat during the 1850s, Clay was arrested in late 1861 for attempting to join a Confederate force in southeast Kentucky. Upon his capture, the *New York Times* observed: "His treacherous tread profanes the soil that Henry Clay's patriotism hallowed."[31]

As the delegates to the Washington conference debated and argued over the next three weeks, growing frustration developed that the assembly was straying from Virginia's original proposition. On February 15 and again on the 26th, Virginia's James A. Seddon introduced Crittenden's proposal as a reminder of where the conference should be heading. James Clay also reintroduced Crittenden's plan for compromise on February 26, including an article he (Crittenden) had added on January 3, providing that the "elective franchise" and the right to hold office "whether federal, State, territorial, or municipal" shall not be exercised by persons who are "in whole or in part, of the African Race." Clay, like Crittenden, wanted to ensure that white supremacy reigned north and south, as his provision would have rendered unconstitutional laws of northern states that permitted free African Americans to vote.[32] The added article further provided that the United States could purchase land in Africa or South America for the colonization of "free negroes and mulattoes, as the several States may wish to have removed from their limits and from the District of Columbia, and such other places as may be under the jurisdiction of Congress."[33]

The Peace Conference's final proposed amendment approved on February 27 was like Crittenden's but differed in substantial ways. It added articles that prohibited the foreign slave trade and provided conditions under which new territory could be acquired. The most notable difference, however, was the omission of a clause Crittenden included in his Article 1 which began, "In all territory of the United States now held, or hereafter acquired, situate north of 36°30' . . ." The words "now held, or hereafter acquired" were designed to authorize slavery in Cuba or parts of Mexico or South America should they eventually be acquired by the United States. Both the southern and northern Democratic platforms of 1860 had recommended the purchase of Cuba from Spain. Republican delegates to the conference were opposed to encouraging in any fashion the acquisition of additional territory for slavery and insisted on the deletion of the clause from the gathering's final amendment before it was sent to the United States Congress.[34] The House of Representatives refused to receive the amendment; the Senate rejected it on March 4 by a vote of 28–7.[35]

Kentucky's delegation to Washington was far from united regarding a solution to the secession problem. Guthrie, Morehead, Bell, and Wickliffe generally accepted the conference amendment despite its differences from Crittenden's resolutions, believing that, once it was submitted for ratification, "the border free States would grant all the guarantees secured by the amendment."[36] Butler and Clay, on the other hand, pressed for more exacting federal protections for slavery. On the territorial issue, they objected to slavery being banned north of the 36°30' parallel and stood firm on the Supreme Court's opinion in the *Dred Scott* case. They wanted more specific language in the "transit" article so that slaves would be protected as "property" by the federal government.

Clay introduced a distinct expansion of the Constitution's fugitive slave clause that would have federalized definitions of "treason, felony, or other crime" to eliminate state interpretation of those terms. Butler and Clay objected to the article dealing with the acquisition of new territory because it would have made the purchase of Cuba "almost impossible." They also objected to the reiteration of the ban on the importation of slaves from outside the United States, arguing that such a ban would prevent Kentucky slave owners who owned plantations in Deep South states from returning "with their slaves" given the reality that those states had already organized themselves as a foreign country.[37] Not surprisingly, the divisions among the delegation mirrored the political divisions in Kentucky itself.

Over the course of Secession Winter, elected officials across the nation debated the future of the institution of slavery and ultimately proposed sixty-eight solutions to the problem posed by the specter of secession—all in the form of amendments to the United States Constitution. As mentioned above, President James Buchanan introduced the idea of a constitutional solution on December 3, 1860, in his opening address to the second session of the Thirty-Sixth Congress with his three-part amendment protecting slavery. Realizing that mere legislation would not adequately address the gravity of the crisis, the elected officials of the country followed Buchanan's lead and proposed their own ideas for a constitutional solution. Most suggestions came from Congress, while others originated in secession conventions, state legislatures, and the Washington Peace Conference. The governors of Kentucky, Tennessee, and Virginia each added their resolutions. Kentucky and Pennsylvania offered six amendments, Tennessee nine, and Virginia, which deliberated longer than any other state and left the longest record of those debates (3,000 pages), contributed sixteen.[38]

The amendments mirrored the political discussion over the future of slavery that had occupied the country since 1846 when Pennsylvania representative David Wilmot introduced his contentious resolution aimed at prohibiting the institution from any lands acquired from Mexico. Although the Compromise of 1850, the Kansas-Nebraska Act, and the Supreme Court's *Dred Scott* decision all aimed at solving the "slavery in the territories" dilemma, none succeeded. The presidential campaign of 1860 resulting in the election of a Republican president brought the issue to a boiling point. By the time of the election, southerners, and Democrats generally, had convinced themselves that Abraham Lincoln was an abolitionist, that the Republican Party was dominated by abolitionists, and that the northern states were largely populated with militant abolitionists of the John Brown stripe. As a result, 90 percent of the proposed constitutional amendments were carefully designed to protect slavery in various ways throughout the country. The largest number attempted to solve the issue of slavery in the territories; others were designed to strengthen the fugitive slave clause of the Constitution and protect slavery in the nation's capital and in federal installations scattered throughout the South. Over half aimed at protecting the transit of slaves with their owners to and through non-slave states and territories, while eleven proposed nationalizing slavery—making bondage, not freedom, the law of the land.

The concerns expressed nationally for the protection of slavery were directly represented in Kentucky's six amendments. All six addressed the ongoing issue of slavery in the territories; four dealt with the return of fugitive slaves and protecting slavery in the District of Columbia and federal forts, shipyards, arsenals, etc., in the South. Three were designed to protect the transit of slaves taken by their owners into free states and territories, and three articulated the popular objective of protecting slavery in the states where it already existed. In fact, of the twenty-seven amendments presented nationally that contained this provision, ten used the exact language proposed by John J. Crittenden on December 18: "No amendment shall be made to the Constitution which shall authorize or give to Congress any power to abolish or interfere with slavery in any of the States by whose laws it is, or may be, allowed or permitted." Of the twenty-eight articles contained in Kentucky's amendments, only Governor Magoffin's effort to protect the "free navigation of the Mississippi river" was not explicitly designed to embed protections for the institution of slavery in the United States Constitution.

By March 4, when Congress passed the Seward/Corwin amendment which would have protected slavery in the fifteen southern states, seven slave states had already left the Union and their delegates had vacated their congressional seats. The resulting Republican majority was unwilling to sanction slavery further at the federal level. Following the fall of Fort Sumter five weeks later, Lincoln's subsequent call for troops to quell the rebellion, and the resulting secession of Arkansas, Tennessee, Virginia, and North Carolina, Kentucky opted for detachment. Hoping to distance herself from the impending war, Kentucky chose, like her sister slave states of Missouri, Maryland, and Delaware, the middle ground of supporting neither the Confederacy nor the United States.

Unlike the three other Border South states, however, the General Assembly declared the Commonwealth neutral in the ensuing conflict. Kentucky "should take no part in the civil war now being waged except as mediators and friends to the belligerent parties," the legislature proclaimed on May 16; the state should instead "occupy a position of strict neutrality."[39] Four days later, Governor Magoffin officially forbad the United States and the Confederate States from "any movement upon the soil of Kentucky or the occupation of any port, post, or place whatever within the lawful boundary and jurisdiction of this State."[40] A subsequent act strengthening the state militia and funding the purchase of arms reiterated neutrality by specifying that the militia could not be used against the "Government of the United States, nor against the Confederate States, unless in protecting our soil from unlawful invasion; it being the intention alone that said arms and munitions of war are to be used for the sole defense of the State of Kentucky."[41] The *New York Times* quickly reacted to the state's declaration calling it a "crude construction," and nothing less than "treason."[42]

In the fateful weeks between Lincoln's inauguration and the Confederate bombardment of Fort Sumter, Kentucky had yet another card to play. While the General Assembly had denied Governor Magoffin's call for a general convention of the states and, later, a convention of the slave states, on April 4, the legislature issued an invitation for a gathering of the border slave states. The delegates who convened in Frankfort on May 27, however, were few. Kentucky's twelve (led by John J. Crittenden) were joined by four representatives from Missouri and one from Tennessee.[43] Maryland and Delaware declined the invitation. The assembly met for seven days, blamed the Deep South slave states for seceding "without any good or sufficient cause," produced yet another plea for a constitutional amendment (Crittenden's, of course), and published an address to the "People of the United States" articulating the delegates' view of the country's condition.[44]

In addition, the gathering, dominated as it was by Kentuckians, produced an "Address to the People of Kentucky" that summed up the state's position in opposition to secession and in favor of Union and the Constitution. "Secession is not a right," the manifesto declared; Kentucky had "no cause of complaint against the General Government, and made none." With war looming (an unnecessary war from their standpoint), the seceded states failed the country by leaving and, moreover, turned a Democratic majority in Congress that would have "controlled" Lincoln, into a Republican majority that enabled him. Southern senators and representatives who "vacated their seats," committed a "great wrong, for which they must answer to posterity."[45]

Kentucky's aloof policy was short lived. Within months, all four Border South states sided in various ways with the United States, although some support for the Confederacy endured. Over the next four years, the four slave states that remained in the Union supplied 216,000 men to the United States Army and 86,000 to the Confederate.[46] Divided loyalties plagued these states throughout, and after, the war.[47]

Secession, constitutional or not, became a reality in the months following Lincoln's election. Ultimately, eleven slave states made the fateful decision to leave the Union and create a new government—the Confederate States of America. The Confederate Constitution, created in the early months of 1861, included many of the measures proposed by Senator Crittenden and other elected officials of the Bluegrass State. It protected slavery beyond the reach of individual states by allowing slave owners to travel unimpeded throughout the newly formed confederacy with their slaves. If the Confederacy acquired new territory, slavery would be protected there as well. Most importantly, however, the expansive constitution emphatically nationalized slavery. By employing the phrases "property in said slaves," "slaves and other property," and "property in negro slaves," the Confederate Constitution-makers protected that form of property, as all other property was protected, by the language of Article I, section 9, part 16: no citizen shall "be deprived of life, liberty, or *property* without due process of law (emphasis added)."[48] Protections for slavery in the Confederate South were deeply lodged in its new constitution. In creating their government, white southerners purposely sacrificed state authority for expanded federal authorities to safeguard their "peculiar institution."

In the aftermath of Lincoln's election, as the nation reacted to the secession of seven Deep South states, Kentuckians considered the developing storm, their place in the nation, and the mediating legacy of Henry Clay. While believing in the rectitude of slavery, they did not believe the institution was inherently threatened by the election of a Republican president. Nor did they believe the institution would be better protected in the new Confederate Constitution. Their middle-of-the-road approach anticipated that peace would result only if the nation's elected officials could agree on a set of compromises clarifying the constitutionality of slavery. Expanding protections for slavery in the United States Constitution, however, was something Republicans—holding a congressional majority after the withdrawal of senators and representatives from seven southern states—could not support. Crittenden's hopes for an amicable settlement based on his resolutions were not to be. As fate would have it, however, the elderly Kentuckian created one of the political bookends for the war. Exactly five years to the day after Crittenden proposed his thirteenth amendment that would have increased slavery's protections in the national charter, Secretary of State William Seward certified the ratification of the Thirteenth Amendment that abolished the institution.[49]

Sources

The political discussions held over Secession Winter were carefully documented in every venue. The debates of the second session of the Thirty-Sixth Congress were captured in the *Congressional Globe* and are easily accessed at: https://memory.loc.gov/ammem/amlaw/lwcglink.html#anchor36. From December 3, 1860, until March 4, 1861, the *Globe* recorded (in 2,000 pages) the speeches and debates of United States senators and representatives. The journals of the Kentucky General Assembly, as it met intermittently during the early months of 1861, provide insights into the political attitudes of Kentucky's elected officials. Facsimile copies can be found at www.hathitrust.org. Lucius E. Chittenden was a delegate from Vermont to the Washington Peace Conference and became its self-appointed scribe. Chittenden carefully noted the conference's deliberations from February 4–27, 1861, and published the proceedings in 1864. As noted, Kentucky's delegates to the Washington gathering were not in full agreement and published their individual reports soon after arriving back in Kentucky. The gathering of the Convention of the Border Slave States, although lasting only a week, provided Kentuckians one last effort at compromise and provides the contemporary student of the war an insightful summary of their thinking on the eve of hostilities. The combined published records of the *Globe*, state legislatures and secession conventions, and the Washington Peace Conference total over 8,000 pages. See bibliography for specific citations of relevant documents.

Editor's Note

Because of the extensive nature of Kentucky's secession documents, I have included only the most germane of them. The speeches have been edited to emphasize the salient points of the debate and to omit redundant or incidental material. Instead of simple ellipses, however, I have given the reader a sense of the omitted material by including explanatory comments within braces, i.e., {}. Many of the documents include brackets in the original to identify individuals or legislative procedures. For clarity, the editor's emendations are therefore also included within braces.

This book would not have seen the light of day had it not been for the early interest and support of Darrell Meadows and Tony Curtis. Patrick Lewis was also "present at the creation" and has provided assistance throughout. Special thanks are extended to Patrick and Jonathan Atkins who read the manuscript and offered extensive and critical comments. Their encouragement and continuing enthusiasm for this project is greatly appreciated. I also need to thank Jane Scott for assistance with legal terms. Scot Danforth and Jon Boggs at the University of Tennessee Press have, yet again, served critical roles in bringing my research to the public.

CHAPTER ONE

Governor Beriah Magoffin

Born in Harrodsburg, Kentucky, Beriah Magoffin (1815–1885) entered politics in 1840 as an appointed police judge. He served in the Kentucky Senate before being elected governor in 1859. Magoffin supported the institution of slavery and believed in the constitutional right of secession although he hoped that a convention of southern states could craft compromise measures that would be acceptable to the North. While leaning toward secession following the fall of Fort Sumter and Lincoln's call for state troops, Magoffin was out of step with the General Assembly which refused to call his recommended convention. Kentucky voters, during the summer of 1861, established the state's anti-secession credentials by filling the state's ten congressional seats with nine Unionists. Following August elections for the General Assembly, Unionists held a majority of 76 to 24 in the House, and a majority of 27 to 11 in the Senate. Magoffin served for another year in a politically diminished capacity until he resigned on August 18, 1862, through a negotiated arrangement that resulted in James F. Robinson being named his successor. After the war, Magoffin served one term (1867–1869) in the Kentucky House where he advocated for the ratification of the Thirteenth Amendment. Kentucky did eventually ratify the amendment—a century later—in 1976 becoming the second to the last state do so. That same year, it became the last state to ratify the Fourteenth Amendment which granted national citizenship to former slaves.

In this public letter written ten days after Lincoln's election, Governor Magoffin presented to the people of Kentucky his assessment of the political situation. He stressed that although the Republican Party clearly intended to abolish slavery throughout the country, Lincoln's election alone was "no cause for secession or rebellion." Most importantly, he argued that because Democrats would control both houses of Congress for the next two years and the Supreme Court remained proslavery in outlook, the incoming Republican administration could do little to "violate our rights."

Governor Magoffin's Letter to the *Kentucky Yeoman*

Frankfort, Kentucky
November 16, 1860

S. I. M. MAJOR, *Esq. Editor of Yeoman:*

DEAR SIR: I am asked by a number of friends, yourself one of them, and have received letters from various parts of the State, all of the same tenor, inquiring of me, *what will Kentucky do, and what ought she to do, now that Lincoln is elected?* I will frankly give you my opinion. I believe she will adhere firmly to her principles. We are defeated, but not conquered. We are beaten, but not dismayed. Kentucky will stand by the positions upon which I was elected in August, 1859. She will stand by the equality and the rights of the States, and the equality and the rights of the people in the States. She will stand by the repeal of the Missouri compromise, by the Dred Scott decision, and by the enforcement of the fugitive slave law. She will stand by every right she has under the Constitution of the United States. She will demand that slavery shall not be interfered with wherever it exists under the Constitution of the United States, and under the laws and Constitutions of the separate States. She will demand that slavery shall not be abolished in the District of Columbia, or wherever it now exists in the Union, and that the slave trade between the States shall not be interfered with by Congress. She will demand her equal rights in all the Territories of this government. She will stand by the position that slave property in the Territories is entitled to the same protection with other property therein, and that no discriminations can be made by the Territorial Legislatures against that property, so as to exclude it directly, or to impair the right of the owners to it, or by unfriendly legislation to render it valueless. She will demand that whenever the people of a Territory having sufficient population shall form a State Constitution, with or without slavery in it, and ask of Congress admission as a State into the Union, she shall be admitted, provided her constitution is Republican in form. She will keep her present status upon the slavery question, believing the laws, the constitution, and the courts afford her adequate protection. She will stand immovably upon the Democratic platform adopted last winter at Frankfort, and upon the one adopted last summer at Baltimore, upon which her noble and gifted son has just been defeated.[1] Entrenched in this position behind the decisions of the Supreme Court of the United States, her rallying cry will be, her rights and her equality in the Union. She will ask nothing she will not concede to her sister States. She wants all her rights under the constitution, and she will neither give up nor compromise a single one of them. She will show her devotion to the Union by standing steadfastly by these, the only principles upon which it can be preserved. She will be, as she has ever been, firm, wise, moderate, and just, and whenever a dominant, reckless, sectional majority, disregarding the idea of her equality, forgetting that the government was made to protect the weak against the strong, and to protect persons, property, and the rights of the States, shall turn it into an engine of oppression instead of protection, by trampling upon her rights, she knows her duty, and she will do it. She will appeal to the ballot box, to the reason, to the justice, and to the patriotism of Congress, of the States, and of the people everywhere; and when everything fails, doubly fortified in her impregnable position, she will calmly and resolutely look the danger in the face, and no matter what the odds may be against her, she will then appeal to the God of battles, and with the constitution in one hand and the sword in the other, and under the flag of the Union, her noble and gallant sons will prove themselves worthy of the glorious heroes from whom they sprung, by striking for their homes and their firesides—for their altars and their rights—for their liberties and the freedom of their children—for the Union under the compact of the constitution—and he who would not do it is a coward and a slave.

I agree with you, that the election of Mr. Lincoln is no cause for secession or rebellion. It is not so regarded by the people of the States. It is true he has been elected by a sectional party, upon sectional ideas, with a reckless sectional hostility to an institution the South will not surrender. The people of the slave States and a large minority of true men in the free States, no matter whether they were the supporters of Mr. Breckinridge, Mr. Bell, or Mr. Douglas, took the ground that if he were elected, and he attempted to carry out his principles and purposes, it would dissolve the Union. Kentucky says, after the election, in my judgment, what all parties here declared before, and that is, she will not submit to the carrying out of his principles. The fathers of the Republic, with General Washington at the head, have warned us against the formation and success of a sectional party as the only danger to the liberties of the people or to the safety of the confederacy. The Republicans have paid no attention to these warnings, but blindly, madly, without regard to consequences, they have declared this government could not exist as part free and part slave, but must be all free. It matters little whether we have to give up our slave property, or whether our children will be compelled to do it. They have made their threats that they intend to deprive us of it sooner or later, and in the free States, as far as they dare or had the power, they have put their threats into execution. They have passed laws in thirteen of the free States, I believe, which prohibit the execution of the fugitive slave law, and have set at naught the Constitution of the United States.[2] Six of these States, New York and Pennsylvania included, deny to the owners of slaves, or to the officers of the government, their jails or public buildings for the protection of this property. Seven of them, including also New York and Pennsylvania, provide defense for fugitive slaves. Many of them declare the slaves free if their owners bring them there; and one State—New Hampshire—declares him absolutely free. Nine of the free States have imposed penalties of imprisonment, and fines of from $1,000 to $5,000 on the officers or persons who may aid in enforcing the laws which have been passed by Congress, and declared to be constitutional by the Supreme Court of the United States. The Legislatures of these States, and the courts of many of them which have passed upon their action, have openly, insultingly, boldly, and defiantly nullified the laws of Congress and the decisions of the Supreme Court. There is no theoretical, but practical disunion in this.

Is it not time all this was arrested? Is it not time we had an *understanding* as to their future action, if we do not intend to be robbed of our slave property? All over the border States they have their agents and emissaries, and many in the other slave States, engaged in stealing and running off our slaves. They avow they will neither give them up when they succeed in getting into the free States, nor will they deliver up the men who steal them. They have elected a man who has avowed, if he did not originate, the doctrine of the irrepressible conflict, and that the States must be all free. He and his party affirm in the most solemn manner they will execute their purposes, so soon as they have the power. They say Mr. Lincoln is a firm and an honest man; and if so, he intends to carry out his principles. The slave States have over four and a half millions of slaves. Kentucky has over $170,000,000 in slave property. She is losing at the rate of over $200,000 per annum of that property. When I stated, in my annual message to the Legislature, the loss was $100,000, few believed it.[3] I have reliable information it is double that sum, and will soon be again doubled, if not in some way arrested. That property, more than one third of all we possess, guaranteed to us by the Constitution of the United States and our laws, worked for, acquired, and left to us by our fathers—that property we are working for, and wish to leave to our children, will soon be rendered valueless, and Kentucky become a free State, if these principles and purposes are carried out. Yet with all these grievances, while no slave State has nullified a law of Congress, or refused a right to a free State under the Constitution—with all this loss of property by Kentucky—with the further fact staring us in the face that the State of Ohio has violated a great constitutional right of the State of Kentucky, in refusing to deliver up upon my demand a fugitive from our State who has been indicted for stealing our slaves—with all these facts and outrages hard to be borne, I would say that the mere election of Lincoln is not sufficient cause for secession or rebellion. He is elected under the forms and according to the Constitution of the United States. We would say to our sister States of the South, we have more cause of grievance than all of the cotton States put together, occupying, as we do, over seven hundred miles of border line. Look at our exposed position—the constant tampering with our negroes by the Abolitionists—the immense annual loss we sustain—the direct infringement of our rights in refusing to execute the fugitive slave law, and in the robbery of our property—in danger to the lives of the owners when they go to the free States to recapture their slaves—in the insults and taunts and injuries to the Federal officers who attempt to do their sworn duty in executing the fugitive slave law, as in the recent mob in Ohio, and in the case of Boothe of Wisconsin—in the wholesale stealing every day going on of our negroes, and the refusal of the people and Governors to deliver up either the property or the thieves: all this, and much more, we complain of, and don't intend to submit to; but we cannot justify you in breaking up the government and going out of the Union on account of the election of a man upon a bad platform, and the worst political principles and purposes.[4]

We say to you and to the Republicans, we stand here as pacificators, as arbitrators. We entreat you of the South not to take this rash step; and to you of the North we say, calmly, but fearlessly and firmly, without threats, you must not encroach upon our constitutional rights as expounded by the highest and purest tribunal in the land. You must stay your arm of fanaticism, of passion, of vengeance, of violence, and of power, for we are resolved to resist unto death any violation of our rights under the Constitution. We will resist aggression; we will defend the Union under the flag of our fathers, following in their footsteps, and encouraged by their example, no matter what the odds may be against us. Mr. Lincoln has been elected according to all the forms under that Constitution which we revere and regard as the depository of our rights and the shield of our safety; and notwithstanding his threats and the danger of carrying out his principles, *he may not do it.* We must wait for an overt act, hoping that truth and reason and justice, embodied in a clear, an impartial delineation of our rights under the Constitution, as expounded by the Supreme Court of the United States, will yet prevent it. A madman or a bad man may stand in the highway adjoining my premises, and he may threaten to burn my house or rob me of my property, and yet I may treat him as a blusterer who would not execute the threat. When he makes the attempt—when he actually crosses my fence and advances upon my property to execute the threat—then will it be time enough, and then will I be justified in shooting down the villain. Let us reason with the Republicans still further; let us remonstrate more earnestly, firmly, and unitedly; let us at all events wait for the overt act, and then Kentucky can and will join her sister slave States. This, it seems to me, is the course of moderation and prudence and wisdom; certainly so, because neither Mr. Lincoln nor his party can pass any law, if the Opposition remain true, that will violate our rights. He can't even get an appropriation bill through Congress to carry on the government. He can't appoint his Cabinet officers who may be offensive to the Democratic party and to the slave States. He can do nothing, with the present House of Representatives and Senate, backed by the Supreme Court, to violate our rights. *Let the anti-Republican members of the Opposition firmly resolve not to discuss the question of slavery any more, and when the Republicans have done let them vote down their measures and proceed to business upon the other important interests of the country.* The question has been discussed too much already, and let them resolve they will discuss it no more. It only produces discord, strife, criminations and recriminations, and sunders all those fraternal ties, socially, politically, and religiously, which bind us together.

I have hope yet, when passion cools and reason resumes its throne, that the North may be brought to see they have as deep a stake in preserving slavery in the South, and the rights of the slave States, as we have. They cannot do without our cotton and sugar, and rice and tobacco, and other staples; and whenever the fanaticism of the people, who have no motive to act but for their own good and the safety of the Republic, shall see this, as see it they will, sooner or later, they will refuse to follow the lead of ambitious, reckless, dangerous, and talented demagogues who are willing to risk fortune, honor, life, and country to gain place and power. They will see that it is not only to their own interest to keep the negro in bondage, but it is to the interest of the slave—*that he is morally, socially, and religiously a better and a happier man than he could be in any other condition.* As a slave, an active, efficient agent in doing great good, as we have him in the slave States; but as a free man, a worthless vagabond, idle, dissipated, miserable—a nuisance and a curse, as they have him in the free States, and are compelled to pass laws to prevent his residence among them. They may see we have other great interests in this country which ought to engage a fair proportion of the time of Congress. Reason and truth and patriotism may yet prevail. Let us hope—hope on and ever, in the absence of an overt act, or until there is no hope for the Union of these States. Great God, let us do nothing! We who have been and are in the right, let us keep in the right, and do nothing to break up this great government. Let us stand upon the right, submitting to nothing wrong. Firmly, unwaveringly, and all together, let us stand upon our constitutional rights, with an unfaltering purpose to make no more concessions—to submit to no more compromises and to resent at once, and to the last extremity, any violation of our rights.

To the States which propose to secede we would say in addition to what we have said, you should not desert us. We are a border State; we have the brunt of the battle; we have more grievances than all of you; we have suffered more wrongs, but we had more forbearance. Even now we have a practical question. It is a wicked, willful, wanton violation of our rights, which lies at the foundation of our Government, and involves the very existence of slavery in Kentucky. It is no abstraction—no Kansas question—no territorial question—but an open, direct violation of our constitutional rights. We don't intend to submit to it. I have demanded of Gov. Dennison, of Ohio, a fugitive now under indictment for stealing our slaves. He has refused to deliver him up.[5]

He and the Republican party of Ohio, and I believe of the whole Union, all concede that the Government could not have been formed but upon the idea that each State must be permitted to regulate its domestic affairs to suit itself, and that unless this idea is fully carried out between the States in their intercourse, the Union is at an end. Yet he refuses to deliver up this fugitive now under indictment in our courts for stealing our negro property, upon the ground, among other reasons, *that the laws of Ohio do not regard it as a felony to steal a slave.* Our laws and constitution, and the constitution of the United States, do recognize negroes as property. They are recognized as such by the Supreme Court of the United States.[6] It has declared it to be a felony to steal a slave, and we will not submit to this violation of our constitutional rights. It is a great practical question now pending between Kentucky and Ohio, and it will test the fact whether or not the Republicans intend to carry out their purposes. I told you on the stump last summer, that I would surrender no constitutional right Kentucky had. This is one of them. If we would surrender this one, it will encourage to wrest from us another and another, until stripped of our rights, our honor, our inheritance, and our manhood, we will have neither the spirit, nor the courage, nor the power to resist.

I shall take this violated right to the courts for the remedy. Failing there, I would take it to Congress, as there is an anti-Republican Congress, and if they give the remedy, Mr. Lincoln will be called on to sign or veto the bill. We will test the question where we have rights whether or not we have remedies. We will test the question whether or not our rights are to be respected under the laws and the decisions of the Supreme Court of the United States. Failing there, I shall tell the people of Kentucky, in the last resort: Here is your violated right. I have done all I can do to obtain the remedy. You are a State's rights people, and now, falling back upon your reserved rights, I will advise such action as I am sure you will take.

To South Carolina, and such other States who may wish to secede from the Union, I would say, the geography of this country will not admit of a division—the mouth and sources of the Mississippi river cannot be separated without the horrors of civil war—we cannot sustain you in this movement merely on account of the election of Lincoln. Do not precipitate us by premature action into a revolution or civil war, the consequences of which will be the most frightful to all of us. It may yet be avoided. There is still hope, faint though it be. Kentucky is a border State, and has suffered more than all of you. She claims that, standing upon the same sound platform, you will sympathize with her, and stand by her, and not desert her in her exposed perilous border position. She has a right to claim that her voice, and the voice of reason and moderation and patriotism, shall be heard and heeded by you. If you secede, your Representatives will go out of Congress, and leave us at the mercy of a Black Republican Government. Mr. Lincoln will have no check. He can appoint his cabinet and have it confirmed. The Congress will then be Republican, and he will be able to pass such laws as he may suggest. The Supreme Court will be powerless to protect us. We implore you to stand by us, and by our friends in the free States, and let us all, *the bold, and true, and just men in the free and the slave States,* with a united front stand by each other, by our principles, by our rights, our equality, our honor, and by the Union under the Constitution. I believe this is the only way to save it, and we can do it.

As it is, a majority of the people are against Mr. Lincoln, although he has been elected.[7] The majority in Congress is against him and his principles. He is in their power, and they would fully represent a majority of the people of the United States, if they would exercise that power in such a manner as to obtain assurances and guarantees that our rights under the Constitution should be respected and preserved. This is what you want and what we want. In this way, we may accomplish it, the Union may be preserved, and we may go on to prosper in the future as we have done in the past. By seceding, by leaving the halls of Congress, by deserting your posts and us now, the government will be broken up, civil war may follow, and God only knows what will be the end. It may yet be averted in some way by not taking this premature step, and we appeal to you by all these considerations, by all the sacred memories which brought the government into existence, and all the ties which should be preserved and strengthened to keep us together as one people—by the battle-fields of the revolution—by the achievements and the blood and the sacrifices and sufferings of the illustrious dead—the martyrs of freedom who died to give us the liberty we now enjoy—by our unparalleled prosperity and progress as a nation—by our commanding position abroad, and, if we continue to be united, our powerful position at home—by all the mortification, ruin, and misery that would attend a failure of our government—by every consideration that should influence an aggrieved, a just, an intelligent, a loyal, a brave, a patriotic, and magnanimous people, to stand by us, by your rights, by the Constitution, and by the Union under the Constitution, in this hour of its greatest danger since it came into existence. Let passion be allayed; let reason assume its throne; let moderation, forbearance, and wisdom guide our counsels, and the country may yet be saved. In any contingency, we believe this government was formed in friendship, affection, and mutual confidence and common interests, and whenever these ties are indissolubly sundered, it is idle to attempt to keep it together by force.

In conclusion, I would say, Kentucky will watch the progress of events, in my opinion, in view of all the tremendous responsibilities that devolve upon her, and take her position calmly, fearlessly, wisely, with her whole heart beating for the Union, and her whole soul overflowing with patriotism and loyalty to that Union under the compact of the Constitution, determined to be just to all sections of this blood-bought confederacy, now the last, best, and brightest hope of freemen and mankind, and with the most perfect confidence when the dread hour of trial comes, if come it must, she has the will, the spirit, the courage, the patriotism, and the manhood, and the ability to defend her inheritance, her honor, and her rights, which have been guaranteed to her by the Constitution of the United States.

Respectfully, your friend and obedient servant,

B. MAGOFFIN.

Source: *Journal of the Called Session of the House of Representatives of the Commonwealth of Kentucky, Begun and Held in the Town of Frankfort, on Thursday the Seventeenth Day of January, in the Year of Our Lord 1861, and of the Commonwealth the Sixty-Ninth* (Frankfort: Printed at the Kentucky Yeoman Office, John B. Major, State Printer, 1861), 12–18.

Stephen Fowler Hale's Letter to Governor Magoffin

December 27, 1860

Born in Crittenden County, Kentucky, Stephen F. Hale (1816–1862) established himself as an attorney in Eutaw, Alabama. Appointed a secession commissioner by Alabama's Andrew B. Moore, Hale attempted to convince Magoffin that Kentucky should not delay in joining the secession movement.[8] Slavery was under constant and increasing attack from the North, he argued, and the "crowning act of insult and outrage upon the people of the South," was the election of Lincoln who opposed the extension of slavery and hoped to effect its ultimate extinction throughout the nation. Hale also hoped to appeal to Magoffin's racist sensibilities by claiming that Lincoln's election meant that southern slave owners would be "degraded to a position of equality with free negroes." "What Southern man," he asked, could contemplate without indignation and horror the triumph of negro equality and white men generally "stripped by the Heaven-daring hand of fanaticism of that title to superiority over the black race which God himself has bestowed?"

To his Excellency B. MAGOFFIN,
Governor of the Commonwealth of Kentucky:

I have the honor of placing in your hands, herewith, a commission from the Governor of the State of Alabama, accrediting me as a Commissioner from that State, to the sovereign State of Kentucky, to consult in reference to the momentous issues now pending between the Northern and Southern States of this Confederacy. Although each State, as a sovereign political community, must finally determine these grave issues for itself, yet the identity of interest, sympathy, and institutions prevailing alike in all the slaveholding States, in the opinion of Alabama, renders it proper that there should be a frank and friendly consultation by each one with her sister Southern States, touching their common grievances, and the measures necessary to be adopted to protect the interest, honor, and safety of their citizens.

I come, then, in a spirit of fraternity, as the Commissioner on the part of the State of Alabama, to confer with the authorities of this Commonwealth, in reference to the infraction of our constitutional rights, wrongs done and threatened to be done, as well as the mode and measure of redress proper to be adopted by the sovereign States aggrieved, to preserve their sovereignty, vindicate their rights, and protect their citizens.

In order to a clear understanding of the appropriate remedy, it may be proper to consider the rights and duties both of the State and citizen under the federal compact, as well as the wrongs done and threatened.

I therefore submit for the consideration of your Excellency, the following propositions, which I hope will command your assent and approval:

1. The people are the source of all political power, and the primary object of all good Governments is to protect the citizen in the enjoyment of life, liberty, and property; and whenever any form of government becomes

destructive of these ends, it is the inalienable right, and the duty of the people, to alter, or abolish it.

2. The equality of all the States of this Confederacy, as well as the equality of rights of all the citizens of the respective States under the Federal Constitution, is a fundamental principle in the scheme of the Federal Government. The Union of these States under the Constitution was formed "to establish justice, insure domestic tranquility, provide for the common defense, promote the general welfare, and secure the blessings of liberty to her citizens and their posterity," and when it is perverted to the destruction of the equality of the States, or substantially fails to accomplish these ends, it fails to achieve the purposes of its creation, and ought to be dissolved.

3. The Federal Government results from a compact entered into between separate sovereign and independent States, called the Constitution of the United States, and amendments thereto, by which these sovereign States delegated certain specific powers to be used by that government, for the common defense and general welfare of all the States and their citizens; and when these powers are abused, or used for the destruction of the rights of any State or its citizens, each State has an equal right to judge for itself, as well of the violations and infractions of that instrument, as of the mode and measure of redress; and if the interest or safety of her citizens demands it, may resume the powers she had delegated, without let or hindrance from the Federal Government, or any other power on earth.

4. Each State is bound in good faith to observe and keep on her part all the stipulations and covenants inserted for the benefit of other States in the constitutional compact—the only bond of Union by which the several Sates {*sic*} are bound together; and when persistently violated by one party to the prejudice of her sister States, ceases to be obligatory on the States so aggrieved, and they may rightfully declare the compact broken, the Union thereby formed dissolved, and stand upon their original rights, as sovereign and independent political communities; and further, that each citizen owes his primary allegiance to the State in which he resides, and hence it is the imperative duty of the State to protect him in the enjoyment of all his constitutional rights, and see to it that they are not denied or withheld from him with impunity by any other State or government.

If the foregoing propositions correctly indicate the objects of this government, the rights and duties of the citizen, as well as the rights, powers, and duties of the State and Federal Government under the Constitution, the next inquiry is, what rights have been denied, what wrongs have been done, or threatened to be done, of which the Southern States or the people of the Southern States can complain?

At the time of the adoption of the Federal Constitution African slavery existed in twelve of the thirteen States. Slaves are recognized both as property, and as a basis of political power, by the Federal compact, and special provisions are made by that instrument for their protection as property. Under the influences of climate and other causes, slavery has been banished from the Northern States, the slaves themselves have been sent to the Southern States, and there sold, and their price gone into the pockets of their former owners at the North. And in the meantime African slavery has not only become one of the fixed domestic institutions of the Southern States, but forms an important element of their political power, and constitutes the most valuable species of their property—worth, according to recent estimates, not less than four thousand millions of dollars—forming, in fact, the basis upon which rests the prosperity and wealth of most of these States, and supplying the commerce of the world with its richest freights, and furnishing the manufactories of two continents with the raw material and their operatives with bread. It is upon this gigantic interest—this peculiar institution of the South—that the Northern States and their people have been waging an unrelenting and fanatical war for the last quarter of a century.

An institution with which is bound up, not only the wealth and prosperity of the Southern people, but their very existence as a political community. This war has been waged in every way that human ingenuity, urged on by fanaticism, could suggest. They attack us through their literature, in their schools, from the hustings, in their legislative halls, through the public press, and even their courts of justice forget the purity of their judicial ermine, to strike down the rights of the Southern slaveholder, and override every barrier which the Constitution has erected for his protection; and the sacred desk is desecrated to this unholy crusade against our lives, our property, and the constitutional rights guaranteed to us by the compact of our fathers. During all this time, the Southern States have freely conceded to the Northern States, and the people of those States, every right secured to them by the Constitution, and an equal interest in the common Territories of the government; protected the lives and property of their citizens of every kind when brought within Southern jurisdiction; enforced through their courts, when necessary, every law of Congress passed for the protection of Northern property, and submitted ever since the foundation of the government, with scarcely a murmur, to the protection of their shipping, manufacturing, and commercial interest, by odious bounties, discriminating tariffs, and unjust navigation laws, passed by the Federal Government to the prejudice and injury of their own citizens.

The law of Congress for the rendition of fugitive slaves, passed in pursuance of an express provision of the constitution, remains almost a dead letter upon the statute book. A majority of the Northern States through their legislative enactments, have openly nullified it, and impose heavy fines and penalties upon all persons who aid in enforcing this law; and some of those States declare the Southern slaveholder who goes within their jurisdiction to assert his legal rights under the constitution, guilty of a high crime, and affix imprisonment in the penitentiary as the penalty. The Federal officers who attempt to discharge their duties under the law, as well as the owner of the slave, are set upon by mobs, and are fortunate if they escape without serious injury to life or limb; and the State authorities, instead of aiding in the enforcement of this law, refuse the use of their jails, and by every means which unprincipled fanaticism can devise, give countenance to the mob, and aid the fugitive to escape. Thus there are annually large amounts of property actually stolen away from the Southern States, harbored and protected in Northern States, and by their citizens. And when a requisition is made for the thief by the Governor of a Southern State upon the Executive of a Northern State, in pursuance of the express provisions of the Federal Constitution, he is insultingly told that the felon has committed no crime, and thus the criminal escapes, the property of the citizen is lost, the sovereignty of the State is insulted, and there is no redress. For the Federal courts have no jurisdiction to award a mandamus[9] to the Governor of a sovereign State, to compel him to do an official executive act, and Congress, if disposed, under the constitution has no power to afford a remedy. These are wrongs under which the Southern people have long suffered, and to which they have patiently submitted, in the hope that a returning sense of justice would prompt the people of the Northern States to discharge their constitutional obligations, and save our common country. Recent events, however, have not justified their hopes; the more daring and restless fanatics having banded themselves together, have put in practice the terrible lessons taught by the timid, by making an armed incursion upon the sovereign State of Virginia, slaughtering her citizens, for the purpose of exciting a servile insurrection among her slave population, and arming them for the destruction of their own masters. During the past summer the Abolition incendiary has lit up the prairies of Texas, fired the dwellings of the inhabitants, burned down whole towns, and laid poison for her citizens, thus literally executing the terrible denunciations of fanaticism against the slaveholder—"Alarm to their sleep; fire to their dwellings, and poison to their food."[10]

The same fell spirit, like an unchained demon, has for years swept over the plains of Kansas, leaving death, desolation, and ruin in its track. Nor is this the mere ebullition of a few half crazy fanatics; as is abundantly apparent, from the sympathy manifested all over the North; where, in many places, the tragic death of John Brown, the leader of the raid upon Virginia, who died upon the gallows a condemned felon, is celebrated with public honors, and his name canonized as a martyr to liberty; and many, even of the more conservative papers of the Black Republican school, were accustomed to speak of his murderous attack upon the lives of the unsuspecting citizens of Virginia, in a half sneering and half apologetic tone. And what has the Federal Government done in the meantime to protect slave property upon the common Territories of the Union? Whilst a whole squadron of the American navy is maintained on the coast of Africa, at an enormous expense, to enforce the execution of the laws against the slave trade—and properly too—and the whole navy is kept afloat to protect the lives and property of American citizens upon the high seas—not a law has been passed by Congress, or an arm raised by the Federal Government, to protect the slave property of citizens from the Southern States, upon the soil of Kansas—the common territory and common property of the citizens of all the States—purchased alike by their common treasure, and held by the Federal Government, as declared by the Supreme Court of the United States, as the trustee for all their citizens; but, upon the contrary, a Territorial government, created by Congress, and supported out of the common treasury, under the influence and control of Emigrant Aid Societies and Abolition emissaries, is permitted to pass laws excluding and destroying all that species of property within her limits; thus ignoring, on the part of the Federal Government, one of the fundamental principles of all good governments—the duty to protect the property of the citizen, and wholly refusing to maintain the equal rights of the States and the citizens of the States upon their common Territories.[11]

As the last and crowning act of insult and outrage upon the people of the South, the citizens of the Northern States, by overwhelming majorities, on the sixth day of November last, elected Abraham Lincoln and Hannibal Hamlin, President and Vice President of the United States. Whilst it may be admitted that the mere election of any man to the Presidency is not, *per se*, a sufficient cause for a dissolution of the Union, yet, when the issues upon, and circumstances under which he was elected, are properly appreciated and understood, the question arises whether a due regard to the interest, honor, and safety of their citizens, in view of this, and all the other antecedent wrongs and outrages, do not render it the imperative duty of the Southern States to resume the powers they have delegated to the Federal Government, and interpose their sovereignty for the protection of their citizens.

What, then, are the circumstances under which and the issues upon which he was elected? His own declarations and the current history of the times but too plainly indicate he was elected by a Northern sectional vote, against the most solemn warnings and protestations of the whole South. He stands forth as the representative of the fanaticism of the North, which, for the last quarter of a century, has been making war upon the South, her property, her civilization, her institution, and her interest—as the representative of that party which overrides all constitutional barriers, ignores the obligation of official oaths, and acknowledges allegiance to a higher law than the Constitution, striking down the sovereignty and equality of the States, and resting its claims to popular favor upon the one dogma, the equality of the races, white and black.

It was upon his acknowledgment of allegiance to a higher law, that Mr. Seward rested his claims to the Presidency, in a speech made by him in Boston before the election.[12] He is the exponent, if not the author, of the doctrine of the irrepressible conflict between freedom and slavery, and proposes that the opponents of slavery shall arrest its further *expansion, and by Congressional legislation exclude it from the common Territories of the Federal Government, and place it where the public mind shall rest in the belief that it is in the course of ultimate extinction.* He claims for free negroes the right of suffrage, and an equal voice in the government—in a word, all the rights of citizenship—although the Federal Constitution, as construed by the highest judicial tribunal in the world, does not recognize Africans imported into this country as slaves, or their descendants, whether free or slaves, as citizens.

These were the issues presented in the last Presidential canvass, and upon these the American people passed at the ballot-box. Upon the principles then announced by Mr. Lincoln and his leading friends, we are bound to expect his administration to be conducted. Hence it is that in high places among the Republican party, the election of Mr. Lincoln is hailed, not simply as a change of administration, but as the inauguration of new principles and a new theory of government, and even as the downfall of slavery. Therefore it is that the election of Mr. Lincoln cannot be regarded otherwise than a solemn declaration, on the part of a large majority of the Northern people, of hostility to the South, her property and her institutions—nothing less than an open declaration of war; for the triumph of this new theory of government destroys the property of the South, lays waste her fields, and inaugurates all the horrors of a San Domingo servile insurrection, consigning her citizens to assassinations, and her wives and daughters to pollution and violation, to gratify the lust of half civilized Africans.[13] Especially is this true in the cotton-growing States, where, in many localities, the slave outnumbers the white population ten to one.

If the policy of the Republicans is carried out, according to the programme indicated by the leaders of the party, and the South submits, degradation and ruin must overwhelm alike all classes of citizens in the Southern States. The slaveholder and non-slaveholder must ultimately share the same fate—all be degraded to a position of equality with free negroes; stand side by side with them at the polls, and fraternize in all the social relations of life; or else there will be an eternal war of races, desolating the land with blood, and utterly wasting and destroying all the resources of the country. Who can look upon such a picture without a shudder? What Southern man, be he slaveholder or non-slaveholder, can without indignation and horror contemplate the triumph of negro equality, and see his own sons and daughters in the not distant future associating with free negroes upon terms of political and social equality; and the white man stripped by the Heaven-daring hand of fanaticism of that title to superiority over the black race which God himself has bestowed? In the Northern States, where free negroes are so few as to form no appreciable part of the community, in spite of all the legislation for their protection they still remain a degraded caste—excluded by the ban of society from social association with all but the lowest and most degraded of the white race. But in the South, where in many places the African race largely predominates, and, as a consequence, the two races would be continually pressing together, amalgamation or the extermination of the one or the other would be inevitable. Can Southern men submit to such degradation and ruin? God forbid that they should.

But, it is said, there are many constitutional conservative men at the North, who sympathize with and battle for us. That is true, but they are utterly powerless, as the late Presidential election unequivocally shows, to breast the tide of fanaticism that threatens to roll over and crush us. With them it is a question of principle, and we award to them all honor for their loyalty to the constitution of our fathers; but their defeat is not their ruin. With us it is a question of self-preservation—our lives, our property, the safety of our homes and our hearthstones—all that men hold dear on earth—is involved in the issue. If we triumph, vindicate our rights and maintain our institutions, a bright and joyous future lies before us. We can clothe the world with our staple—give wings to her commerce, and supply with bread the starving operative in other lands, and at the same time preserve an institution that has done more to civilize and Christianize the heathen than all human agencies beside—an institution alike beneficial to both races, ameliorating the moral, physical, and intellectual condition of the one, and giving wealth and happiness to the other. If we fail, the light of our civilization goes down in blood, our wives and our little ones will be driven from their homes by the light of our own dwellings. The dark pall of barbarism must soon gather over our sunny land, and the scenes of West India emancipation, with its attendant horrors and crimes, (that monument of British fanaticism and folly) be reenacted in our own land upon a more gigantic scale.[14]

Then is it not time we should be up and doing like men who know their rights and dare maintain them? To whom shall the people of the Southern States look for the protection of their rights, interests, and honor? We answer, to their own sons and their respective States. To the States, as we have seen, under our system of Government, is due the primary allegiance of the citizen, and the correlative obligation of protection devolves upon the respective States—a duty from which they cannot escape; and which they dare not neglect, without a violation of all the bonds of fealty that hold together the citizen and the sovereign.

The Northern States and their citizens have proved recreant to their obligations under the Federal Constitution; they have violated that compact, and refused to perform their covenants in that behalf.

The Federal Government has failed to protect the rights and property of the citizens of the South, and is about to pass into the hands of a party pledged for the destruction, not only of their rights and their property, but the equality of the States ordained by the Constitution and the heaven-ordained superiority of the white over the black race. What remains then for the Southern States and the people of these States if they are loyal to the great principles of civil and religious liberty, sanctified by the sufferings of a seven-years' war, and baptized with the blood of the revolution? Can they permit the rights of their citizens to be denied and spurned; their property spirited away; their own sovereignty violated, and themselves degraded to the position of mere dependencies instead of sovereign States? Or, shall each for itself, judging of the infractions of the constitutional compact, as well as the mode and measure of redress, declare that the covenants of that sacred instrument in their behalf, and for the benefit of their citizens, have been willfully, deliberately, continuously, and persistently broken and violated by the other parties to the compact, and that they and their citizens are therefore absolved from all further obligations to keep and perform the covenants thereof, resume the powers delegated to the Federal Government, and as sovereign States, form other relations for the protection of their citizens and the discharge of the great ends of government? The Union of these States was one of fraternity as well as equality; but what fraternity now exists between the citizens of the two sections? Various religious associations, powerful in numbers and influence, have been broken asunder, and the sympathy that bound together the people of the several States at the time of the formation of the Constitution has ceased to exist, and feelings of bitterness, and even hostility, have sprung up in its place. How can this be reconciled and a spirit of fraternity established? Will the people of the North cease to make war upon the institution of Slavery, and award to it the protection guaranteed by the Constitution? The accumulated wrongs of many years; the late action of their members in Congress refusing every measure of justice to the South, as well as the experience of all the past, answer, *No, never!*

Will the South give up the institution of slavery and consent that her citizens be stripped of their property, her civilization destroyed, the whole land laid waste by fire and sword? It is impossible; she cannot, she will not. Then why attempt longer to hold together hostile States under the stipulations of a violated constitution? It is impossible; disunion is inevitable. Why then wait longer for the consummation of a result that must come? Why waste further time in expostulations and appeals to Northern States and their citizens, only to be met, as we have been for years past, by renewed insults and repeated injuries? Will the South be better prepared to meet the emergency when the North shall be strengthened by the admission of the new Territories of Kansas, Nebraska, Washington, Jefferson, Nevada, Idaho, Chippewa, and Arizona, as non-slaveholding States, as we are warned from high sources will be done within the next four years, under the administration of Mr. Lincoln? Can the true men at the North ever make a more powerful or successful rally for the preservation of our rights and the constitution than they did in the last Presidential contest? There is nothing to inspire a hope that they can.

Shall we wait until our enemies shall possess themselves of all the powers of the government? until Abolition judges are on the Supreme Court bench, Abolition collectors at every port, and Abolition postmasters in every town, secret mail agents traveling the whole land, and a subsidized press established in our midst, to demoralize the people? Will we be stronger then, or better prepared to meet the struggle, if a struggle must come? No, verily! When that time shall come, well may our adversaries laugh at our folly and deride our impotence. The deliberate judgment of Alabama, as indicated by the joint resolutions of her General Assembly, approved February 24, 1860, is, that prudence, patriotism, and loyalty to all the great principles of civil liberty incorporated in our Constitution, and consecrated by the memories of the past, demand that all the Southern States should now resume their delegated powers, maintain the rights, interests, and honor of their citizens, and vindicate their own sovereignty.[15] And she most earnestly but respectfully invites her sister sovereign State, Kentucky, who so gallantly vindicated the sovereignty of the States in 1798, to the consideration of these grave and vital questions, hoping she may concur with the State of Alabama in the conclusions to which she has been driven by the impending dangers that now surround the Southern States. But if, on mature deliberation, she dissents on any point from the conclusions to which the State of Alabama has arrived, on behalf of that State I most respectfully ask a declaration by this venerable Commonwealth of her conclusions and position on all the issues discussed in this communication. And Alabama most respectfully urges upon the people and authorities of Kentucky the startling truth, that *submission or acquiescence on the part of the Southern States, at this perilous hour, will enable Black Republicanism to redeem all its nefarious pledges, and accomplish all its flagitious ends*; and that hesitation or delay in their action will be misconceived and misconstrued by their adversaries, and ascribed not to that elevated patriotism that would sacrifice all but their honor to save the Union of their fathers, but to division and dissension among themselves and their consequent weakness; that prompt, bold, and decided action is demanded alike by prudence, patriotism, and the safety of their citizens.

Permit me, in conclusion, on behalf of the State of Alabama, to express my high gratification at the cordial manner in which I have been received as her Commissioner by the authorities of the State of Kentucky, as well as the profound personal gratification which, as a son of Kentucky, born and reared within her borders, I feel, at the manner in which I, as the Commissioner from the State of my adoption, have been received and treated by the authorities of the State of my birth. Please accept assurances of the high consideration and esteem of

Your obedient servant, &c., S. F. HALE,

Commissioner from the State of Alabama.

Frankfort, December 27, 1860.

Source: *Journal of the Called Session of the House of Representatives of the Commonwealth of Kentucky, Begun and Held in the Town of Frankfort, on Thursday the Seventeenth Day of January, in the Year of Our Lord 1861, and of the Commonwealth the Sixty-Ninth* (Frankfort: Printed at the Kentucky Yeoman Office, John B. Major, State Printer, 1861), 20–28.

Governor Magoffin's Letter to Stephen Fowler Hale

December 28, 1860

Governor Magoffin quickly responded to Commissioner Hale's letter agreeing with him on his (Hale's) characterization of the "grave political issues" confronting the country, but disagreeing with him that secession was the answer. The "war" waged by the North on the South's peculiar institution was serious and needed to be addressed collectively rather than individually. Magoffin reiterated his belief that the logical solution was to be found in a "full and free conference of all the Southern States." Such a conference, he argued, would result in an amendment to the Constitution that would bring "explicit definition and final recognition" to the "rights of African slavery in the United States, and the relations of the Federal Government to it."

EXECUTIVE DEPARTMENT,
Frankfort, Ky., Dec. 28, 1860.

To HON. S. F. HALE, *Commissioner from the State of Alabama:*

Your communication of the 27th inst., addressed to me by authority of the State of Alabama, has been attentively read.

I concur with you in the opinion that the grave political issues yet pending and undetermined between the slaveholding and non-slaveholding States of the confederacy are of a character to render eminently proper and highly important a full and frank conference on the part of the Southern members, identified, as they undoubtedly are, by a common interest, bound together by mutual sympathies, and with the whole social fabric resting on homogeneous institutions. And coming, as you do, in a spirit of fraternity, by virtue of a commission from a sister Southern State, to confer with the authorities of this State in reference to the measures necessary to be adopted to protect the interests and maintain the honor and safety of the States and their citizens, I extend you a cordial welcome to Kentucky.

You have not exaggerated the grievous wrongs, injuries, and indignities to which the slaveholding States and their citizens have long submitted, with a degree of patience and forbearance justly attributable alone to that elevated patriotism and devotion to the Union which would lead them to sacrifice well nigh all, save honor, to recover the government to its original integrity of administration, and perpetuate the Union upon the basis of equality established by the founders of the Republic. I may even add, that the people of Kentucky, by reason of their geographical position and nearer proximity to those who seem so madly bent upon the destruction of our constitutional guarantees, realize yet more fully than our friends farther South the intolerable wrongs and menacing dangers you have so elaborately recounted. Nor are you, in my opinion, more keenly alive than are the people of this State to the importance of arresting the insane crusade so long waged against our institutions and our society by measures which shall be certainly effective. The rights of African slavery in the United States, and the relations of the Federal Government to it, as an institution in the States and Territories, most assuredly demand at this time explicit definition and final recognition by the North. The slaveholding States are now impelled by the very highest law of self-preservation to demand that this settlement should be concluded upon such a basis as shall not only conserve the institution in localities where it is now recognized, but secure its expansion under no other restrictions than those which the laws of nature may throw around it. That unnecessary conflict between free labor and slave labor but recently inaugurated by the Republican party as an element in our political struggles, must end; and the influence of soil, of climate, and local interests, left unaided and unrestricted save by constitutional limitations, to control the extension of slavery over the public domain. The war upon our social institutions and their guaranteed immunities, waged through the Northern press, religious and secular, and now threatened to be conducted by a dominant political organization through the agency of State Legislatures and the Federal Government, must be ended. Our safety, our honor, and our self-preservation, alike demand that our interests be placed beyond the reach of further assault.

The people of Kentucky may differ variously touching the nature and theory of our complex system of government; but when called upon to pass upon these questions at the polls, I think such an expression would develop no material variance of sentiment touching the wrongs you recite, and the necessity of their prompt adjustment. They fully realize the fatal result of longer forbearance, and appreciate the peril of submission at this juncture. Kentucky would leave no effort untried to preserve the Union of the States upon the basis of the Constitution as we construe it; but Kentucky will never submit to wrong or dishonor, let resistance cost what it may. Unqualified acquiescence in the administration of the government upon the Chicago platform,[16] in view of the movements already inaugurated at the South, and the avowed purposes of the representative men of the Republican party, would, I feel assured, receive no favor in this State, whether her citizens shall in the last resort throw themselves upon the right of revolution as the inherent right of a free people never surrendered, or shall assert the doctrine of secession, can be of little practical import. When the time for action comes—and it is now fearfully near at hand—our people will be found rallied as a unit under the flag of resistance to intolerable wrong; and being thus consolidated in feeling and action, I may well forego any discussion of the abstract theories to which one party or another may hold to cover their resistance.

It is true that, as sovereign political communities, the States must determine, each for itself, the grave issues now presented; and it may be that when driven to the dire extremity of severing their relations with the Federal Government, formal independent separate State action will be proper and necessary. But resting, as do these political communities, upon a common social organization, constituting the sole object of attack and invasion, confronted by a common enemy, encompassed by a common peril, in a word, involved in one common cause, it does seem to me that the mode and manner of defense and redress should be determined in a full and free conference of all the Southern States, and that their mutual safety requires full co-operation in carrying out the measures there agreed upon. The source whence oppression is now to be apprehended is an organized power, a political Government in operation, to which resistance, though ultimately successful—and I do not for a moment question the issue—might be costly and destructive. We should look these facts in the face, nor close our eyes to what we may reasonably expect to encounter. I have therefore thought that a due regard to the opinions of all the slaveholding States would require that those measures which concern all alike, and must ultimately involve all, should be agreed upon in common convention, and sustained by united action.

I have before expressed the belief and confidence, and do not now totally yield the hope, that if such a convention of delegates from the slaveholding States be assembled, and, after calm deliberation, present to the political party now holding the dominance of power in the Northern States, and soon to assume the reins of national power, the firm alternative of ample guarantees to all our rights and security for future immunity, or resistance, our just demands would be conceded, and the Union be perpetuated stronger than before. Such an issue so presented to the Congress of the United States, and to the Legislatures and people of the Northern States—and it is practicable in abundant time before the Government has passed into other hands—would come with a moral force which, if not potent to control the votes of the representative men, might produce a voice from their constituents which would influence them. But if it fail, our cause would emerge, if possible, stronger, fortified by the approbation of the whole conservative sentiment of the country, and supported by a host of Northern friends who would prove in the ultimate issue most valuable allies. After such an effort, every man in the slaveholding States would feel satisfied that all had been done which could be done to preserve the legacy bequeathed us by the patriots of '76 and the statesmen of '89, and the South would stand in solid unbroken phalanx, a unit. In the brief time left, it seems to me impracticable to effect this object through the agency of commissioners sent to the different States. A convention of authorized delegates is the true mode of bringing about co-operation among the Southern States, and to that movement I would respectfully ask your attention, and through you solicit the co-operation of Alabama. There is yet another subject upon which the very highest considerations appeal for a united southern expression.

On the 4th of March next, the Federal Government, unless contingencies now unlooked for occur, will pass into the control of the Republican party. So far as the policy of the incoming administration is foreshadowed in the antecedents of the President elect, in the enunciations of its Representative men, and the avowals of the press, it will be to ignore the acts of sovereignty thus proclaimed by Southern States, and of coercing the continuance of the Union, its inevitable result will be civil war of the most fearful and revolting character. Now, however the people of the South may differ as to the mode and measure of redress, I take it that the fifteen slaveholding States are united in opposition to such a policy, and would stand in solid column to resist the application of force by the Federal authority to coerce the seceding States. But it is of the utmost importance that before such a policy is attempted to be inaugurated, the voice of the South should be heard in potential, official, and united protest. Possibly the incoming administration would not be so dead to reason as, after such an expression, to persist in throwing the country into civil war, and we may thereby avert the calamity. An attempt "to enforce the laws" by blockading two or three Southern States would be regarded as quite a different affair from a declaration of war against thirteen millions of freemen, and if Mr. Lincoln and his advisers be made to realize that such would be the issue of the "force policy," it will be abandoned. Should we not realize to our enemies that consequence and avert the disastrous results? But if our enemies be crazed by victory and power, and madly persist in their purpose, the South will be better prepared to resist.

You ask the co-operation of the Southern States in order to redress our wrongs; so do we. You have no hope of a redress in the Union. We yet look hopefully to assurances that a powerful reaction is going on at the North. You seek a remedy in secession from the Union. We wish the united action of the slave States assembled in convention within the Union. You would act separately; we unitedly. If Alabama and the other slave States would meet us in convention, say at Nashville or elsewhere, as early as the 5th day of February, I do not doubt that we would agree in forty-eight hours upon such reasonable guarantees, by way of amendment to the Constitution of the

United States, as would command at least the approbation of our numerous friends, in the free States, and by giving them time to make the question with the people there, such a reaction in public opinion might yet take place as to secure us our rights, and save the government. If the effort failed, the South would be united to a man, the North divided, the horrors of civil war would be averted—if any thing can avert the calamity; and if that be not possible, we would be in a better position to meet the dreadful collision. By such action, too, if it failed to preserve the government, the basis of another confederacy would have been agreed upon, and the new government would in this mode be launched into operation much more speedily and easily than by the action you propose.

In addition to the foregoing, I have the honor to refer you to my letter of the 16th ult., to the Editor of the Yeoman, and to my letter to the Governors of the slave States, dated the 9th December, herewith transmitted to you, which, together with what I have said in this communication, embodies, with all due deference to the opinions of others, in my judgment, the principles, policy, and position which the slave States ought to maintain.

The Legislature of Kentucky will assemble on the 17th of January, when the sentiment of the State will doubtless find official expression. Meantime, if the action of Alabama shall be arrested until the conference she has sought can be concluded by communication with that department of the government, I shall be pleased to transmit to the Legislature your views. I regret to have seen in the recent messages of two or three of our Southern sister States a recommendation of the passage of laws prohibiting the purchase by the citizens of those States, of the slaves of the border slaveholding States. Such a course is not only liable to the objection so often urged by us against the Abolitionists of the North of an endeavor to prohibit the slave trade between the States, but is likewise wanting in that fraternal feeling which should be common to States which are identified in their institutions and interests. It affords me pleasure, however, to add, as an act of justice to your State, that I have seen no indication of such a purpose on the part of Alabama. It would certainly be considered an act of injustice for the border slaveholding States to prohibit, by their legislation, the purchase of the products of the cotton-growing States, even though it be founded upon the mistaken policy of protection to their own interests.

I cannot close this correspondence without again expressing to you my gratification in receiving you as the honored Commissioner from your proud and chivalrous State, and at your courteous, able, dignified, and manly bearing in discharging the solemn and important duties which have been assigned to you.

I have the honor to be, with sentiments of high consideration,

Your friend and obedient servant,
B. MAGOFFIN.

Source: *Journal of the Called Session of the House of Representatives of the Commonwealth of Kentucky, Begun and Held in the Town of Frankfort, on Thursday the Seventeenth Day of January, in the Year of Our Lord 1861, and of the Commonwealth the Sixty-Ninth* (Frankfort: Printed at the Kentucky Yeoman Office, John B. Major, State Printer, 1861), 28–32.

Governor Magoffin's Address to the Kentucky General Assembly

January 17, 1861

When Magoffin addressed Kentucky's general assembly on January 17, South Carolina, Mississippi, Florida, and Alabama had already declared their independence from the United States. The withdrawal of the eight senators and nineteen representatives from those four states effectively turned control of both the Senate and the House of Representatives over to the Republican Party for the remainder of the Thirty-Sixth Congress. With secession now a reality, the governor reiterated his belief that a "convention of the slaveholding States," could arrest the dismemberment of the Union if it adopted Crittenden's proposed amendment.

Magoffin could not help but engage in a bit of hyperbole when he announced that with Lincoln's election "the Federal Government will be committed to the control of the Republican Party." Magoffin had apparently forgotten that in his November letter to the editor of the *Yeoman* he had reminded his readers that Republicans had won the executive branch but lost both houses of Congress to the Democrats. It was not Lincoln's election that gave Republicans control of the federal government (except, of course, over the Supreme Court), but the secession of southern states. In addition, while invoking the threat posed by the Chicago platform adopted by the Republican Party, Magoffin failed to mention that that platform contained a plank reiterating the party's conviction that each state had the constitutional right to "order and control its own domestic institutions, to its own judgment exclusively."

Gentlemen of the Senate and House of Representatives:

When in March last the Legislature adjourned, and with kind remembrances of the winter's association you separated for your respective homes, I did not apprehend that alarming complication of our federative system which has rendered imperative upon me your convocation in extraordinary session. The Republic seemed then launched upon a career of limitless national prosperity, while its citizens enjoyed an aggregate of domestic and social happiness unequaled in the condition of any other people. Covering twenty-three degrees of latitude, and sixty degrees of longitude, our territory was nearly equal to that of all Europe, and embraced a soil of unsurpassed fertility, adapted by every pleasing variety of climate to all the products of the earth. Our commerce, sustained by an extended system of internal improvements reaching, through the media of turnpikes, canals, rivers, and inland seas, to the very heart of every section of the country, and finding its outlets upon the Atlantic and Pacific oceans, and upon the Gulf of Mexico, may be said to have commanded the markets of the world. The keels of our steamers plowed every ocean, and the seas and navigable streams of the most remote regions were whitened by the sails of our merchant vessels. Our people, numbering thirty millions of freemen of all nations and races, and realizing as the fruit of their industry, $2,000,000,000 in annual productions; by their great and thriving cities; by their magnificent churches, school-houses, colleges, and charitable institutions; by their progress in agriculture and manufactures; by their advance in the arts and sciences, gave unmistakable evidence of a degree of internal prosperity not reached by the same number of people under any other form of government. In view of these great blessings and encouraging signs, the glorious results of less than a century's growth of the Republic, I had fondly hoped the union of the States would be perpetual, and did not doubt that the next cycle of fifty years would more than realize the poet's wildest dream.

With a heavy heart I turn to contemplate the present condition of our once happy country. At the very time when every industrial pursuit was yielding its highest remuneration, we have witnessed a stagnation in trade. The earth has responded with an abundant harvest to the enlightened cultivation of the agriculturalists; but while the crop awaits transportation to market, commerce is paralyzed, and the laws of exchange disordered. The business of the country was never in a more healthy condition, nor our people in the main more prosperous; yet credit is destroyed, confidence lost, and financial ruin imminent. These phenomena can only find their explanation in the troubled condition of our political affairs. We, the people of the United States, are no longer one people, united and friendly. The ties of fraternal love and concord, which once bound us together, are sundered. Though the Union of the States may, by the abstract reasoning of a class, be construed still to exist, it is really and practically, to an extent at least, fatally impaired. The confederacy is rapidly resolving into its original integral parts, and its late loyal members are intent upon contracting wholly new relations. Reluctant as we may be to realize the dread calamity, the great FACT OF REVOLUTION stares us in the face, *demands recognition*, and will not be theorized away. Nor is the worst yet told. We are not yet encouraged to hope that this revolution will be bloodless. A collision of arms has even now occurred between the Federal Government and the authorities of a late member of the Union, and the issue threatens to involve the whole country in fratricidal war.[17] It is under these circumstances of peculiar gloom that you have been summoned. To your trust must now be committed, in great measure, the destinies of our beloved State, and upon you devolves the solemn responsibility of so wielding the accorded influence of Kentucky in this momentous crisis, as shall conserve the honor and happiness of our people and promote the good of all. I can only beseech you, by all you hold dear in this sad hour of our country's peril, to cast aside old party affiliations, and, looking facts full in the face as they actually exist, to address yourselves earnestly to the great work before you.

Our present unfortunate political complications are the legitimate scions of underlying causes against which all the great conservative statesmen of the age have solemnly warned their countrymen. A political organization based upon the one idea of hostility to the institution of African slavery, and embodying as one of its material elements of strength, an intolerant sectional fanaticism, has been for years steadily gathering power in the non-slaveholding States, and has at last exhibited national ascendancy in the election of Abraham Lincoln, its faithful exponent, to the Presidency of the United States. It is true that triumph was reached through all the forms of law, but it was effected by the agency of purely sectional votes, and rests upon sectional animosity. By virtue of that election, the Federal Government will be committed to the control of the Republican party, and administered upon a platform of principles destructive to our rightful equality as States and citizens, and fatal to the stability and security of our whole social organization.

Receiving the verdict pronounced on the 6th of November last as the deliberate expression of the sentiments of the citizens of the North, and as indicative of the settled purpose of the dominant party to administer the Government detrimentally to their vital interests, the people of several Southern States, immediately upon its announcement, initiated movements looking to the speedy severance of their relations with the other States and with the General Government. These movements progressed with startling rapidity, and were sustained by such unanimity of feeling in the several States as rendered all resistance idle and useless. Meantime patriotic efforts have not been wanting to effect an adjustment of the difficulties and restore the former friendly relations of the States; but I regret to say, to this hour with little hope of success.

My humble endeavors have been earnestly addressed to the work of bringing about a convention of the slaveholding States, believing that their united voice in demanding just and reasonable guarantees against the future invasion of their constitutional rights by the dominant power would achieve the object and reunite the States. Had such a movement been early initiated in the border States, I am assured it would have been favorably responded to by the whole South, in which event I firmly believe our embarrassments would ere this have presented fair prospect of adjustment. But the proposition met with limited favor here, was violently assailed, and the time passed. It is now too late. The revolution has progressed beyond that point.

Soon after the election of Mr. Lincoln, in order to place Kentucky, as far as I could, in her true position, and in answer to continued inquiries for my views, I addressed a letter to the Editor of the Kentucky Yeoman, which is herewith transmitted to you as embodying a more elaborate expression of my opinions.

On the 9th of December last, believing there was still a hope of bringing about united action on the part of the slaveholding States, I addressed a letter to the Governors of the Southern States, urging a conference with a view to an adjustment on the basis therein presented. That paper is herewith submitted to your consideration.[18]

On the 27th of December the Hon. S. F. Hale, a commissioner from the

State of Alabama, called upon me at the seat of Government and communicated to me in writing the purpose of his commission. I responded in writing, again urging the importance of conference by the slaveholding States, and still clinging to the hope that such action would elicit a patriotic response from the Northern people, if not from the Representative men of that section. That correspondence is also now transmitted to you.

A Commissioner from the State of Mississippi, Hon. Mr. Featherston,[19] also called upon me in December, on a similar mission. I gave him verbally the same response.

In Congress the efforts of the friends of the Union have not been more successful. Various propositions for adjustment have been made, and measures without number submitted to the Republican members for their approbation, as alternatives of a disruption of the Government. But a radical difference of principle was found to be an insurmountable obstacle to every proposed scheme. The recognition by the government of property in slaves, its inviolability in the States, and protection in the Territories, constituted the basis of the demands of the South. The Republicans maintain towards this principle an unyielding opposition. And herein lies the great impediment to all compromise. Parties resting upon principles so directly antagonistic can not, without material concession, unite upon any measure involving the subject of difference.

Among other propositions of compromise offered, I beg to call your attention to the constitutional amendments proposed by our own distinguished Senator, the Hon. John J. Crittenden, and ask for them an expression of your approbation. While they do not secure to the slave States the full measure of their constitutional equality, I should be willing, in view of their practical value, to accept them rather than dissolution. Certainly these guarantees, asked by the resolutions of Mr. Crittenden, are the least security the South can with safety accept; and their distinguished author estimated aright the sentiment of our people when he expressed the opinion that Kentucky would not be content with less. But I regret to say that even these fair, just, and moderate demands have been sternly rejected by the dominant party. Insensible to the direful calamity impending over us, crazed by power or blinded by fanaticism, the representative men of the Republican party, leaders whose words control the opinions of millions of misguided disciples, voted in a body against every proposition embodied in the amendments moved by Mr. Crittenden. They have gone even further. They announce in the halls of

Congress and through the press, in public places and in private circles, that they have no compromise to make, no concessions to offer, and no assurances to give other than that the Federal Government will be administered by Mr. Lincoln in accordance with the principles of the Republican (Chicago) platform.

Thus firm in position, obstinate in spirit, and sullen in temper, the Republicans have thwarted every scheme devised to restrain the seceding States. Instead of retarding, their unsuccessful efforts at adjustment have rather precipitated disunion. The secession feeling has gathered strength every day, extended throughout the cotton and sugar-growing States, and is now encroaching upon those nearer the confines of the non-slaveholding sections. On the 20th of December, South Carolina, by the unanimous vote of a Convention of Delegates fresh from the people, passed an ordinance of secession, severing her relations with the United States, and reassuming her original sovereignty. On the ——day of January, the State of Mississippi, by a vote of her people approaching unanimity, assumed a like position among the nations of the world.[20] Alabama and Florida, a few days after, announced to the world similar action.[21] Georgia, Louisiana, Arkansas, and Texas have unmistakably indicated their purpose to assume like independence.

It now seems inevitable, that before your deliberations will probably close, eight States will have withdrawn from the confederacy, and most probably will be in consultation touching the organization of a new Federative Government. It cannot be successfully responded in refutation of this presentation of facts, that the secession ordinances are nullities. I have no disposition at such a time to indulge a discussion touching the abstract questions which might be raised. We have to deal with facts as actually existing, and have no use for hair-splitting theories. I assume, that in a very few days eight States will have declared their sovereign independence, and that, to that extent at least, our Union will have ceased to exist, inasmuch as no power on earth can coerce their unwilling allegiance to the Federal Government. In that contingency, now so imminent as to be almost a certainty upon which you may safely project your action, what attitude shall Kentucky assume, and by virtue of what authority shall her external relations be hereafter determined?

Kentucky will not submit to the degradation of inequality in the Union. Conscious of the will and ability of her citizens to maintain their honor, their rights, and freedom, she will protect them in the Union or out of it. Kentucky has to this hour borne herself with the dignity, the forbearance, and the moderation becoming her historic character. She has borne much, and will bear much for the cause of the Union. But in my opinion the people of Kentucky will never consent to remain in this confederacy, now abandoned by a large portion of the slaveholding members, with no guarantees of protection from the anti-slavery power now dominant. Kentucky will not and ought not to submit to the principles and policy avowed by the Republican party, but will resist, and resist to the death, if necessary.

But I recall the suggestive inquiry just put. In view of the partial disruption of the Union, the secession of eight or ten States, the establishment of a Southern Confederated Republic, and the administration of this Government upon the principles of the Chicago platform—a condition of our country most likely near at hand—what attitude will Kentucky hold, and by virtue of what authority shall her external relations be determined? Herein are involved issues of momentous consequence to the people. It is of vital importance to our own safety and domestic peace that these questions be solved in accordance with the will of the majority of our people. How have our neighboring States prepared to meet this emergency? Tennessee has, through the action of her Legislature, referred the whole subject to her people, to be passed upon in their sovereign capacity.[22] Virginia and North Carolina are discussing the propriety of a similar course, and will most probably authorize the people, through sovereignty conventions, to dispose of questions so deeply and vitally concerning their interests.[23] Missouri seems likely to adopt a similar policy.[24] These States wisely recognize the fact that the country is in a state of revolution, and it seems to me there is an eminent propriety, at such a time, in a direct appeal to the people. The ordinary departments of the Government are vested with no power to conduct the State through such a revolution. Any attempt by either of these departments to change our present external relations, would involve a usurpation of power, and might not command that confidence and secure the unanimity so essential to our internal safety. Thus encompassed by embarrassment, complication, and doubt, assailed by a diversity of counsels, and encountering much variety of opinion, it seems to me that the wisest, as certainly the safest mode of meeting the extraordinary emergency, is to adopt the course pursued by our neighboring States, and refer these great questions to the arbitrament of the people, whose happiness and destinies they so deeply affect. We should in this mode secure unity among ourselves, and attract the cordial loyalty of all our citizens to Kentucky wherever she may cast her lot. I therefore submit to your consideration the propriety of providing for the election of delegates to a convention, to be assembled at an early day, to whom shall be referred, for full and final determination, the future Federal and inter-State relations of Kentucky.

Meantime I would leave no expedient untried which promises, however faintly, the restoration of fraternal relations between the States, and offers even remote hope of again reuniting the members and rescuing the Union from its present peril. We seem to be drifting in a gale upon the rocks of disunion. Let us make one more, one united, one last effort to save the old ship. Although she has never encountered such a tempest, she has weathered many fearful storms. Anchor after anchor has been thrown out to save her, but she still drifts before the swelling waves upon the fearful breakers—hull and cabin and deck are creaking and cracking, and every joint and bolt and timber is strained to its utmost tension. There should be no divided counsels now. Let us throw overboard former jealousies, past party affiliations, passions, and personal ambition. Let us make one more effort to save her all together; and if she is lost, let us cling to the noble wreck, and reconstruct the vessel from the staunch old timbers of the Constitution. There is hope that an adjustment, honorable to all, may be effected through the action of the border slave States, including Tennessee and North Carolina. Their approval of the amendments to the constitution proposed by Senator Crittenden, with security for their future observance, presented to Congress, to the free States in legislative session, and to the people if practicable, as an ultimatum, may yet secure the guarantees we require, and possibly in the end bring back all the States in one Union. To this last effort a convention of these States is necessary. I would, therefore, recommend to you the adoption of resolutions inviting a conference of these States, and of such others as may choose to co-operate, at Baltimore, for an early day in February. It will then devolve upon you to provide for the appointment of Commissioners to represent Kentucky. The conjoint declaration of these States against coercion might do much to avert impending war. Their united co-operation in any event, would materially promote their future safety and peace.

The relations of the Federal Government with the seceding States have occasioned the most anxious solicitude with those who have at heart the peace and tranquility of the country. I had hoped that when the secession movement or the revolution, had assumed its present aspect, when four sovereign States, by the almost unanimous vote of their people,[25] had announced their purpose to close their past federal relations, and likely soon to be joined by four others, there would be found none so mad, none so blind to the dire results, as to advise or countenance the employment of military force in futile resistance to their action. Such a proposition, whether it be called plainly coercion and subjugation, or be disguised under the specious phrases of "enforcing the laws" and "protecting public property," means civil war, and war of the most frightful and abhorrent character. I can but regard the action of the Federal Government in refusing to recognize the *fact* of secession, and its proposed attempt to maintain the supremacy of its laws within the borders of the seceding States, as a policy more utterly barren of good result, and more certainly fraught with calamity, than any step yet taken in the drama. This government stands upon the consent of the governed: its internal strength springs from the voluntary allegiance of the citizens; it is sustained by the common affection, the mutual confidence, and fraternal feelings of the people. It cannot be held together by force, and the attempt so to sustain it will not only fail, and fail in blood, but will destroy the last hope of reconstruction. Kentucky cannot and will not be an indifferent observer of the "force policy." The seceding States have not in their hasty and inconsiderate action our approval; but their cause is our rights, and they have our sympathies. The people of Kentucky will never stand by with arms folded while those States struggling for their constitutional rights and resisting oppression are being subjugated to an anti-slavery Government. Thousands of our gallant citizens would fly to the conflict. Moreover, the idea of coercion, when applied to great political communities, is revolting to a free people, contrary to the spirit of our institutions, and if successfully prosecuted, would endanger the liberties of the people. I cannot believe that these threats of coercion, nor these denunciations of treason against the people of the South, coming as they do from men who have for years habitually violated the Constitution, elicit any sympathy in the hearts of Kentuckians, no matter what may be their opinions touching the abstract right or present policy of secession. I trust, therefore, you will at once declare by resolution the unconditional disapprobation of Kentucky of the employment of force in any form against the seceding States.

It becomes my duty to call your attention to another subject, if possible, affecting more nearly the safety of our people, the importance of which is suggested by the political complications hereinbefore presented. I allude to the subject of our State military organization. I have the gratification to communicate to you that, under the admirably drawn and well adapted "Militia Law" enacted by you at your regular session in March last, an organization of companies, battalions, and regiments has been effected, than which I can recommend none more reliable and efficient. Copies of this law have been sought for by those having in charge the military organizations of other States, and it now constitutes the basis of the system in more than one State. I was particularly fortunate in securing the services of Gen. S. B. Buckner,[26] a native Kentuckian, in the responsible position of Inspector General. He has brought to the position an amount of experience, ability, and patriotic labor, to which I attribute, in a great measure, the present highly encouraging condition of the corps. His report, giving full information on the subject, will be communicated to you, and to it your attention is invited. Our people seem thoroughly aroused to the importance of a thorough and effective military corps, sufficient for any and all emergencies. You will readily perceive the necessity of extending them all proper aid and encouragement.

An appropriation of money for the purpose of more efficiently arming, equipping, uniforming, and providing munitions of war for this corps of volunteer soldiers, now constituting the main defense of our people, will be regarded by you as among your first and most imperative duties. No man can foresee the issue of our present political troubles. It becomes our duty to prepare for the worst, and look carefully to the security and safety of our citizens. But this subject is of such manifest importance as to need no argument from me. I refer to the report of the Inspector General for full information touching the condition of our military defenses at this time, and the further provision needed.

Accompanying the message you have a statement from the Auditor, showing the financial condition of the State on the 15th day of this month. I have caused this exhibit to be made, that you may understand the necessity of providing for a revenue sufficient to meet the extraordinary expenditures likely to become unavoidable.

While I would appreciate your disinclination to permit your attention to be diverted at this time from the grave subjects already presented, by any matters of ordinary legislation, I cannot forego the mention to you of a calamity which, since your last adjournment has withdrawn from a large number of unfortunates the munificent provision made for them by the State. On the —— day of——— last the large building devoted to the care of the insane at Hopkinsville was completely destroyed by fire. Fortunately the calamity was attended with little loss of life, but the inmates were subjected to no small discomfort. The report of the commissioners, giving full information on the subject, will, in a few days, be submitted to you. You will see the necessity of rebuilding the asylum and providing for the comfort and support of the patients. No matter how pressed by the burdens of government, the people of Kentucky will never complain of taxation when levied for the support of the unfortunate insane.

Since your last adjournment, a controversy has arisen between this State and the State of Ohio, touching the rendition of a fugitive from the justice of the laws of Kentucky, escaped into Ohio. The questions arising in the controversy are novel and interesting, and of a character affecting very nearly the rights of our State, and the security of the citizens. The facts will appear from the correspondence between the Governor of Ohio and myself, to which you are referred. On the 23d of December, at my direction, a petition was filed in the Supreme Court of the United States, praying a mandamus or a rule to show cause, directed to the Governor of Ohio, the argument of which, I am advised, will be heard on the 8th of February. I have employed learned and competent counsel, who will guard well and ably the interests of the State. An appropriation of $—— will be necessary to meet the cost and necessary expenses of the case.

Feeling, in this day of our country's trial and calamity, the necessity of Divine assistance, invoking His aid in shaping your deliberations and beseeching His blessing upon your efforts to save the country, I will take pleasure in co-operating with you in any just measures calculated to bring about this result.

B. MAGOFFIN.

Source: *Journal of the Called Session of the House of Representatives of the Commonwealth of Kentucky, Begun and Held in the Town of Frankfort, on Thursday the Seventeenth Day of January, in the Year of Our Lord 1861, and of the Commonwealth the Sixty-Ninth* (Frankfort: Printed at the Kentucky Yeoman Office, John B. Major, State Printer, 1861), 4–11.

CHAPTER TWO

Constitutional Amendment Proposed by Senator John Jordan Crittenden

John J. Crittenden (1786–1863), at age seventy-four, was the elder statesman of the Thirty-Sixth Congress. He had served as the governor of Kentucky, United States Attorney General (twice), and intermittently in the United States Senate being elected a second time in 1842 to fill Henry Clay's vacated seat. Crittenden had opposed the annexation of Texas, the subsequent war with Mexico, and the Kansas-Nebraska Act. In 1860, he helped found the Constitutional Union Party.

Throughout his political career, Crittenden was associated with fellow Kentuckian Henry Clay who was ten years his senior. Unfettered by Clay's lust for the presidency, Crittenden benefitted from Clay's mentoring in their home state as well as in Congress where they served together as Kentucky's senators between 1835 and 1842. Clay was nationally recognized as the "Great Compromiser" because of his ability to craft political solutions to the 1820 Missouri statehood issue, the tariff controversy of the 1830s, and the 1850 debate over slavery in the land acquired from Mexico. Over Secession Winter, Crittenden hoped to emulate Clay in finding a skillful solution to the secession crisis.

Crittenden first proposed his amendment on December 18, 1860, with a long introductory speech to the full Senate. Four days later he proposed the same amendment to the Senate's Committee of Thirteen, chaired by Kentucky's Lazarus Powell. On January 3, 1861, Crittenden introduced Senate Resolution 54 that included his original proposal with an added seventh article that would have 1) prohibited all "persons who are, in whole or in part, of the African race," from voting or holding elected office at all levels of government, and 2) given Congress the authority to acquire land in Africa and South America for the colonization of "free negroes and mulattoes." The added article, Crittenden acknowledged, had been borrowed from Senator Stephen A. Douglas's proposed amendment submitted to the Committee of Thirteen on Christmas Eve 1860. Crittenden's Senate Resolution 54 was recommended to the Washington Peace Conference by Kentucky delegate James B. Clay on February 26, 1861, and is reproduced in chapter 6.

Senator Crittenden's Speech to the US Senate (Whig/American/Unionist)

December 18, 1860

Compromise of the Slavery Question.

Mr. CRITTENDEN. I am gratified, Mr. President, to see in the various propositions which have been made, such a universal anxiety to save the country from the dangerous dissensions which now prevail; and I have, under a very serious view and without the least ambitious feeling whatever connected with it, prepared a series of constitutional amendments, which I desire to offer to the Senate, hoping that they may form, in part at least, some basis for measures that may settle the controverted questions which now so much agitate our country. Certainly, sir, I do not propose now any elaborate discussion of the subject. Before presenting these resolutions, however, to the Senate, I desire to make a few remarks explanatory of them, that the Senate may understand their general scope.

The questions of an alarming character are those which have grown out of the controversy between the northern and southern sections of our country in relation to the rights of the slaveholding States in the Territories of the United States, and in relation to the rights of the citizens of the latter in their slaves. I have endeavored by these resolutions to meet all these questions and causes of discontent, and by amendments to the Constitution of the United States, so that the settlement, if we can happily agree on any, may be permanent, and leave no cause for future controversy. These resolutions propose, then, in the first place, in substance, the restoration of the Missouri compromise, extending the line throughout the Territories of the United States to the eastern border of California, recognizing slavery in all the territory south of that line, and prohibiting slavery in all the territory north of it; with a provision, however, that when any of those Territories, north or south, are formed into States, they shall then be at liberty to exclude or admit slavery as they please; and that, in the one case or the other, it shall be no objection to their admission into the Union. In this way, sir, I propose to settle the question, both as to territory and slavery, so far as it regards the Territories of the United States.

I propose, sir, also, that the Constitution shall be so amended as to declare that Congress shall have no power to abolish slavery in the District of Columbia so long as slavery exists in the States of Maryland and Virginia; and that they shall have no power to abolish slavery in any of the places under their special jurisdiction within the southern States.

These are the constitutional amendments which I propose, and embrace the whole of them in regard to the questions of territory and slavery. There are other propositions in relation to grievances, and in relation to controversies, which I suppose are within the jurisdiction of Congress, and may be removed by the action of Congress. I propose, in regard to legislative action, that the fugitive slave law, as it is commonly called, shall be declared by the Senate to be a constitutional act, in strict pursuance of the Constitution. I propose to declare, that it has been decided by the Supreme Court of the United States to be constitutional, and that the southern States are entitled to a faithful and complete execution of that law, and that no amendment shall be made hereafter to it which will impair its efficiency. But, thinking that it would not impair its efficiency, I have proposed amendments to it in two particulars. I have understood from gentlemen of the North that there is objection to the provision giving a different fee where the commissioner decides to deliver the slave to the claimant, from that which is given where he decides to discharge the alleged slave; the law declares that in the latter case he shall have but five dollars, while in the other he shall have ten dollars—twice the amount in one case than in the other. The reason for this is very obvious. In case he delivers the servant to his claimant, he is required to draw out a lengthy certificate, stating the principal and substantial grounds on which his decision rests, and to return him either to the marshal or to the claimant to remove him to the State from which he escaped. It was for that reason that a larger fee was given to the commissioner, where he had the largest service to perform. But, sir, the act being viewed unfavorably and with great prejudice, in a certain portion of our country, this was regarded as very obnoxious, because it seemed to give an inducement to the commissioner to return the slave to the master, as he thereby obtained the larger fee of ten dollars instead of the smaller one of five dollars. I have said, let the fee be the same in both cases.

I have understood, furthermore, sir, that inasmuch as the fifth section of that law was worded somewhat vaguely, its general terms had admitted of the construction in the northern States that all the citizens were required, upon the summons of the marshal, to go with him to hunt up, as they express it, and arrest the slave; and this is regarded as obnoxious. They have said, "in the southern States you make no such requisition on the citizen;" nor do we, sir. The section, construed according to the intentions of the framers of it, I suppose, only intended that the marshal should have the same right in the execution of process for the arrest of a slave that he has in all other cases of process that he is required to execute—to call on the *posse comitatus* for assistance where he is resisted in the execution of his duty, or where, having executed his duty by the arrest, an attempt is made to rescue the slave. I propose such an amendment as will obviate this difficulty and limit the right of the master and the duty of the citizen to cases where, as in regard to all other process, persons may be called upon to assist in resisting opposition to the execution of the laws.

I have provided further, sir, that the amendments to the Constitution which I here propose, and certain other provisions of the Constitution itself, shall be unalterable, thereby forming a permanent and unchangeable basis for peace and tranquility among the people. Among the provisions in the present Constitution, which I have by amendment proposed to render unalterable, is that provision in the first article of the Constitution which provides the rule for representation, including in the computation three fifths of the slaves.[1] That is to be rendered unchangeable. Another is the provision for the delivery of fugitive slaves. That is to be rendered unchangeable.

And with these provisions, Mr. President, it seems to me we have a solid foundation upon which we may rest our hopes for the restoration of peace and good-will among all the States of the Union, and all the people. I propose, sir, to enter into no particular discussion. I have explained the general scope and object of my proposition. I have provided further, which I ought to mention, that, there having been some difficulties experienced in the courts of the United States in the South in carrying into execution the laws prohibiting the African slave trade, all additions and amendments which may be necessary to those laws to render them effectual should be immediately adopted by Congress, and especially the provisions of those laws which prohibit the importation of African slaves into the United States. I have further provided it as a recommendation to all the States of this Union, that whereas laws have been passed of an unconstitutional character, (and all laws are of that character which either conflict with the constitutional acts of Congress, or which in their operation hinder or delay the proper execution of the acts of Congress,) which laws are null and void, and yet, though null and void, they have been the source of mischief and discontent in the country, under the extraordinary circumstances in which we are placed; I have supposed that it would not be improper or unbecoming in Congress to recommend to the States, both North and South, the repeal of all such acts of theirs as were intended to control, or intended to obstruct the operation of the acts of Congress, or which in their operation and in their application have been made use of for the purpose of such hindrance and opposition, and that they will repeal these laws or make such explanations or corrections of them as to prevent their being used for any such mischievous purpose.

I have endeavored to look with impartiality from one end of our country to the other; I have endeavored to search up what appeared to me to be the causes of discontent pervading the land; and, as far as I am capable of doing so, I have endeavored to propose a remedy for them. I am far from believing that, in the shape in which I present these measures, they will meet with the acceptance of the Senate. It will be sufficiently gratifying if, with all the amendments that the superior knowledge of the Senate may make to them, they shall, to any effectual extent, quiet the country.

Mr. President, great dangers surround us. The Union of these States is dear to the people of the United States. The long experience of its blessings, the mighty hopes of the future, have made it dear to the hearts of the American people. Whatever politicians may say; whatever of dissension may, in the heat of party politics, be created among our people, when you come down to the question of the existence of the Constitution, that is a question beyond all party politics; that is a question of life and death. The Constitution and the Union are the life of this great people—yes, sir, the life of life. We all desire to preserve them, North and South; that is the universal desire. But some of the southern States, smarting under what they conceive to be aggressions of their northern brethren and of the northern States, are not contented to continue this Union, and are taking steps, formidable steps, towards a dissolution of the Union, and towards the anarchy and the bloodshed, I fear, that are to follow. I say, sir, we are in the presence of great events. We must elevate ourselves to the level of the great occasion. No party warfare about mere party questions or party measures ought now to engage our attention. They are left behind; they are as dust in the balance. The life, the existence of our country, of our Union, is the mighty question; and we must elevate ourselves to all those considerations which belong to this high subject.

I hope, therefore, gentlemen will be disposed to bring the sincerest spirit of conciliation, the sincerest spirit and desire to adjust all these difficulties, and to think nothing of any little concessions of opinions that they may make, if thereby the Constitution and the country can be preserved.

The great difficulty here, sir—I know it; I recognize it as the difficult question, particularly with the gentlemen from the North—is the admission of this line of division for the territory, and the recognition of slavery on the one side, and the prohibition of it on the other. The recognition of slavery on the southern side of that line is the great difficulty, the great question with them. Now, I beseech them to think, and you, Mr. President, and all, to think whether, for such a comparative trifle as that, the Union of this country is to be sacrificed. Have we realized to ourselves the momentous consequences of such an event? When has the world seen such an event? This is a mighty empire. Its existence spreads its influence throughout the civilized world. Its overthrow will be the greatest shock that civilization and free government have received; more extensive in its consequences; more fatal to mankind and to the great principles upon which the liberty of mankind depends, than the French revolution with all its blood, and with all its war and violence. And all for what? Upon questions concerning this line of division between slavery and freedom? Why, Mr. President, suppose this day all the southern States, being refused this right; being refused this partition; being denied this privilege, were to separate from the northern States, and do it peacefully, and then were to come to you peacefully and say, "let there be no war between us; let us divide fairly the Territories of the United States:" could the northern section of the country refuse so just a demand? What would you then give them? What would be the fair proportion? If you allowed them their fair relative proportion, would you not give them as much as is now proposed to be assigned on the southern side of that line, and would they not be at liberty to carry their slaves there, if they pleased? You would give them the whole of that; and then what would be its fate?

Is it upon the general principle of humanity, then, that you [addressing Republican Senators] wish to put an end to slavery, or is it to be urged by you as a mere topic and point of party controversy to sustain party power? Surely I give you credit for looking at it upon broader and more generous principles. Then, in the worst event, after you have encountered disunion, that greatest of all political calamities to the people of this country, and the disunionists come, the separating States come, and demand or take their portion of the Territories, they can take, and will be entitled to take, all that will now lie on the southern side of the line which I have proposed. Then they will have a right to permit slavery to exist in it; and what do you gain for the cause of anti-slavery? Nothing whatever. Suppose you should refuse their demand, and claim the whole for yourselves: that would be a flagrant injustice which you would not be willing that I should suppose would occur. But if you did, what would be the consequence? A State north and a State south, and all the States, north and south, would be attempting to grasp at and seize this territory, and to get all of it that they could. That would be the struggle, and you would have war; and not only disunion, but all these fatal consequences would follow from your refusal now to permit slavery to exist, to recognize it as existing, on the southern side of the proposed line, while you give to the people there the right to exclude it when they come to form a State government, if such should be their will and pleasure.

Now, gentlemen, in view of this subject, in view of the mighty consequences, in view of the great events which are present before you, and of the mighty consequences which are just now to take effect, is it not better to settle the question by a division upon the line of the Missouri compromise? For thirty years we lived quietly and peacefully under it. Our people, North and South, were accustomed to look at it as a proper and just line. Can we not do so again? We did it then to preserve the peace of the country. Now you see this Union in the most imminent danger. I declare to you that it is my solemn conviction that unless something be done, and something equivalent to this proposition, we shall be a separated and divided people in six months from this time. That is my firm conviction. There is no man here who deplores it more than I do; but it is my sad and melancholy conviction that that will be the consequence. I wish you to realize fully the danger. I wish you to realize fully the consequences which are to follow. You can give increased stability to this Union; you can give it an existence, a glorious existence, for great and glorious centuries to come, by now setting it upon a permanent basis, recognizing what the South considers as its rights; and this is the greatest of them all: it is that you should divide the territory by this line and allow the people south of it to have slavery when they are admitted into the Union as States, and to have it during the existence of the territorial government. That is all. Is it not the cheapest price at which such a blessing as this Union was ever purchased? You think, perhaps, or some of you, that there is no danger, that it will but thunder and pass away. Do not entertain such a fatal delusion. I tell you it is not so. I tell you that as sure as we stand here disunion will progress. I fear it may swallow up even old Kentucky in its vortex—as true a State to the Union as yet exists in the whole Confederacy—unless something be done; but that you will have disunion, that anarchy and war will follow it, that all this will take place in six months, I believe as confidently as I believe in your presence. I want to satisfy you of the fact.

Mr. President, I rise to suggest another consideration. I have been surprised to find, upon a little examination, that when the peace of 1783 was made, which recognized the independence of this country by Great Britain, the States north of Mason and Dixon's line had but a territory of one hundred and sixty-four thousand square miles, while the States south of Mason and Dixon's line had more than six hundred thousand square miles. It was so divided. Virginia shortly afterwards ceded to the United States all that noble territory northwest of the Ohio river, and excluded slavery from it.[2] That changed the relative proportion of territory. After that, the North had four hundred and twenty-five thousand square miles, and the South three hundred and eighty-five thousand. Thus, at once, by the concession of Virginia, the North, from one hundred and sixty-four thousand, rose to four hundred and twenty-five thousand square miles, and the South fell from six hundred thousand to three hundred and eighty-five thousand square miles. By that cession the South became smaller in extent than the North. Well, let us look beyond. I intend to take up as little time as possible, and to avoid details; but take all your subsequent acquisitions of Florida, of Louisiana, of Oregon, of Texas, and the acquisitions made from Mexico. They have been so divided and so disposed of that the North has now two millions, two hundred thousand square miles of territory, and the South has less than one million.

Under these circumstances, when you have been so greatly magnified—I do not complain of it, I am stating facts—when your section has been made so mighty by these great acquisitions, and to a great extent with the perfect consent of the South, ought you to hesitate now upon adopting this line which will leave to you on the north side of it nine hundred and odd thousand square miles, and leave to the South only two hundred and eighty-five thousand? It will give you three times as much as it will give her. There is three times as much land in your portion as in hers. The South has already occupied some of it, and it is in States; but altogether the South gets by this division two hundred and eighty-five thousand square miles, and the North nine hundred thousand. The result of the whole of it is, that the North has two million two hundred thousand square miles and the South only one million.

I mention this as no reproach, as no upbraiding, as no complaint—none at all. I do not speak in that spirit; I do not address you in that temper. But these are the facts, and they ought, it seems to me, to have some weight; and when we come to make a peace-offering, are we to count it, are we to measure it nicely in golden scales? You get a price, and the dearest price, for all the concession asked to be made—you have the firmer establishment of your Union; you have the restoration of peace and tranquility, and the hopes of a mighty future, all secured by this concession. How dearly must one individual, or two individuals, or many individuals, value their private opinions if they think them more important to the world than this mighty interest of the Union and Government of the United States!

Sir, it is a cheap sacrifice. It is a glorious sacrifice. This Union cost a great deal to establish it; it cost the yielding of much of public opinion and much of policy, besides the direct or indirect cost of it in all the war to establish the independence of this country. When it was done, General Washington himself said, Providence has helped us, or we could not have accomplished this thing. And this gift of our wisest men; this great work of their hands; this work in the foundation and the structure of which Providence himself, with his benignant hand, helped—are we to give it all up for such small considerations? The present exasperation; the present feeling of disunion, is the result of a long-continued controversy on the subject of slavery and of territory. I shall not attempt to trace that controversy; it is unnecessary to the occasion, and might be harmful. In relation to such controversies, I will say, though, that all the wrong is never on one side, or all the right on the other. Right and wrong, in this world, and in all such controversies, are mingled together. I forbear now any discussion or any reference to the right or wrong of the controversy, the mere party controversy; but in the progress of party, we now come to a point where party ceases to deserve consideration, and the preservation of the Union demands our highest and our greatest exertions. To preserve the Constitution of the country is the highest duty of the Senate, the highest duty of Congress—to preserve it and to perpetuate it, that we may hand down the glories which we have received to our children and to our posterity, and to generations far beyond us. We are, Senators, in positions where history is to take notice of the course we pursue.

History is to record us. Is it to record that when the destruction of the Union was imminent; when we saw it tottering to its fall; when we saw brothers arming their hands for hostility with one another, we stood quarreling about points of party politics, about questions which we attempted to sanctify and to consecrate by appealing to our conscience as the source of them? Are we to allow such fearful catastrophies {*sic*} to occur while we stand trifling away our time? While we stand thus, showing our inferiority to the great and mighty dead, showing our inferiority to the high positions which we occupy, the country may be destroyed and ruined; and to the amazement of all the world, the great Republic may fall prostrate and in ruins, carrying with it the very hope of that liberty which we have heretofore enjoyed; carrying with it, in place of the peace we have enjoyed, nothing but revolution and havoc and anarchy. Shall it be said that we have allowed all these evils to come upon our country, while we were engaged in the petty and small disputes and debates to which I have referred? Can it be that our name is to rest in history with this everlasting stigma and blot upon it?

Sir, I wish to God it was in my power to preserve this Union by renouncing or agreeing to give up every conscientious and other opinion. I might not be able to discard it from my mind; I am under no obligation to do that. I may retain the opinion, but if I can do so great a good as to preserve my country and give it peace, and its institutions and its Union stability, I will forego any act upon my opinions. Well now my friends [addressing the Republican Senators,] that is all that is asked of you. Consider it well, and I do not distrust the result. As to the rest of this body, the gentlemen from the South, I would say to them, can you ask more than this? Are you bent on revolution, bent on disunion? God forbid it. I cannot believe that such madness possesses the American people. This gives reasonable satisfaction. I can speak with confidence only of my own State. Old Kentucky will be satisfied with it, and she will stand by the Union and die by the Union if this satisfaction be given.

Nothing shall seduce her. The clamor of no revolution, the seductions and temptations of no revolution, will tempt her to move one step. She has stood always by the side of the Constitution; she has always been devoted to it, and is this day. Give her this satisfaction, and I believe all the States of the South that are not desirous of disunion as a better thing than the Union and the Constitution, will be satisfied and will adhere to the Union, and we shall go on again in our great career of national prosperity and national glory.

But, sir, it is not necessary for me to speak to you of the consequences that will follow disunion. Who of us is not proud of the greatness we have achieved? Disunion and separation destroy that greatness. Once disunited, we are no longer great. The nations of the earth who have looked upon you as a formidable Power, a mighty Power, and rising to untold and immeasurable greatness in the future, will scoff at you. Your flag, that now claims the respect of the world, that protects American property in every port and harbor of the world, that protects the rights of your citizens everywhere, what will become of it? What becomes of its glorious influence? It is gone; and with it the protection of American citizens and property. To say nothing of the national honor which it displayed to all the world, the protection of your rights, the protection of your property abroad is gone with that national flag, and we are hereafter to conjure and contrive different flags for our different republics according to the feverish fancies of revolutionary patriots and disturbers of the peace of the world. No, sir; I want to follow no such flag. I want to preserve the union of my country. We have it in our power to do so, and we are responsible if we do not do it.

I do not despair of the Republic. When I see before me Senators of so much intelligence and so much patriotism, who have been so honored by their country, sent here as the guardians of that very union which is now in question, sent here as the guardians of our national rights, and as guardians of that national flag, I cannot despair; I cannot despond. I cannot but believe that they will find some means of reconciling and adjusting the rights of all parties, by concessions, if necessary, so as to preserve and give more stability to the country and to its institutions.

Mr. President, I have occupied more time than I intended. My remarks were designed and contemplated only to reach to an explanation of this resolution.

The PRESIDING OFFICER, (Mr. FITZPATRICK,[3] in the chair.) Does the Senator desire the resolution to be read?

Mr. CRITTENDEN. Yes, sir; I ask that it be read to the Senate.

Mr. GREEN.[4] The hour has arrived for the consideration of the special order.

Mr. CRITTENDEN. I desire to present this resolution now to the Senate; and I ask that it may be read and printed.

The PRESIDING OFFICER. The Secretary will report the resolution.

The Secretary read it, as follows:

A JOINT RESOLUTION (S. NO. 50) PROPOSING CERTAIN AMENDMENTS TO THE CONSTITUTION OF THE UNITED STATES.

Whereas serious and alarming dissensions have arisen between the northern and southern States, concerning the rights and security of the rights of the slaveholding States, and especially their rights in the common territory of the United States; and whereas it is eminently desirable and proper that these dissensions, which now threaten the very existence of this Union, should be permanently quieted and settled by constitutional provisions, which shall do equal justice to all sections, and thereby restore to the people that peace and good-will which ought to prevail between all the citizens of the United States: Therefore,

Resolved by the Senate and House of Representatives of the United States of America in Congress assembled, (two thirds of both Houses concurring,) That the following articles be, and are hereby, proposed and submitted as amendments to the Constitution of the United States, which shall be valid to all intents and purposes, as part of said Constitution, when ratified by conventions of three-fourths of the several States:

ARTICLE 1. In all the territory of the United States now held, or hereafter acquired, situate north of 36°30', slavery or involuntary servitude, except as a punishment for crime, is prohibited while such territory shall remain under territorial government. In all the territory south of said line of latitude, slavery of the African race is hereby recognized as existing, and shall not be interfered with by Congress, but shall be protected as property by all the departments of the territorial government during its continuance. And when any territory, north or south of said line, within such boundaries as Congress may prescribe, shall contain the population requisite for a member of Congress according to the then Federal ratio of representation of the people of the United States, it shall, if its form of government be republican, be admitted into the Union, on an equal footing with the original States, with or without slavery, as the constitution of such new State may provide.

ART. 2. Congress shall have no power to abolish slavery in places under its exclusive jurisdiction, and situate within the limits of States that permit the holding of slaves.

ART. 3. Congress shall have no power to abolish slavery within the District of Columbia, so long as it exists in the adjoining States of Virginia and Maryland, or either, nor without the consent of the inhabitants, nor without just compensation first made to such owners of slaves as do not consent to such abolishment. Nor shall Congress at any time prohibit officers of the Federal Government, or members of Congress, whose duties require them to be in said District, from bringing with them their slaves, and holding them as such during the time their duties may require them to remain there, and afterwards taking them from the District.

ART. 4. Congress shall have no power to prohibit or hinder the transportation of slaves from one State to another, or to a Territory in which slaves are by law permitted to be held, whether that transportation be by land, navigable rivers, or by the sea.

ART. 5. That in addition to the provisions of the third paragraph of the second section of the fourth article of the Constitution of the United States, Congress shall have power to provide by law, and it shall be its duty so to provide, that the United States shall pay to the owner who shall apply for it, the full value of his fugitive slave in all cases when the marshal or other officer whose duty it was to arrest said fugitive was prevented from so doing by violence or intimidation, or when, after arrest, said fugitive was rescued by force, and the owner thereby prevented and obstructed in the pursuit of his remedy for the recovery of his fugitive slave under the said clause of the Constitution and the laws made in pursuance thereof. And in all such cases, when the United States shall pay for such fugitive, they shall have the right, in their own name, to sue the county in which said violence, intimidation, or rescue was committed, and to recover from it, with interest and damages, the amount paid by them for said fugitive slave. And the said county, after it has paid said amount to the United States, may, for its indemnity, sue and recover from the wrong doers or rescuers by whom the owner was prevented from the recovery of his fugitive slave, in like manner as the owner himself might have sued and recovered.

ART. 6. No future amendment of the Constitution shall affect the five preceding articles; nor the third paragraph of the second section of the first article of the Constitution; nor the third paragraph of the second section of the fourth article of said Constitution;[5] and no amendment shall be made to the Constitution which shall authorize or give to Congress any power to abolish or interfere with slavery in any of the States by whose laws it is, or may be, allowed or permitted.

And whereas, also, besides those causes of dissension embraced in the foregoing amendments proposed to the Constitution of the United States, there are others which come within the jurisdiction of Congress, and may be remedied by its legislative power; and whereas it is the desire of Congress as far as its power will extend, to remove all just cause for the popular discontent and agitation which now disturb the peace of the country, and threaten the stability of its institutions: Therefore,

1. *Resolved by the Senate and House of Representatives of the United States of America in Congress assembled*, That the laws now in force for the recovery of fugitive slaves are in strict pursuance of the plain and mandatory provisions of the Constitution, and have been sanctioned as valid and constitutional by the judgment of the Supreme Court of the United States; that the slaveholding States are entitled to the faithful observance and execution of those laws, and that they ought not to be repealed, or so modified or changed as to impair their efficiency; and that laws ought to be made for the punishment of those who attempt by rescue of the slave, or other illegal means, to hinder or defeat the due execution of said laws.

2. That all State laws which conflict with the fugitive slave acts of Congress, or any other constitutional acts of Congress, or which, in their operation, impede, hinder, or delay the free course and due execution of any of said acts, are null and void by the plain provisions of the Constitution of the United States; yet those State laws, void as they are, have given color to practices, and led to consequences, which have obstructed the due administration and execution of acts of Congress, and especially the acts for the delivery of fugitive slaves, and have thereby contributed much to the discord and commotion now prevailing. Congress, therefore, in the present perilous juncture, does not deem it improper, respectfully and earnestly to recommend the repeal of those laws to the several States which have enacted them, or such legislative corrections or explanations of them as may prevent their being used or perverted to such mischievous purposes.

3. That the act of the 18th of September, 1850, commonly called the fugitive slave law, ought to be so amended as to make the fee of the commissioner, mentioned in the eighth section of the act, equal in amount in the cases decided by him, whether his decision be in favor of or against the claimant. And to avoid misconstruction, the last clause of the fifth section of said act, which authorizes the person holding a warrant for the arrest or detention of a fugitive slave, to summon to his aid the *posse comitatus*, and which declares it to be the duty of all good citizens to assist him in its execution, ought to be so amended as to expressly limit the authority and duty to cases in which there shall be resistance or danger of resistance or rescue.

4. That the laws for the suppression of the African slave trade, and especially those prohibiting the importation of slaves in the United States, ought to be made effectual, and ought to be thoroughly executed; and all further enactments necessary to those ends ought to be properly made.

Source: *Congressional Globe*, 36th Cong., 2nd Sess., 112–14, (Joint Resolution No. 50).

(Also submitted to the Senate's Committee of Thirteen on December 22, 1860; 36th Cong., 2nd Sess., Senate Report 288, 3–4.)

CHAPTER THREE

Crittenden Debated: Pro-Crittenden

Southern support for John Crittenden's six-part compromise package stemmed directly from the nation's experience over the previous decade. Specifically the failure of the Kansas-Nebraska Act to extend slavery convinced many that the popular sovereignty solution to organizing the western territories needed to be abandoned. Crittenden's proposal reinstating the "time-honored" Missouri Compromise line that would prohibit slavery above the 36°30' line and protect it below appeared far more sensible. Over the course of the decade, slavery had not progressed into the Nebraska Territory, and slavery was not moving into the Utah Territory although the Mormon-dominated legislature had passed a protective (although very mild) slave code.[1]

The only territory south of the compromise line was that of New Mexico which stretched from Texas to California. While its climate and topography seemed to invite the institution more than the plains and mountainous areas to the north, Crittenden described it as "the most sterile and worthless of its extent upon this whole continent." Crittenden believed his envisioned division of the West would appeal to moderate Republicans as well as moderate Democrats. Republicans, he hoped, would find value in the prohibition of slavery north of the line, while Democrats, he hoped, would find security of knowing slavery was protected to the land west of Texas. One of his inducements to northern support for his plan was to remind Republicans that because slavery had already been introduced into New Mexico via the popular sovereignty provision of the Compromise of 1850 (approximately two dozen slaves had been taken there, mostly by military officers), Republicans would not be giving up anything. Crittenden hoped Republicans would also see his solution south of 36°30' as symbolic: his amendment would permit slavery to expand into a land inhospitable to slavery. In addition, if they could tolerate the existence of slavery where it already existed in the states (which Republicans supported in their 1860 platform), why not tolerate it where it already existed in the territories?

Moderate southerners also thought that Crittenden's arrangement would bring northern support because they were giving up more than northerners. According to Taney's decision in the *Dred Scott* case, slave owners had a constitutional right to venture with their slaves into any part of the western territories and have their property protected there at least until the territory applied for statehood. In accepting the 36°30' line of division, southerners were formally giving up a right authorized by the Supreme Court of the United States. As several of the speeches that follow indicate, free territory had expanded over the course of the previous seventy years 1,000 percent, while slave territory had expanded only 33 percent. Agreement on Crittenden's division of the West would still leave the lion's share of the country slave free.

Senator John Jordan Crittenden

US Senate
January 7, 1861

Senator Crittenden's proposed amendment to the Constitution quickly became the most popular of the sixty-eight offered as solutions to the secession crisis largely because of its scope, but also because of its presumed reasonableness. It was promoted in Congress, the Washington Peace Conference, state legislatures, and several of the secession conventions.

On multiple occasions, Crittenden took to the floor of the Senate to defend his resolutions. On January 7, 1861, he argued vigorously for his "compromise" in the territories. Creating a political division along the 36°30' meridian prohibiting slavery above and protecting it below would force both Republicans and Democrats to give up something. Republicans would need to abjure their "no extension" position while

Democrats would need to disregard the *Dred Scott* decision and accept as sufficient the toehold slavery already had in the Territory of New Mexico. Generally, Crittenden announced that he did not believe in the right of secession, calling it "nothing but a lawless violation of the Constitution." His obligation, as he saw it, was to save the Union by engineering concessions from both sides.

SLAVERY QUESTION.

Mr. CRITTENDEN:
Mr. President, I rise now for the purpose of moving to take up the resolution which I offered some few days ago. I hope the Senate will now proceed to its consideration; and I trust that we shall continue to consider it until it is finally disposed of, to the exclusion of all other business; and I desire that to be considered as my motion.

The VICE PRESIDENT. The Senator from Kentucky moves to take up for consideration the joint resolution (S. 54) proposing certain amendments to the Constitution of the United States, offered by him.[2]

{Senator Crittenden began his remarks by commenting on the "extraordinary condition of the country," and hoping that amendments could be proposed by Congress and adopted by the states by "convention or by Legislature . . . restore quiet to the country."}

Then, sir, as to the constitutional amendments which are proposed for the sanction of the people, and upon which they are to give their opinion, I had occasion some time ago to make a few remarks, and I intend now to add only a few more. I do not intend to go very much at large into this question. I do not know that I shall at any time—certainly not now, when I am not fully apprised, perhaps, of the various objections that may be made to them. The first remedy proposed consists in a new article to be added to the Constitution, and which proposes for its object to settle the question of territory, and the question of slavery in respect to territory, and to settle that—how? Simply to provide that all the territory north of 36°30' shall be free from slavery; that on the south slavery shall be recognized and protected, as it now exists by the laws existing there for its protection, and to continue so until that territory, or any suitable proportion of it, shall be formed into a State and admitted into the Union. Then they are to be admitted with such provision as they may choose to make in their constitution in respect to slavery—excluding it or admitting it. This is all. To the North all is given; to the South it is only provided that things shall remain as they are until the territory becomes a State, and then it is to adopt this institution of slavery or not, according to the wish of the people that are interested in the new State. It seems to me there is something very just and very fair on the face of this proposition.

We are a great nation, composed now of thirty-three States. Fifteen of these have this peculiar institution of slavery; the others have excluded it, each acting according to its own free choice under the Constitution. Slavery existed in these and more States when the Constitution was formed. The Constitution took things as they were, recognized them as they were, and left them as they were, to the exclusive jurisdiction of the several States. Those who had the institution of slavery were left to the sole dominion over it; those who were without it were left to the free and full course of their own will and of their own wisdom upon the subject, on the one side to continue to exclude it, or on the other side to continue to retain it. This was the broad, general, reciprocal justice which the Constitution did to all sections of the country.

Now, sir, I ask the same standard and the same measure of justice. Let us take things as they are; that is the object. To the north of 36°30' slavery has been excluded. I say, therefore, slavery is excluded. To the south, slavery exists as a matter of fact. I ask you to recognize it. That was the principle upon which the framers of our Constitution went, recognizing the *status* existing at the time, adopting that, accepting that as a basis. This is what I understand in respect to all the States. This is all now that I ask; all that this proposition is. There are south of that line, the Indian territory, and the Territory of New Mexico; that is all. Of the Indian territory I need say nothing; that is appropriated to others, and upon the terms of that appropriation it rests. By those terms, however, slavery may be recognized as existing there; for the fact is, it does exist. So in all New Mexico; and how comes it to exist in New Mexico? It exists potentially in New Mexico in virtue of the decision of the Supreme Court of the United States in the so-often quoted case of Dred Scott. They say that all the people of the United States have the right equally to go into the common territory of the United States, and carry with them any species or description of property recognized as such in the States from which they emigrate. Potentially, then, slavery does exist there; but more than that: by the great compromise measures of 1850, a territorial government was formed for New Mexico; and one of the compromises, one of the adjustments on that great occasion, was to give this Territory, which was a subject of dispute in respect to the question of slavery, power to "legislate on all rightful subjects of legislation." It was intended to cover this case; it did cover the case of slavery by the broad and distinct terms in which the power was given to the Territorial Legislature. That was the agreement between the North and South: "We will say nothing about slavery ourselves, but we will constitute a territorial government, and we will give to that territorial government, representing the local interests, representing the local population, the power to dispose of this subject according to the wishes and according to the interests of the people of the Territory." In the exercise of that power, the people of the Territory did pass an act authorizing and regulating slavery in every particular; and that act now exists.[3] Slavery only to a very limited extent exists there; but it exists by law actually.

Now, what does this amendment of mine propose? Not that gentlemen shall agree that slavery may exist there; not that they shall concede any principle; not that they shall concede any policy; but simply that they shall recognize a fact, a fact that they cannot dispute—the fact of the actual existence of slavery under actual law, emanating from that Territory under power granted in the compromise of 1850, which was intended to settle the affairs of the country, and to relieve us from the troubles which have now returned. It was hailed by the whole people, accepted as a peace offering on all sides, and has been continued from that day. Under the power given by that act of Congress of 1850, slavery has been admitted into that Territory, and all that is proposed by my amendment is, as I said, simply to recognize that; and furthermore, the fact being recognized, that it shall be recognized that that state of things, that fact, shall continue as it is, until the Territory shall have acquired a sufficient population, according to the ratio of representation for Representatives, to entitle it to one member in Congress, and then to be admitted into the Union on an equal footing with the rest of the States, and with a constitution adopting or excluding slavery, according to the judgment of the people themselves.

This is the whole proposition in that respect. Well, I confess, sir, it seems to me that it is very little to grant. Some gentlemen are averse to compromise. Well, gentlemen, you may call this a compromise. May it not with equal propriety be called an honest adjustment of rights? But if it were a compromise, is it not a fair compromise? And upon what principle are we opposed to compromise? All human life is but a compromise, From {*sic*} the cradle to the grave, every step of it is a compromise between man and society. And when peace is the reward of compromise, it has been usually blessed. A man, it is said, in respect to the compromise of a lawsuit, must be allowed to purchase his peace. A man can purchase nothing better, nothing dearer than his peace, even in private transactions. How is it in relation to divisions between great communities, different countries, or great sections of the same country? Are they not more necessary there? Are they not more demanded by the interests of society, more demanded by humanity itself, than in any other condition of life? Just as much more demanded as the consequences are greater and more momentous, and more destructive ordinarily. If there were no compromise, parties would have to settle, by force or by war, these questions.

Is there in this compromise anything repulsive to any section of this country? I know the great Republican party of this country have declared themselves against the extension of slavery. Is this, in the sense of that declaration, is this, in the sense of that tenet of their faith, an extension of slavery? I have before shown, what is the indisputable fact that slavery does exist here by law, which covers the whole Territory. It is not extending slavery into a Territory where no slavery exists. Slavery does exist there; and the question is, whether you will let it exist, according to the laws under which it does exist, until the Territory becomes a State, and decides for itself whether slavery shall continue longer or not. Is there such stringency in the doctrine of the party upon this subject, that neither for weal nor for woe, neither for peace nor for war, will they, mediately or immediately, on a principle of compromise or on a principle of justice, recognize the existence of slavery in the Territory of New Mexico?

What gentleman, as a statesman, can stand upon that ground? What Senator can stand upon that ground? Say that we are here, as I verily believe we are, upon the brink of intestine and civil war, that that war can be prevented by recognizing the fact of the existence of slavery, and agreeing that it shall continue for ten or fifteen years, until the Territory shall become prepared to enter the Union as a State, and that Senators had rather encounter civil war, had rather encounter the destruction of this Union, and of this Government, than to agree to these terms—upon what grounds? Upon any grounds of public welfare? Upon any avowed grounds of policy or patriotism? Can any Senator stand upon that ground? What is his ground, then? The Republican party sees that by possibility, under this adjustment, that State, if it chooses slavery, may come into the Union hereafter as a slave State. Are they pledged against that under all circumstances? Are there general rules, rules that admit of no exceptions? The old maxim is, that the exception proves the rule. If the rule be reasonable, there always are exceptional circumstances that may occur, which would prevent the application of the rule; but here are general rules that admit of no exception; and civil war, pestilence, famine, and everything else, are to be encountered, rather than to recede one single hair's breadth from a particular, prescribed doctrine. I cannot conceive it possible.

But suppose, Mr. President, that this proposition does make such provision that the ultimate result of it may be, if the people of the Territory choose, that it may hereafter be entitled, under this amendment of the Constitution, to come in as a slave State. What do gentlemen say to that? Is it a dogma that no slave State ever shall hereafter be admitted into this Union; and will they, for the maintenance and preservation of that dogma, sacrifice the country? Will they encounter civil war and disunion and all its fearful consequences, rather than yield up in a single instance this dogma of no more slave States? Surely if that dogma were to be pressed with ever such heartfelt conviction, and such heartfelt zeal, it could not be but that, in the hearts that had so adopted and embraced it, such an exception might be made as this. When the fate of my country is on the one side and my dogma on the other, let the dogma go rather than the country be prostrated. Is any member of the Senate prepared to say, in the face of this country and of the world, that rather than yield up his dogma in a single instance, he will see the country go to ruin, or he will attempt to enforce his opinion by the sword? Is there any man who would do such a thing as that, so contrary to the law and teachings of the Almighty, and contrary to all humanity?

Sir, we are one people. I glory in the thought. Will one half of the people undertake to say, we have a conscientious scruple about admitting a slave State, and we intend to substitute that scruple in place of all your territorial rights? This Government, as made by our fathers, was made by States who held slaves and States who did not. We now stand in the same attitude. Then, in their time, most or all of the States held slaves, and now a minority of them only hold slaves. Shall the present majority, holding no slaves, plead, as an apology for usurping all the common territory of the country, a conscientious scruple, a dogma upon their part that no more slave States shall be admitted? I ask my honorable friends on this side of the Chamber if that is the political system or ethics upon which they intend to act; if it is that which they can avow, as a party, for monopolizing that which is common property? Will they plead a conscientious scruple? Sir, it is a great nursery for conscientious scruples, indeed, if men can make titles in themselves to common property in that way. I do not know why a man who held with me a tract of land might not take the same scruple against me, and say that I was heretical, and violated all his dogmas, in politics and religion; that his scruples would not allow him to be in such communion with me as to hold property in common. And how does he gratify his conscience, and how does he dissolve this question of casuistry? By taking the whole property to himself and turning me out. I say it is a great nursery for scruples of this sort, if an argument of that kind is to be found here.

And now, Mr. President, see how exactly the very territory in dispute comes within the line of all that reasoning which would show that every part of the country ought to be considered as equally entitled to share in the enjoyment of it. That country was but recently acquired from Mexico; and it was acquired by conquest. Is it not as plain a case that every section of the country paid its proportionate part of the consideration, as if it had been bought with money and each citizen had contributed the number of pence that his interest amounted to? Did not the South contribute her part of the treasure which bore the expense of that purchase? Did she not contribute her portion of the blood that was shed in obtaining it? Did she not do even a little more of it than our northern brethren, because of their remote situation? We were nearer the scene of action, could get to it more easily, and therefore, perhaps, there were more southern than northern men engaged in the war. The millions of money that it cost were paid, not out of a sectional purse, but out of a national purse, to which all contributed. We fought, one as well as another, and all sections did their duty.

I do not recur to these things for reproach upon any section of our country. No, sir. I love it all too well. It is all my country. I am not the man to degrade any portion of it by any language I have to use.

This territory, then, plainly and clearly, was acquired by us all. It is but the work of yesterday. Now, a portion attempt to take it. They have scruples about allowing us to our full and unrestricted and unreserved equal right in the territory. Can this be proper? We are but one community, with diverse institutions in relation to domestic slavery, as well as in relation to many other subjects. We have grown up in, and cultivated habits suitable to, all the circumstances surrounding us, just as every people on earth have. The institution of slavery has given a variety to the form of society in which it exists. The absence of it has given form to a somewhat different condition of society, but equally adapted to its people. So it will be everywhere. You say, then, for instance, by way of mitigating the wrong done, that you only exclude slaveholders; you only exclude three hundred thousand—not a section of the country; not States; not fifteen States; but three hundred thousand slaveholders in those States. Whether that is a correct computation of them I do not know; nor is it of the least importance to this argument. No; the wrong does not stop there. All the millions that have been reared in the society formed, and receiving its character, and receiving its complexion from that institution, though they may not be the owners of slaves, have been brought up and habituated to the habit and form of society which that institution has given birth to. That makes a difference in the habits of a people not to be worn off in a day or a minute—transient, I admit; but they are, for the present, their habits. Their feelings and their habits go along together; and neither would you northern men prefer to go into the society of these people under circumstances equal; nor would the southern man, with his habits and his feelings, prefer to go into northern society, simply because of changes in the custom and habits; that is all. By restraining the slaveholders from going into any Territory, then you restrain the formation of any such habits as this other man, who is not a slaveholder in the southern States, has formed. You do not expel him, you erect a barrier; not an insuperable one; you create a new difficulty in his way in going there, where he is to meet with strangers, and strangers of somewhat different habits from himself.

{Crittenden here observed that "ordinary equity and justice" established in the Constitution argue against the Republican position of excluding slavery from the western territories.}

It is through a long train of events, of party controversies, that the country has been brought to its present deplorable condition. It would be idle to say that in the course of that long controversy all the blame has been on one side, and all the right on the other. Right and wrong have never been so exclusively divided in any human controversy. We have all contributed to excite those passions and those feelings which now bring our country into the most imminent peril. I shall not attempt to balance this account, and show clearly which has been in the wrong. That would be an idle attempt, and would do no good, if successful. It is not to the past so much that I would allude as to the present and the future. No matter whether I have been the wrong doer or whether I have received the wrong, when the question comes as to the safety of the country, as to the safety of the Constitution, I should act with a reference to that object, and not to any past or present controversies that I may have with parties or with individuals.

Mr. President, I am not here as the advocate of slavery. I am here as the advocate of the Union, honestly, sincerely, zealously. I am pleading for that; and I am pleading with the Senate to do that which I believe will preserve the Union and stop the course of revolution and of war, and which alone I believe will do it. If I plead for this solution of territorial difficulties, it is because I believe it is necessary to save the Union. Is it possible that any Senator could believe, with respect to this arid and sterile Territory, it could be an object with any gentleman to desire the extension of slavery? I do not believe myself that slavery can ever be invited there. Climate, soil, its remoteness from all the great avenues of commerce, all tend, in my opinion, to interpose natural barriers against it. That, however, is not so much the question as our right to go there at all. You have no more right to take away poor land than you have rich land, from our settlement. Upon the principles of the Constitution, you have no more right to take away one than the other; and it is not so much the violation of territorial authority as it is the violation of that principle of equality, that principle of equal right upon which every section stands.

That the South has received some wrong in the course of our party action, is, I think, most clear. There has been introduced into this country, it has grown up, forced on by party principles step by step, without any man perhaps comprehending the whole conclusion and the whole extent of it, until it has appeared in all its fearful proportions, a great power, said to be the ruling power of this country, that has introduced an anti-slavery system of policy in the United States. In the original Constitution—and my friends from the North look to that fact, and cherish it—the word "slave" is not to be found. How often have we heard that repeated here, my friends? You cling to it with tenacity, as a great fact; and yet what have you done? Your system of policy, that upon which you have triumphed—upon which your platform rests—is nothing but anti-slavery alone. Is this right? The opinions may be right as private opinions; but under the Constitution of the United Sates, upon the great principles and policies which it contemplated, was it ever to be imagined, or is it ever to be justified, that a great party should stand alone upon a system of anti-slavery, making war by one section upon another section—a war of opinion, if no more?

It is in vain that you endeavor to mitigate this war of opinion, this war of denunciation, one against another, one system against another, by saying: "We do not lay our hands upon you; we do not touch slavery in the States." But you abuse and denounce the institution of one half the States of your great country, and you know where it must strike. That that has given great alarm to some portions of the southern States, ought not to surprise you. It is quite natural. It will be something more than a mere common inference, if, after having succeeded, if, after having commenced the formation of your great party, for the avowed purpose of retrieving what you supposed you had lost by the repeal of the Missouri compromise, you now refuse not only to restore that line, and to accept all the territory north of it, and only to yield up that the present state of things shall continue in the territory south until that territory becomes a State.

You have just succeeded in a great contest upon your anti-slavery system of policy. If now, just at this critical time, in the moment of your great victory, in the moment, as it may be supposed, when you are confident, elated by that victory, you refuse to give this security, and plant yourselves proudly and sternly upon platforms and dogmas, and say: "We will take no step backward," have not the South some little cause to complain? But, as generous men, as American statesmen, as Americans, having an interest throughout this whole great continent, are not these motives sufficient to induce you to make, if necessary, a compromise, and a liberal compromise? Now that you are the victors, be just; and not only just, but liberal. Less than this will create more dissatisfaction, more misapprehension. Will you not do all in your power to quiet and to put an end to these troubles?

I hope I shall not be understood as addressing you with any language in a spirit of offence. I do not. I appeal to you as my countrymen; I appeal to you as statesmen; I appeal to you as victors in a great political strife; and I implore you to make your victory useful to your country and honorable to yourselves, by that greatest of all acts which you can ever have the power or the opportunity to do, of saving that country by settling this question. You are called upon to make no concessions. I do not concede that I ask any concession in this proposition. It is nothing more than justice, bare justice.

Allow me to recount here for a moment what has been our history in relation to territorial acquisitions from the peace of 1783 down to this time. As

I read from the book the other day, you had at that time one hundred and sixty-six thousand square miles, and the South six hundred and fifty thousand square miles. How is it now? The first change in these proportions was produced by the cession made by Virginia of all the territory northwest of the Ohio, with a provision excluding slavery. That changed the proportion, and made the North over four hundred thousand square miles, and the South over three hundred thousand square miles. The North, at this early period, and by means of this voluntary cession, become {*sic*} the greater in point of territory. We went on to acquire Florida, Louisiana, and what we conquered and purchased from Mexico. All these various acquisitions have been so divided out that, at this day, the North has two million two hundred thousand square miles, and the South less than one million square miles, even when you have given her this Territory of New Mexico. Given her, did I say? You only agree that the present state of law there, in respect to persons held to servitude, shall continue until it becomes a State—that is all. The condition it is now in was not produced by force, or by any fraud. It has obtained its present condition by law, passed with the consent of the Senate of the United States. The act of September 18, 1850, gave authority to the Legislature to authorize and sanction slavery.

Then, if we can settle this matter of difficulty in relation to the Territories, there is, I think, in all the other propositions, nothing that anybody can complain of. As to the fugitive slave law, it is only changed and altered so as to make it less obnoxious to our fellow-citizens of the North. That is the whole extent of the amendment. Therefore that can be no ground of complaint on the part of our northern friends.

As to the prohibition to abolish or prohibit slavery in the District of Columbia, and the places under the special jurisdiction of Congress within the slave States, it seems to me that stands upon a ground that no man can deny. These Territories have been ceded to the General Government by slave States. It could not be expected or apprehended that it was supposed that Congress would abolish slavery in little spots within the midst of the slaveholding States. At the time this cession was made, was any such thing contemplated by any one? Is it to be presumed it was? If not, would it not be bad faith on the part of the Government, to say the least of it, to use its jurisdiction for purposes which they supposed injurious to them, and not contemplated by any of the parties at the time of the cession? Good faith requiring that these things should not be done, would it be too much to ask you, as an assurance that it shall not be done, to declare that the Constitution ought not to be so construed as to give power to do it? I think there can be no question about that.

I do not intend to go more particularly or precisely into the argument on this question at this time, and I hope it will never be required at my hands hereafter. There are some questions involved in this matter in relation to the country, upon which I desire merely to give my opinion. I have said that all parties have been to blame in these controversies. It is so of necessity. Our infirmities necessarily lead to that in all long-continued controversies. It has been so here. Who can say that the South has not acted rashly? Who can say that the South is not now acting unwisely? I cannot. To say nothing of the past political errors which they have committed, but to look to the present, I do not believe in this right of secession. It is a new doctrine. It has sprung up and grown wonderfully in a very few years. It is not named in the Constitution. It has no name anywhere in all our code of laws. If it means anything at all, it is revolution; and notwithstanding the attempts to secede from the bold front and character of revolution, it is nothing but a lawless violation of the Constitution. That is my opinion. I do not intend to argue it; but I wish to take the responsibility of saying, in these momentous times, when the Constitution of the country is apt to be run down, and trodden down; when a right of secession is urged; a right to go off, and to take with them forts and arsenals, and everything prepared for the common defense, that I cannot agree with it. It is new to me. It is of modern growth.

But, sir, I do not desire to be carried off into that question. I want only to bear my testimony for the Constitution of my country. I want it to be known—and, as far as my poor voice can go, it shall go—that this Constitution, so far from its being liable to be broken by any body that chooses to secede, as they call it, is a grand and inviolable instrument upon which no man should lay his unhallowed hand, or attempt to withdraw himself. If he is oppressed, let him take the responsibilities of revolution; let him defy the war; let him proclaim himself a revolutionist, and not attempt to hide his revolution in the little subtilties of law, and the little subtilties with which he surrounds secession, as it is called. I do not believe in it. It is no justification. My honorable friend from Louisiana [Mr. BENJAMIN][4] quotes Mr. Madison and Mr. Webster as authority for this doctrine.[5] Why, sir, if the gentleman had extended his inquiry a little further, he would have seen that no doctrine was ever repudiated more precisely, exactly, and sternly, than this doctrine of secession was by Mr. Madison; and Mr. Webster's name and fame are identified with the argument by which he was supposed to have destroyed every pretext on which such a doctrine could stand. If it is intended merely as another name for revolution, be it so. I do not know that gentlemen have not a right to so denominate their actions if they please; but a constitutional right to break the Constitution—a constitutional right to destroy the Union—would be indeed a strange form of government.

I am for the Union; but, my friends, I must be also for the equal rights of my State under this great Constitution and in this great Union. You must be prepared to grant them. I hope you will be. You desire to maintain the Union. You say you do. I believe it. I do. But we must preserve it on the proper terms of equal respect and equal regard. The dogma of my State is, that she has as much right to go into the Territories with her slaves as you, who do not choose to hold such property, have to go without them. That is their dogma. Would it not be best for both of us to renounce the pretension to go on its own dogma at the expense of the other, and let us make that odious thing, if it must be called so—a compromise—again to restore our fellowship and our brotherhood. Balance the consequences of a civil war and the consequences of your now agreeing to the stipulated terms of peace here, and see how they compare one with another. I will not repeat again what is asked of you. It is but a trifle in point of territory, a trifle in point of any material value that can be assigned to it, and there is no breach of any principle. It is an exception, and a fair exception upon exceptional grounds, to the principle you avow. On the the {*sic*} other side, you have civil war—

{In response from a question from Senator Lyman Trumbull from Illinois, Crittenden offered a few remarks to the extent that it was his belief that if Congress accepted his amendment, peace would be preserved. It may not satisfy South Carolina, he added, because hers "is a peculiar case." Senator Robert Toombs from Georgia followed with a long speech listing his "demands," all of which proposed increased federal protections for the institution of slavery including an agreement that slaves be protected as property under the Constitution.}

Source: *Congressional Globe*, 36th Cong., 2nd Sess., 264–67.

Representative William Ellis Niblack (Democrat)

US House of Representatives
January 31, 1861

William E. Niblack (1822–1893) had been admitted to the Indiana bar in 1843, elected to the Indiana House of Representatives in 1849 and 1850, and served in the Indiana Senate from 1850 to 1853. He was elected to the Thirty-Fifth and Thirty-Sixth Congresses, did not run for reelection, but returned to Congress and served five terms from 1865 to 1875.

Mr. NIBLACK. Mr. Speaker, the powers and duties of the Government, in relation to the Territories of the United States, has been, for several years past, the overshadowing question in national politics. It has been the central idea upon which old political parties have been reorganized, and around which new ones have been formed. With the discussions upon it, the whole subject of African slavery on this continent has become involved. Divisions and differences in relation to it afford the occasion, if they are not the cause, of the unhappy condition of things now existing in the country.

In the few remarks I have to offer, I shall feel myself obliged, however reluctant I may be, and however familiar to the public mind the whole subject may be, to refer, as preliminary to some conclusions at which I desire to arrive, to a few of the salient points in the history of this territorial question.

The proper organization and government of these Territories has been a source of trouble and embarrassment to the Federal Government from the first territorial acquisition to the present day. The eminent men who framed the Constitution of the United States, and who, with much prophetic wisdom, provided so well for most of the contingencies which have arisen, seem never to have realized the importance which this subject was destined to assume, and hence omitted to make such specific provisions for the acquisition and government of new districts of country as experience has since shown to be highly desirable.

As to the constitutional powers of this Government, in these respects, we have had to rely mainly upon references from the grant of other powers more clearly defined.[6]

The first idea seemed rather to be to hold and govern the Territories as provinces, Congress to enact all the laws necessary for this purpose. The next proposition was to organize them as incipient and *quasi*-independent States outside of the Union, to be admitted into the Confederacy as soon as they were deemed to have a sufficient population. This has been usually known as Mr. Jefferson's plan; finally, however, the policy was adopted of organizing temporary or provisional governments for them, at the discretion, and to exist during the pleasure of Congress. This policy was inaugurated in the adoption of the ordinance of 1787, and has been continued, with varying amendments and modifications, to the present day. Under this system the Federal Government, as a general proposition, appoints the executive and judicial officers of the Territories. These things occurred, however, during the old Congress of the Confederation, and before the adoption of the Constitution of the United States, and hence do not furnish precedents of binding authority, if found at all in conflict with any of the provisions or principles of the existing Constitution.

Early in the history of this territorial system the question of slavery became one of some interest. Yielding, however, to the natural laws destined, to a great extent, to govern the question of slavery in this country at all times—that is, the laws of climate, of soil, and of production—almost by common consent this institution was first discouraged, and its extension into the northwestern Territories prohibited; but it was encouraged and protected in its extension into the Territories on the southwest. Thus, in a friendly and fraternal spirit, means were provided by which both systems of labor in use under our Government had a natural outlet. At that time, therefore nothing more seemed to be demanded on either side. Thus the policy of dividing the common Territories of the United States between the two systems of labor, seemed, though informally, to be tacitly acknowledged.

When Missouri applied for admission, lying as she does on both sides of what was regarded as a natural boundary between the free and the slave States, though, in my judgment, clearly entitled to unconditional admission as a slave State, by the terms of the Louisiana purchase, a determined and even furious opposition was made to her admission, because of her toleration of slavery. Then, for the first time, was the question of slavery in the Territories presented in that angry and excited form which has since given us so much trouble and anxiety.

After much angry feeling and discussion on both sides, as a preliminary measure, it was enacted by Congress, that, north of a certain line, slavery or involuntary servitude should thereafter be prohibited. With this, much of the opposition to the application of Missouri was withdrawn, and provisions were made by which she was admitted as one of the States of this Confederacy. These measures were acquiesced in; and thus again was the slavery question disposed of, by acting upon the idea of a division of territory between those who desired to tolerate and those who desired to prohibit slavery.

As one result of the Mexican war, we acquired a very large new district of country. As preliminary to this acquisition, it was proposed in Congress to forever exclude slavery from all territory to be thus acquired.[7] If I read the history of the country correctly, this is the first time a proposition was ever seriously urged to exclude slaveholders from all the Territories of the United States. Those who now contend that such a policy is in accordance with the practices of the fathers of the Republic, certainly do not read history impartially. That many of them entertained anti-slavery views, I readily grant; but they never went so far as to attempt, either by constitutional provision or constitutional enactment, to exclude slavery from all common Territories. As before remarked, theirs was rather a policy of division, and not of total prohibition or exclusion.

The proposition thus to exclude slavery from the proposed newly-acquired territory failed. After its acquisition, a proposition was brought forward to extend the Missouri line through this territory to the Pacific ocean. That also failed. In 1850, as a part of the compromise measures of that year, and as one of the necessities of the times, a new policy in relation to slavery in the Territories was inaugurated. It was provided that the people interested should determine whether they would have slavery, or not, without the intervention of Congress; thus abandoning the older policy of division. This plan seemed to be so much in accordance with the genius of our Government, and of such easy and universal application to all Territories, wherever situated, that it was embraced by both of the leading political parties of the day. It but remained to repeal the act which established the Missouri line, to make this principle applicable to all then existing Territories, and this was accordingly done in 1854.

Notwithstanding the opposition which followed the repeal of the Missouri line, I, in common with thousands of other friends of that measure, never doubted that the principle on which it was done would be again sanctioned by the people. Such I believe to be the opinion of a majority of the American people to-day on the abstract question alone. But other questions have now overshadowed this one; and it is with the exigencies of the hour that the practical statesman must deal.

Bearing upon this question of popular sovereignty, as it is termed, in opposition to the theory of congressional sovereignty and of congressional intervention, the decision of the Supreme Court of the United States, in the Dred Scott case, has played an important part. Whatever differences of opinion may prevail, either among my political friends or my political opponents, in relation to this decision, it is due to frankness to say that I was taken by surprise by it; and that, from the first, I very cheerfully acquiesced in it. In the first place, I felt it my duty, as a good citizen, to yield obedience to the tribunal which pronounced this decision. In the next place, the reasons assigned by a majority of the judges who concurred in it, were, to me, satisfactory as to the conclusions to which the court arrived. I have not time to review that decision now; but I will remark, in passing, that if it be conceded that the right of the master in the services of his slave be, under any State law, a vested property right, then, none but a sovereign power can divest this right. It follows, therefore, that to enable any legislative body to do this, the power must be conferred by some grant of the Constitution under which it is held. If no such grant has been given, then the power does not exist in the Legislature. This principle has been recognized, though in a different sort of case, by the supreme court of my own State. I refer to the case of Beebe *vs.* the State, (6 Indiana Reports, p. 501.)[8] How far the Territorial Legislature may, under its police and regulating powers, encourage or discourage any particular class of property without an unwarranted infringement of vested rights, I will not now stop to inquire. This I regard as still an unsettled question.

Practically, sir, I do not regard the points involved in this decision of as much importance to any section as many seem to have done. After all that may be said and done, a majority of the people in each distinct and sovereign political community ultimately settle for themselves the kind of domestic institutions under which they will live. But as a constitutional question, and as an exposition of the law of the case in this territorial question, I have, from the first, accepted this decision, and have only to regret that the country generally, has not been willing to do so also. I would much prefer, even now, as a common platform upon which all might stand, the conservative doctrines contained in it. Other theories, however, prevailed in the contest through which we have just passed. Though, by a minority vote, yet under the forms of the Constitution, a President has been elected on a platform denying to slaveholders any participation as such in the common Territories, and insisting upon the power and duty of Congress to exclude slavery from all those Territories. This is in direct conflict with the decision to which I have referred, upon any construction placed upon it, and, in my opinion, offensively unjust to the people of the southern States. There is no denying the fact that this result, whether well founded or not, has filled the southern mind with feelings of the deepest apprehension, and has already produced a most disastrous effect in many of the southern States. For myself, sir, I deeply regret the course which several of the southern States have taken. As an abstract proposition, I do not concede the right of secession, in the sense in which it is claimed by the seceding States. I can but regard their proceedings as revolutionary, and subversive of the Constitution; but it is of no use now to argue these abstract propositions. King George III thought that our fathers had no right to secede from him; and technically, according to the theories of his Government, they had not. But still, they did it. In spite of British bayonets they claimed to be the exclusive judges of the extent of their grievances, and of mode of redress. Many of the southern States are evidently intending to act on the same theories. Their success is a question for the future to solve.

When a revolution is successful, its heroes are voted patriots; when it fails, its leaders are denounced as rebels. In this, as in all other hazards, success is everything.

{Representative Niblack then offered the opinion that Congress still had the authority to "arrest" the secession movement. "Let us not," he implored, "commence an indiscriminate slaughter of friends and foes; let us first exhaust every effort at the peaceful settlement of the impending troubles."}

Another very curious fact in this connection is, that many of those most belligerent towards the seceding States have long been noted for their hostility to the admission of any more slave States. Thus, it seems that a slave State cannot get *into* this Union, nor *out* of it, without a fury of indignation and of epithets from them. Why, sir, if they hate slavery half as badly as they profess to, I should think they would be glad to get rid of the States in which it exists on almost any terms. Can it be that it is only for power to govern the slave States that they have been all the time struggling?

But, sir, I will not pursue this branch of my remarks further. With the great mass of the people of the State which I have the honor to represent in part, next, after the preservation of the rudest elements of liberty, is the maintenance of the American Union of States. Differing as we may as to the manner of accomplishing this result, I presume there is little difference in agreeing that to effect this all reasonable efforts ought to be persistently made.

Whether the southern States are entitled to them or not, a large portion of their people feel that they ought to have some additional guarantees. They assure us that, without them, they no longer feel secure. Concede, for the sake of the argument, that they are all in the wrong and need no new guarantees; yet, let us, as generous men, offer something which will afford to those who have left a decent pretext for their return to us. They only desire that we will put in writing, in some solemn and irrevokable form, that which we have so frequently assured them in our speeches and at the hustings. They want the questions now so important to them, since they have permanently become a minority section, placed beyond the contingencies of mere construction or inference, but so written that he who runs may read.

Sir, I believe it to be the interest of all sections that new guarantees be at once offered, and that some fair and honorable adjustment should be at once made. I feel satisfied that the northern States can offer to the South such additional guarantees as will, in the end, satisfy the great mass of its people, without changing in the least the form of our Government or the principles upon which it was founded. The great question of the day is, shall we try the experiment? Most unhesitatingly I answer, yes.

The next question is, how are these new guarantees to be tendered? It is conceded by all of those who are willing to make concessions, that additional amendments to the Constitution be proposed; and that whatever shall be finally agreed to shall be locked up in the Constitution as a part of it, and thus placed beyond the contingencies of an ordinary presidential canvass. I believe now, that some such plan is, in every point of view, the most desirable, as it would be in practice the most efficient. The Constitution as it is is good enough for me personally, and I regret any supposed necessity for amending it; yet I cheerfully yield to what seem to be the emergencies of the hour. We want peace, we want a restoration of confidence, and we want increased stability to the Government. For those I am willing to concede everything which honor and patriotism will permit.

All legislative and judicial compromises having failed to accomplish a withdrawal of this vexed question of slavery from the halls of Congress—which all conservative men have so much and so long desired—let us make one more, and, if need be, last effort to this end, by amending the Constitution. A portion of the proposed amendments is objected to by some because the word "slave" in contained in them. I appreciate, sir, the motives which induced the omission of that word in the old Constitution; but a crisis has arisen in our Government which requires us to look this whole question fully and squarely in the face; when all mere speculative theories ought to be abandoned; when we ought to deal with it as becomes practical men dealing with stubborn facts. As has been well said, elsewhere, why cavil about the name in the Constitution, when the thing itself is clearly contained within it? Many of our treaties with foreign nations, together with numerous acts of Congress, all constituting a part of the supreme law of the land, contain the word "slave" within them. Why not, also, call things by their proper names in the Constitution itself, when, by failing to do so, misconstructions and misunderstandings are the result?

So far as the territorial branch of this controversy is concerned, I would very much prefer, of course, to adhere to and to act upon my own peculiar theories in relation to it. If no others be adopted, I presume I shall still adhere to them, as, in principle, I regard them as the fairest and best. I would much prefer to see the common Territories of the United States occupied and enjoyed in common by the people of all the States upon terms of equality, and in the spirit of fraternal harmony; but, sir, so bitter and so determined has been the opposition of those who object to this plan of settlement from the first, that I now despair of its being allowed to go into successful operation with that promptness necessary to meet the crisis. I hold myself ready, therefore, to embrace any proposition which carries with it the appearance of justice and equality, and I will endeavor to accommodate myself to the view of others in matters of detail. So great, sir, is my attachment to the present form of Government, and so anxious am I to preserve and perpetuate its blessings, that if I cannot save this Union upon my own terms which will be effectual, and not in flagrant violation of the rights of those whom I have the honor to represent. I have been as much a partisan in matters within the legitimate range of party politics, as, perhaps, any man ought to be; but, sir, I am willing to yield all mere party considerations, and all thoughts of mere personal consistency, in at least one more earnest effort to do something to reunite the country.

I have been satisfied, ever since I have had an opportunity of consulting with persons from the different sections of the Confederacy, after the opening of the present session of Congress, that some plan for a fair and equitable division of the Territories of the United States, as between the sections, accompanied with suitable guarantees, would command more strength, and, at the same time, be more efficient in the end, than any other plan. By this, I mean the establishment of a line something like the old Missouri line, north of which slavery shall be prohibited, and south of which it shall be recognized, and, if necessary, protected. By making this constitutional by the requisite amendments, and by specifically defining the rights of the parties on both sides of this line, the most serious objections to the old Missouri line will be removed.

It follows, therefore, sir, that I am inclined to favor the plan substituted by Mr. Crittenden, in the Senate some time since, or something similar to it, in preference to any other now pending before Congress. First, I think it more feasible and complete than any other; and second, I am led to believe that it will be more effectual, and command more real strength all over the country, than any other. If I cannot get that, then I am willing to aid in supporting what may be next best. So far as the report of the committee of thirty-three is concerned, there is much in it which I commend. It seems to look in the right direction; but as a whole, sir, I think it falls short of what the country had a right to expect under existing circumstances. There are but few of the propositions contained within it that I can sustain. It is no time for any mere temporizing policy. If we concede at all, why not cover the whole ground in controversy, and thus make final work of it; if possible, leave nothing more to mere inference or construction in relation to slavery.

It is objected by many of our Republican opponents to the plan of Mr. Crittenden, or to any similar plan, that it runs counter to the Chicago platform. This, sir, to a certain extent, I frankly admit; but what of it? Is not the preservation of the peace and integrity of the country of greater moment that all party platforms? Away with such considerations in times like these. This plan affords common middle ground; why cannot all the Union men come together upon it? It is but a return to the old idea of dividing what it seems we cannot enjoy in common, in peace. This will still leave the new States to be formed on both sides of the proposed line free to adopt whatever domestic institutions they choose when they throw off the territorial condition. Besides, sir, the proposition to absolutely exclude the southern people, or rather the slaveholders, as such, from all participation in the common Territories of the United States, has always seemed to me so manifestly unjust, that I never could bring myself to believe that the great mass of the fair-minded men of the Republican party have intended rigorously to insist on the ultimate enforcement of such a dogma. I have ever regarded it more as a device to carry an election with than anything else. In this view of it, it has already served its purpose. Whenever, therefore, any gentleman insists upon a rigorous enforcement of this policy in the present temper of the country, and is unwilling to concede anything on this point, I cannot but regard him as a practical disunionist.

Sir, if the southern people were a race of cannibals, so long as we were in the Union with them, and living under a common Constitution, I would be willing to divide the common benefits and common property with them fairly and equally. How much more strongly is this obligation imposed when they are kindred, our friends and our brethren? Whenever I shall determine that I will not consent to recognize any claim on the part of the southern people, including, of course, the slaveholders, to any of the Territories, or other common property of all the States, I will not then even claim to be a Union man. To those who stand in this category I ask, why not say at once to the people of the South, "Stand and deliver. This Government is ours; not yours!" Why do you cry "Peace, peace, when there is no peace," and when none is intended? Why continually proclaim that you are for the Constitution and the Union, when you are not willing to concede anything to preserve them?

If, sir, by the exercise of a wise forbearance, a resort to arms can be avoided, and a peaceful and honorable settlement of existing troubles can be effected, nations will yet rise up to call us blessed. If, however, by any rash or reckless act of ours, this country shall be involved in a desolating civil war, then the sooner the curtain of oblivion is thrown over the present exciting and terrible chapter in our history as a nation, the better for us in the eyes of posterity.

I am proud to be able to say that, so far as my own, my native State is concerned, she has been true to her constitutional obligations. In nothing vital can the southern people justly complain of her. It is no use to deny the fact, however, that towards some of the northern States the South has just cause of complaint. Let those offending States make the *amende honorable*,[9] as Rhode Island has done;[10] then let us tender some fair and honorable mode of adjustment of the whole controversy; and, if all overtures shall be rejected, then new questions will arise and new responsibilities intervene. I do not, however, fear such a result, and will not discuss so remote a contingency. "Sufficient unto the day is the evil thereof."

If, nevertheless, sir, after all peaceful means shall be exhausted, we find that a final and inexorable separation must take place, I cannot, in any view of the case which I have been able to take, see what good can result from a resort to arms. War, as between the different sections or the different States, would be, *ipso facto*,[11] dissolution. States at war are, necessarily, foreign to each other. While I would cling to the Union so long as there is a fragment of it left worth preserving, yet, if we must part, in the name of humanity let us do so like Christian and reasonable men. Let us say to those who will not remain with us, as Abraham said to Lot:

> Let there be no strife, I pray thee, between me and thee, and between my herdmen and thy herdmen, for we be brethren.
>
> Is not the whole land before thee? Separate thyself, I pray thee, from me: if thou wilt take the left hand, then I will go with the right; or if thou depart to the right hand, then I will go to the left.[12]

Sir, the theme is too mournful a one, and I will not dwell upon it.

May He who controls the destiny of nations rule all things for the best.

Source: *Congressional Globe*, 36th Cong., 2nd Sess., 677–80.

John White Brockenbrough

Virginia Secession Convention
March 6, 1861

John W. Brockenbrough (1806–1877), born in Hanover County, Virginia, and educated at the College of William and Mary and the University of Virginia, established himself as a lawyer and later judge in Lexington. In early 1861, he served as one of five commissioners from Virginia to the Washington Peace Conference. Elected to the Confederate Provisional Congress in Montgomery, Alabama, he chose not to run for the Regular Confederate Congress, and became, instead, a Confederate district judge for Western Virginia.

Two days after the inauguration of President Lincoln, George W. Summers[13] presented Brockenbrough's report on the deliberations of the Washington Peace Conference to Virginia's secession convention. In the report, Judge Brockenbrough carefully examined each article of the conference's final amendment to the Constitution and determined that Senator Crittenden's solution was "far preferable to that of the late Peace Conference." (The complete text of the Washington Peace Conference's amendment is included in chapter 8.)

The Hon. JOHN TYLER, *ex-President of the United States, and Hon.* GEORGE W. SUMMERS*:*

Gentlemen: I beg leave to address you, as two of the Commissioners representing the State of Virginia in the late Peace Conference at Washington, and also as members of the State Convention, now sitting in Richmond, and to state, as briefly as I can, my views in reference to the results of that Conference.

The act of the General Assembly of Virginia which originated the Conference, declares the patriotic purposes which impelled the Legislature in resorting to this extraordinary mode of adjusting the unhappy controversy which now divides the States of this Confederacy, and declares that unless it be satisfactorily adjusted, "a permanent dissolution of the Union is inevitable; and the General Assembly, representing the wishes of the people of this Commonwealth, is desirous of employing every reasonable means to avert so dire a calamity, and determined to make a final effort to restore the Union and the Constitution in the spirit in which they were established by the fathers of the Republic." The act further declared the opinion of the General Assembly to be, that the resolutions submitted to the Senate of the United States by Mr. Crittenden, with several specified modifications, constitute the basis of such an adjustment of the controversy as would be accepted by the people of Virginia.

The plan of adjustment agreed upon by a majority of the Conference differs in many important particulars from the scheme of Mr. Crittenden. The main difficulty we had to contend with in the controversy, was in a satisfactory adjustment of the Territorial question. The Crittenden plan distinctly recognizes slavery of the African race South of 36 30 as existing, and precludes Congress from interfering therewith: and declares that it shall be *protected as property* by all the departments of the territorial government during its continuance. The Conference plan contains no such recognition, *eo nomine*,[14] but declares that "the status of persons held to involuntary service or labor; as it now exists, shall not be changed: nor shall any law be passed by Congress or the Territorial Legislature to hinder or prevent the taking of such persons from any of the States to said territories, nor to impair the rights arising from said relation; but the same shall be subject to judicial cognizance in the federal courts, according to the course of the common law."

Whether this provision is substantially equivalent to the corresponding clause of the Crittenden plan is a question of interpretation. The language of the latter is clear and perspicuous; of the former, vague and ambiguous. Whatever the true construction of it be, it is a most weighty objection to it, that it admits of various interpretations. The rights arising from the relation of master and slave are expressly recognized, and the Federal Courts are required to take cognizance of them; but neither the Executive or Legislative departments are, *in terms*, required to protect them. Its advocates in the Conference insisted that while the rights arising, from the relation are referred to the judicial determination of the Courts, the recognition of them in the article, by a just implication, imports that it is the duty of the Legislature to afford them ample protection by positive enactment of laws necessary to accomplish the end. If this be the proper construction of the clauses, and in my opinion it is—the guarantee of protection of the rights of property in slaves in the territories, is equivalent to that contained in the Crittenden scheme. But we have to resort to implication to deduce it. The terms employed, to secure protection of the rights growing out of the relation of master and slave, are negative only; they shall not be changed, or the introduction of slaves hindered, or the rights of the master impaired by legislation. No duty is prescribed to hedge them round with proper enactments. It is for this reason that I made a most strenuous effort to amend the section by interpolating the words—"and it shall be the duty of the Territorial Government, in all its departments, to protect the rights arising from said relation." The effort was repeatedly and most earnestly made. It was ineffectual, but it is fair to say that the sense of the Conference was not tested on this particular question—the consideration of the amendment being precluded by the ruling of the Chair, that the section was not then amendable.

The rights of the master are made subject to judicial cognizance *according to the course of the common law!* How far can the *courts* afford protection to the rights of the master to his slave, according to the course of the common law? Where legal rights exist, that most wise and flexible system of law known as the common law always supplies the appropriate remedies for their enforcement. The invasion of a right is an injury, for the redress of which a suitable remedy was always afforded; for the common law knows no such anomaly as a wrong without a remedy. Any civil injury, therefore, to the rights growing out of the relation of master and slave would be redressed, according to the course of the common law, by supplying the appropriate remedy of detinue, trover, case, &c.[15] It is said that at common law, slavery was not recognized—that at common law, man could not have property in man; and the celebrated Somerset case, and the late Anderson case are cited, in support of the proposition; to which may be added the imposing authority of W. H. Seward himself.[16] But the common law is not referred to here to determine *rights*, but simply to furnish *remedies* for injuries to rights recognized by the section in explicit terms. The principle that rights always draw after them at common law the remedy for injuries to those rights, does not apply to public wrongs or crimes. These are not punishable until defined and appropriate penalties are deduced either by the common law or by statute. But we cannot look to the common law as a source of criminal jurisdiction in the Federal Courts where those rights are made cognizable, for those tribunals have no such jurisdiction, and can only take cognizance of crimes specially created or defined by statute. Statutes prescribing police regulations are indispensable in a slaveholding country; but the duty of enacting them is not enjoined by this section, unless it be implied from the recognition of the rights arising from the relation of master and slave. Is it a fair implication from the language in this section, that it is the duty of the Territorial Legislature of New Mexico to protect the rights of slave owners by all proper enactments? In my judgment, it admits of no other fair or reasonable construction. There is much circumlocution to avoid the use of the terms "slave" and "slavery"; but the *status* of persons held to involuntary service or labor there, is that of slavery, and the persons so held are slaves; that *status*—that is, the state or condition of slavery—shall not be changed, nor the importation or introduction of such persons from any of the States prevented, nor the rights arising from such relation impaired. They would be impaired without proper legislation for their protection, and the duty of such protection may therefore be inferred, since the failure to legislate may as effectually impair the rights recognized, as positive hostile legislation. But, in point of fact, there is no necessity for such legislation in New Mexico. It exists already in very ample measure, as I learn from undoubted authority. The *status* of such persons, as it now exists, is recognized as a status of slavery, and of slavery only; the rights of the master are already fully protected by law, and to repeal those laws would be a clear violation of the spirit and very words of this section, as it would certainly impair, most probably destroy, those rights. Upon every sound principle of interpretation, I think that the rights of the master to his slaves, *as property*, are protected by this section.

The second section introduces a new, and as I think, valuable principle. So far as the acquisition of future territory is concerned, it creates a dual Senate, by an equal partition of power between the two sections of the Senate. This is a practical guarantee of equal power to the weaker section, by which the South can exclude any future territory, if the conditions of an admission are disadvantageous to her. But the Northern section may equally checkmate her, in her attempts to acquire future territory. True, but the only territory South of 36 deg. 30 min. which can be hereafter acquired, is Cuba and the Northern part of Mexico. Cuba is a slaveholding island already, and its great resources can only be developed by slave labor.[17] The North is more eager to possess it than the South. If any portion of Mexico is hereafter acquired, it will be on the principle of a fair and equitable partition of the territory between the sections. This section was approved by four of the Commissioners from Virginia.

The third section embodies, substantially, I think, the provisions of the second, third and fourth sections of the Crittenden plan. It prohibits Congress from interfering with slavery within any State or Territory; or in the District of Columbia, without the consent of Maryland and of the owners, or making the owners just compensation; or with representatives or others bringing slaves for personal service with them and taking them away; or in places within the exclusive jurisdiction of the United States within those States and Territories where slavery exists; or the removal or transportation of slaves from one State or Territory to any other where slavery exists; or the right during transportation, by sea or river, of *touching* at ports, shores and landings, and of landing in cases of distress. The right of *transit* through States where slavery does not exist, is not confirmed. The provision that no higher rate of taxation shall be imposed on slaves than on land, is of some value to the South.

The action prohibiting the foreign slave trade by Constitutional amendment is objectionable, simply because it is wholly unnecessary. Even the confederated States of the South now constituting an independent Government of slave States, *de facto*, if not *de jure*, have prohibited this traffic. The advocates for the re-opening of it in any one of the border slave States are very few, and there was no sort of necessity for interpolating this provision, which had no connection with the pending controversy, into this scheme of adjustment.

The seventh and last section of the Conference scheme is very much less satisfactory than the corresponding one in Mr. Crittenden's plan. Each provides for the payment of the full value of fugitive slaves by the United States in all cases where the officer, charged with the duty of making the arrest, is prevented from so doing by violence or intimidation, or when after arrest, the slaves are rescued. But the former {the seventh section} is defective in not providing for re-imbursement to the United States by clothing it with power to impose and collect a tax on the county or city where the outrage was committed, equal to the principal, interest and costs, as is provided in the Crittenden resolutions. There is a double advantage in this feature. In the first place it is more just and equitable to cast the burthen on those who committed the wrong than upon the public treasury. The South is thus made, by its omission in the Conference scheme, to pay its full proportion of a charge resulting from a wrong committed against herself. But by far the most important consideration is, that such a requirement would tend powerfully to restrain such wicked outrages by making it the interest of the offending locality to suppress all mobs and riotous assemblages, to rob and plunder the citizens of the South for no other cause than asserting an undoubted constitutional right.

I have thus endeavored to run a parallel between the two plans of adjustment. On the whole, it is clear that the Crittenden plan is far preferable to that of the late Peace Conference. It is necessary to say how earnestly, yet ineffectually, we struggled to come up to the very letter of our commission by obtaining an adjustment on the basis of the former plan, and in every variety of form. We were uniformly voted down by that inexorable majority! At length, all rival schemes being rejected, the naked question came up of the adoption or rejection of the present Conference scheme. The vote was by sections, and Virginia voted against the most important sections, particularly the first and seventh of the series; and they were all adopted *seriatim*.[18] It was supposed that, as a matter or course, the vote would be taken upon the scheme as an entirety, and I then announced to one of you that after the most anxious deliberation, I had come to the conclusion that, distasteful as the scheme was to me, I felt it to be my duty to cast a representative vote, and sustain the measure as a whole. I was convinced that Western Virginia, which I in part represented, would have so voted by an immense majority, if her voice could be heard within that hall, and, acting under that strong conviction, I would have done homage to that great principle of representative government which demands that the representative yield his individual sentiments, and give utterance to those of his constituents. But no vote was taken on the plan, as a whole, the Chair having ruled that each section being successively adopted, the entire plan was adopted, and no farther vote was necessary or admissible, under the parliamentary rule.

The most solemnly momentous issue that ever agitated the councils of our dear old Commonwealth is now fairly made up and must soon find its solution in the deliberations of the Convention now assembled to give expression to her sovereign will. My earnest prayer is that true wisdom may conduct her safely and honorably out of this great crisis. Every loyal son of hers awaits the issue with intense solicitude, and for myself I will say that my destiny is bound up indissolubly with hers!

I am, gentlemen, most cordially,
Your friend,
JOHN W. BROCKENBROUGH.

Source: Reese, George H., ed. *Proceedings of the Virginia State Convention of 1861: February 13-May 1.* 4 vols. (Richmond: Virginia State Library, 1965), I, 419–24.

Delegate James H. Moss

Missouri Secession Convention

March 11, 1861

James H. Moss[19] was a thirty-five year old lawyer from Liberty, Clay County, Missouri when he was elected a delegate to Missouri's secession convention. Both town and county were established in 1822: the town named for the concept of American liberty, and county after Kentucky statesman Henry Clay. Missouri convened a secession convention on

February 28 and on March 19 voted, with only one dissenting vote, against secession.

On March 9, the convention's Committee on Federal Relations delivered its report to the assembled delegates. The committee prefaced its findings by observing that the South had "well-grounded" complaints against the North, but that it was "equally true that heretofore there has been no complaint against the action of the Federal Government in any of its departments, as designed to violate the rights of the Southern States." The report contained seven resolutions beginning with one that confirmed the State's stand against secession. "That at present," it stated, "there is no adequate cause to compel Missouri to dissolve her connection with the Federal Union." Another supported Senator Crittenden's amendment as the solution to the "causes of difference" between the sections. The fifth resolution begged both the federal government and the seceding states to "stay the arm of military power, and on no pretense whatever bring upon the nation the horrors of civil war." To this section, Delegate Moss offered an amendment that stated that Missouri would not aid any seceding state, nor would it "furnish men and money" to assist the federal government to "coerce a seceding State."

Mr. MOSS. Well, I will not say anything about this amendment {his amendment mentioned above} at present, but confine myself to the majority report. I agree with the position taken in that report—the position taken by my worthy friend who is before me, as the Chairman of the Committee. I believe, gentlemen, that the hopes of the people of Missouri—yes, of the Union, of the Border States as well as of the Northern States—I say, I believe that their only hope of salvation now is with the people; and the sooner we go to them the better. And for that reason I am opposed to all preliminary proceedings by bodies of men whose work, when it is finished, amounts to nothing. I tell you the people have got tired of such things. They are sick, and they want a physician who can heal them. They do not want to be compelled to swallow any more quack medicine.

It is urged by some of the friends of the Border State propositions, that it would be advantageous to decline, for the present, holding a National Convention. And why? They say, in order that we might present an unbroken front. They say, fix upon an ultimatum. Well, now, gentlemen, I disagree with my friends in that respect. I disagree with them for this reason: if I am dealing with an enemy—for the sake of illustration, I will call those gentlemen who are advocating "irrepressible conflict" our enemies—and I propose to him to compromise, and I have four or five different plans of compromise; then, if I see that he indicates that he is in favor of a certain one of those plans, and that plan suits me to the letter, I believe that good policy is to meet him at once, and not waste my time discussing the advantages of the other propositions. If I see that he will give me all that I ask, then, gentlemen, I feel it to be my duty as well as my interest, and the dictates of common sense, to accede to it at once. Now, how do we stand in regard to this? Missouri says that she proposes the Crittenden resolutions as the proper basis for a settlement of the question. Do you doubt, that the Border States all indorse that proposition? I presume not. How is it in the North? Why, the Crittenden resolutions stand without a rival. Look at the memorials and petitions that have flooded our National Legislature.[20] What object have they been presented for? Look at the 14,000 names from the city of Boston praying for the adoption of those resolutions.

Now, my idea of the policy of Missouri is this: lead out in this great conciliatory movement. Tell your brothers of the Border States that, believing that a majority of the citizens of the United States are agreed that the Crittenden resolutions present a fair and equitable basis of settlement, Missouri plants herself upon that position, and calls upon the Border States to follow her. There is no doubt but the Northern States can be made to accede to them; and I tell you, gentlemen, we will go into that National Convention with four-fifths of her delegates instructed to occupy them as a basis. That is what we will do, and we will do it without holding a Border State Convention; and I believe, honestly, we will reach that point more successfully by Missouri's taking this ground right at the start, as she has a right to do, and determining that she is not going to hold any further consultation with sister States except in National Convention, and that she will instruct her delegates to the National Convention to stand upon that platform, and will call upon her sister Border States to do likewise. Then, gentlemen, I believe we will go into a National Convention—I mean the friends of compromise—I mean the delegates that come from the people, from whom we look for salvation, will go there as a unit, and I believe all will go virtually satisfied with the Crittenden compromise.

As I remarked before, the impatient people—they are in the habit of traveling by railroad, and talking by telegraph, and they wish to see the great difficulty we have to contend with settled with dispatch. They are impatient. They have forgotten that it took eight long years of bloodshed, and suffering, and trial, to build up this magnificent edifice; and now, because they cannot stay its tottering walls, and re-instate it upon its ancient foundations in an hour, they get impatient and cry out for revolution. Gentlemen, the sooner we can get to the people the better.

If I thought that in advocating a National Convention, I should be instrumental in bringing about a conflict between delegates from the Border States and from Northern States, I would have different views about the matter. I should not advocate it; but I believe our delegates will go there, and the Northern delegates will go there, and a great majority of all will be instructed to vote for the Crittenden resolutions.

Although it may be a little tiresome for me now to discuss the merits of the Crittenden resolutions, much as they have been discussed, yet I hope I shall be indulged, for this reason: that we have these battles to fight over again with the people; and I know the skill and ingenuity and masterly management of our enemies in Missouri; (when I say our enemies, I mean the secessionists *per se*, these gentlemen who think that Missouri's salvation depends upon going out *now*.[21] I want the people of Missouri to understand the force of our position here. I know it will be contended by our enemies, when we have passed these resolutions, that we have done nothing—that what we have done amounts to nothing—and that Missouri has taken no position whatever; that we are submissionists, and all that sort of thing; and, recollecting these facts, recollecting the history of the canvas, and the fight made heretofore, I think it not inappropriate, in this connection, in a short way, to speak of the peculiar merits of the Crittenden resolutions as the basis of settlement.

In order to appreciate these merits, let us ask ourselves, in the first place, what are we seeking to remedy? What is it that has terrified the South in regard to the danger of her institutions? Is it the mere squabble about the Territories? Far from it. It is the announcement of the celebrated doctrine that Mr. LINCOLN claims to be the father of the "irrepressible conflict." I know that Republicans interpret that one way, but the South—the men of the South—the men of the slave States—all interpret it another way, and I think their interpretation is right. How do they interpret it? They interpret it, gentlemen, to mean, not only the exclusion of Southern men from the Territories, and the hedging in of slavery with a wall of fire, as has been remarked by some other gentleman. They may be wrong in this interpretation; but whether it be right or wrong, the general opinion entertained in the South is, that it means eternal and unceasing warfare upon the institution, and that, whilst the Republican party now, under our present Constitution, acknowledge that Congress has no power to invade a Southern State by legislation for the purpose of interfering with the institution in the States, yet, when in some future time they have acquired sufficient strength, they will institute such interference. Whether that idea be erroneous or correct, is a matter I do not propose to investigate. Suffice it to say, that the great object in the outset of this conciliatory movement, is to give the Southern mind peace upon this great question. It is to satisfy them that they need no longer look with anxiety and dread to their Northern brethren.

Now, let us see whether the Crittenden resolutions reach that point. How does Mr. Crittenden propose to remedy the evil? How does he propose to give peace and safety to the South? He says we will amend the Constitution in a certain way, so as to deprive Congress of the power ever to interfere with the question of slavery in a State; and for a further guarantee, we will make that provision in the Constitution like a law of the Medes and Persians, *unalterable.*

Gentlemen, if there be any in this Convention, who are secessionists, (and I hope there are none;) if there is a man here with a true Southern heart in his bosom, who is honest and candid, I ask whether he would propose to offer amendment to that? Could we ask for a stronger guarantee than the one contained in the Crittenden resolutions reaching to that point? I believe, gentlemen, that no other statesman has offered an amendment to the Constitution that suits the people of the South better.[22] We think it is as strong an amendment as we can get.

What is the next point? The next point, gentlemen, is to give protection to the four thousand millions of slave property in the States. You may talk about principles, your Territorial questions, the theory of the Government, and all that sort of thing, but I tell you the men who have labored for a lifetime to build up a little fortune, and have got half of it in slave property, will not rest satisfied for a moment without sufficient guarantees that they can lie down at night and sleep quietly and in safety, and know that no robber dare break in and take their property from them. They want protection for the four thousand millions of dollars of slave property. Now, how does Mr. Crittenden propose to reach that point? Is there any improvements which has ever been suggested upon his plan? What does he propose to do? Gentlemen, you are aware that we have upon our statute book, passed by our National Legislature, the Fugitive Slave Law. What has been the trouble in the South? It was, that when a Southern man undertook to pursue a slave into a free State a mob would arise and take his property from him, and he had no remedy—he was powerless. That needs rectifying. We need a stronger guarantee in regard to that point than we have had heretofore. How are we to get it? Mr. Crittenden proposes that the General Government shall come in with her strong arm and deal with the Northern robber who dares to violate the law. He does not leave the individual to struggle with the law; but he proposes that the General Government should pay the value of the stolen property to the owner, and that she shall undertake to deal with the offender according to his deserts.

Men of Missouri—slave holders—can you suggest an improvement on that? I believe none has ever been suggested that was more satisfactory to the South than that.

Then, gentlemen of the Convention, the two great points are now disposed of. Peace and quiet are restored to the South. They no longer look upon their Northern brethren as enemies, because they have not the *power* to do them injury.

All those startling fears upon which artful and designing men worked in order to carry themselves into power, without reference to the effect that it is to have upon the nation, and which have in a great measure led us to our present unfortunate condition, they are rid of. We put an impassible barrier between the enemies of slavery and the owners of slave property in the States. We deprive the Abolitionist of the power ever to alter the American Constitution, so as to give Congress the power to invade a Southern State by legislation; and we give full and ample protection to the four thousand millions of dollars worth of property in the States.

Well, those two material points are satisfactorily disposed of. The next question, and, gentlemen, the only question remaining to be considered (for I believe that the people of the North agree that we are entitled, under the Constitution, to all those guarantees and to all the protection that we ask, so far as slavery is concerned in the States,) is that of the Territories. Well, what of the Territories? It is unnecessary for me to argue this question at length before this Convention; but, gentlemen, as that is the point upon which our enemies hang the fate of Missouri, I will argue it. That is the great weapon of war in the hands of our enemies. They say all is very well about the States, but the danger lies in the Territories. Well, now, this is not a question entirely of principle, but a question of fact—a question of practicability. You go on to demonstrate to them that the God of Nature has put his veto on the introduction of slavery north of 36 degrees 30 minutes. Yet they will argue with you a day, and say they don't care whether that is true or false—whether the laws of nature have placed impassable barriers between them and that Territory or not; they will maintain that the abstract principle is right, and that there should be no concession upon that point. They say the Revolution was fought on a preamble, and they talk about a *principle*. Well, I apprehend, whenever the people can understand this principle in a practical light, they will make but poor headway with that principle. They insist that they have the right of going into any Territory and occupying every foot of ground that the God of Nature will allow them to occupy, and that they are not willing to abandon that right in any instance whatever. That is the argument of the secessionists.

Well, what does that amount to? it {*sic*} amounts to just this—our Northern brethren now, and I believe it sincerely, will give us the Crittenden Resolutions whenever we can get at the sense of the people in a National Convention; they will give us guarantees for the protection of slavery in the States; they will give us this impassable barrier to prevent men, hereafter, from carrying the war into Africa; they will give us protection for every foot of territory where you can take slavery according to the laws of Nature; but the Secessionists say we will surrender all these guarantees offered us, and for what? for {*sic*} the sake of asserting an abstract principle that is barren—a right that is a barren abstraction—and they say further, that they consider this compromise altogether on one side, that we give up every thing, and that we get nothing.—Why, gentlemen, is that the manner in which the thing suggests itself to you; and right here, at the risk of being—as I remarked before—a little tedious, I will go slightly into the past political history of our country on the subject of slavery, and shall take, to some extent, the same line of argument pursued a day or two since by the gentleman from Clinton—Judge Birch.[23] Let us look to the national legislation of the past, and see whether or not this is not a compromise we are getting. It will be remembered, and I will pass very rapidly over the history, that in 1820, Missouri sought to come in as a slave State but was opposed, but at last she did come in with her magnificent domain. Time rolled on, and Texas with her magnificent empire sought to come into the Union. It was still opposed by men of the North, with the exception of those of our Northern friends who have always been willing to stand by our Constitutional rights, and they agreed to admit her. How? Texas has a territory of three hundred millions of acres of land. And what were the conditions prescribed by Texas? They were that she should be admitted with the right to divide her territory into four great States, and she has the right to-day if she is not out of the Union. It was a part of the contract, as you will observe by reading the proceedings of Congress in 1845, and further, by reading WEBSTER'S great speech on the compromise measures of 1850, where he takes that ground and says: "Texas to-day has the right to divide her magnificent Territory into four slave States, and that it is a part of the contract under which she was admitted." Well, gentlemen, time rolled on, and New Mexico and California sought to come in. The same enemies in the Northern States attempted to prevent the admission of those Territories, and what then took place? Why, the immortal Clay came fortward {*sic*} and offered a resolution which embodied the celebrated doctrine of non-intervention, by means of which men of the slave States, with their property, could go into those territories and stand side by side the men of the free States. By and by our Southern brethren said to the North, this will not satisfy us. Your citizens have been encroaching upon us, and making war upon our institutions, and robbing us of our property, and we have no remedy. Give us the Fugitive Slave Law. They did so. And while a Northern man[24] was in the Presidential chair they executed that law. That was not all. Time rolled on again, and in 1854, when Kansas and Nebraska sought to come in, what was done then? Our Southern brethren said this celebrated doctrine which was enunciated in the compromise measures of 1850, the doctrine of non-intervention, is cramped and trammeled in its full operation on account of the old Missouri Compromise, and we now ask you to do what by right and justice you should do to us. We ask you to remove the old Missouri restriction and give the people of the South the right to go into the common territory and say what institutions they shall have. Did they refuse? No, they gave it to us. What was done then? It was then sought to take the power of legislating on this subject of slavery in the Territories, as I before remarked, out of the hands of Congress. Our Southern brethren said: Take this away from Congress, and give us all a fair opportunity—Kentucky, Louisiana and Arkansas—and give us an opportunity to go there and take an equal chance with our Northern brethren, and let the people decide. We did go into Kansas Territory and passed laws for the protection of the slave, as we did in New

Mexico, and which now stands on our statute book. That is the way the thing stands. I am now reciting this history for the purpose of showing that this is a compromise. I understand a compromise to mean a yielding up on the part of both sides. Now, all this was right. I do not claim that the North has given us anything that we are not entitled to; but this Kansas-Nebraska bill was given to us upon our solicitation, and upon that platform we elected James Buchanan, a sworn friend of the South, by an overwhelming majority,[25] and the astonishing spectacle is now presented that notwithstanding all this seven of our Southern brethren have deserted us and gone out of the Union. I undertake to show you that the propositions contained in the Crittenden resolutions in reference to the territory are, in the truest sense of the word, a compromise, and I think I can demonstrate it. We have asked the fugitive slave law, and it was put upon our statute book. We asked that the power to regulate slavery in the territories be given to the people from Congress, and what do we find? We find that we cannot be protected in the territories—that the arm of the territorial legislature is too weak—that our Northern enemies, those who are really our Northern enemies, have three men to our one, and that they can fill the territories and rob us of our protection. Now, what do we ask? We ask that this power shall be placed back in Congress; that it shall once more be restored to the General Government that she by her strong arm shall give us protection. Suppose they do it, don't they give us something? Don't they yield us something? Certainly; and, I contend, just what we are entitled to. We now ask that we shall not be left to our enemies who get the power in the Territories, but that the Government shall come to our rescue. Suppose they give it to us, is it nothing? But they tell us about the guarantees they gave us for slavery in the States. There is the Fugitive Slave Law, and all you can ask. We are not responsible for its execution. The President has the power to execute it, and we have done all we can. We say we admit that, and ask you to do more—to give us a remedy that will be of some practical utility to us. We ask you to let us go into this Territory with our slave property, and claim protection of the General Government. I do not know what other men's ideas of compromise are, but that fills my idea exactly. And mind you, when I say all this, I don't mean to say that they yield one thing that we are not entitled to. We are entitled to it all, and we should take it in the spirit of compromise. I have deemed it proper, gentlemen of the Convention, to detain you thus long in the discussion of my views in regard to the Crittenden propositions.

{Moss concluded his remarks by observing that there were sufficient Union men in the South, in spite of the efforts of Jefferson Davis, to support some sort of compromise measure. Missouri, he pronounced, will not supply troops to "make war" upon the federal government. "Now, if I do not mistake the feeling of Missouri, as between South Carolina and Major Anderson [Robert Anderson, commander of Fort Sumter], the sympathies of Missouri are in favor of Major Anderson."}

Source: *Journal and Proceeding of the Missouri State Convention, Held at Jefferson City and St. Louis, March, 1861* (St. Louis: George Knapp & Co., Printers and Binders, 1861), 69–73.

CHAPTER FOUR

Crittenden Debated: Anti-Crittenden

With very few exceptions, Republicans opposed any constitutional compromise on the slavery issue for several reasons. Primarily they argued that the subject of slavery in the territories had been formally put before the voting public in the election of 1860 and conclusively decided. The presidential contest, they reasoned, had offered three options for slavery in the territories: popular sovereignty (Douglas), protection by the federal government (Breckinridge), and no extension (Lincoln). Lincoln's victory in an incontestable democratic election should have settled the matter. Why, they asked, should Republicans compromise on the very issue upon which Lincoln had been elected? Additionally they argued that white southerners complained not against the federal government, but against northern interference with the rendition of fugitive slaves, a subject properly decided by courts.

The federal government had not restricted slavery in any way over the past decade. In fact, Republicans argued, in 1850, Congress had acceded to southern demands in expanding federal responsibility in returning runaway slaves, and, in that same year, opened the New Mexico and Utah territories to the possibility slavery: before the decade was out, both territories had enacted positive slave codes. Furthermore, Congress, as Delegate James H. Moss made clear in his speech in the previous chapter, had reversed the Missouri Compromise line in 1854 so that southerners had a chance of establishing slavery in the northern portion of the Louisiana Purchase, and, three years later, the Supreme Court had rendered a decidedly pro-southern, proslavery opinion in the case of Dred Scott. As a result of federal action, slavery had expanded over the previous decade, not contracted. The South was seceding because of fears of what the executive branch under Lincoln might do, not because of what the federal government had done.

The rush to secession baffled many Republicans because while Lincoln had won the presidency, Democrats had emerged from the election of 1860 holding majorities in both the House and the Senate, and Roger B. Taney still presided over a proslavery Supreme Court. Republicans did not, in spite of what many Democrats argued, control the federal government. Moreover, as some of them pointed out, southern demands for protections for slavery in the Constitution turned democratic tradition on its head. Instead of respecting the time-honored tradition of slavery being local and freedom national, Democratic compromise measures intended to make slavery national and freedom local.

As the following speeches reveal, the southern charge that the "Black" Republican Party consisted of abolitionists and that the incoming president was determined to abolish slavery was baseless. The party of Lincoln (and, of course, Lincoln himself) opposed any extension of slavery into the territories, but upheld the constitutional right of states to determine for themselves whether to support or prohibit the institution. The federal government, under the Constitution, had no more right to interfere with slave labor in the South than it did to interfere with free labor in the North, lectured Massachusetts's Republican Daniel Gooch. Interestingly, this Bostonian compared northern abolitionists to southern disunionists observing that both wished to "give to this Government greater powers; the one that it may abolish and prohibit slavery everywhere in all the States; the other that it may establish and protect slavery everywhere in all the States."

In addition, some of the suggested amendments infringed on northern states' rights. Crittenden's fourth article regarding transit of slaves, for example, would have forbidden northern states from prohibiting slaveowners from bringing their slaves with them when doing business in the North as New York had done in 1841. Furthermore, as Representative Gooch points out below, Crittenden's seventh article prohibiting free blacks from voting or holding elective office impinged on a state's right to determine citizenship and who shall exercise the elective franchise. Representative Gooch wryly observed, "I find that those men who have always claimed to be the especial guardians of State rights, value them only as they make in favor of slavery."

Representative James Wilson (Republican)

US House of Representatives
February 1, 1861

James Wilson (1825–1867) practiced law in Crawfordsville, Indiana. He served in the United States Army during the Mexican War from June 1846 until June 1847. He was elected as a Republican to the Thirty-Fifth and Thirty-Sixth Congresses and served in the House of Representatives from 1857 to 1861. He again entered the United States Army as captain of volunteers and served from 1862 until 1865.

Representative Wilson introduced his comments by observing that "the Federal Government is to-day as it was last year, and as it has been for four years." He then turned to the "revolution" taking place in the country and the reasons supporting secession. He specifically discussed South Carolina's declaration of secession and its complaints about northern personal liberty laws and the concern that slavery will be excluded from the western territories. Wilson rebutted the declaration's stated fears that slavery would be prohibited from the territories by restating the decision of the *Dred Scott* case and by adding, "How is it with New Mexico? It was free when acquired from the Republic of Mexico. Is it not a slave Territory now?" The Indianan also voiced the common Republican opposition to the "hereafter acquired" clause in Senator Crittenden's compromise proposal. Wilson was well aware on February 1, that the withdrawal of six southern states from the Union (and their senators and representatives from Congress) meant that Republicans controlled both houses throughout the remainder of the Thirty-Sixth Congress.

Sir, the whole complaint of South Carolina is unjust. It has no foundation whatever. It is absurd. Here I leave this question. It is useless to proceed any further. I will only say, whatever may be the result of the action of South Carolina; whatever may be the result of the action of the other States who now stand in open opposition to the Government of the United States, still, I believe that the judgment of mankind and the judgment of posterity will declare and indelibly stamp it on the pages of history that there never was so causeless, so unnatural, and so unjustifiable a rebellion, as this which now convulses the country.

I come now to the question immediately before the House. On the second day of this session of Congress, the President of the United States made an especial reference to the alarming state of public affairs, in his annual message. On the same day, on motion of the honorable gentleman from Virginia, [Mr. BOTELER][1] a special committee of thirty-three was appointed to consider the disturbed condition of the country. In the Senate of the United States, the distinguished Senator from Kentucky [Mr. CRITTENDEN] brought forward a series of measures for the permanent adjustment of the question of slavery. All of these plans of adjustment are before us and the people. We have the plan of the President, the plan of the Senator from Kentucky, and the plan of the committee of thirty-three. What of these plans of adjustment? What is their object? Sir, we are informed that it is to conciliate the South. Why conciliate? Has the South been wronged? Wherein, I ask? Has the South been oppressed by any act of the Federal Government? Where is the evidence? Where is the act? If any such act of the General Government exists, let it be produced. If there is none, then there is nothing to concede or conciliate. But we are told that these are all measures of peace. With whom? With the loyal States? Let the seizure of Fort Moultrie, let the affair of the Star of the West, let the environment of Fort Pickens answer. Peace measures indeed! We had a peace measure in 1820; we had a peace measure in 1850. Where are they? Both have been swept aside. Can we expect, is it reasonable to expect, that any adjustment we may now agree upon will share any better fate? Let us not be precipitate in this matter. Let us not be in haste to adopt measures for which we may be justly reproached forever. Sir, after all, the difficulty is not in Congress nor in the people. It is in slavery itself, and nowhere else. But let us consider these plans. What, then, is the plan of the President? It is this: an explanatory amendment of the Constitution on three special points:

1. An express recognition of the right of property in slaves in the States where it now exists or may hereafter exist.

2. The duty of protecting this right in all the common Territories throughout their territorial existence, and until they shall be admitted as States into the Union, with or without slavery, as their constitutions may prescribe.

3. A like recognition of the right of the master to have his slave who has escaped from one State to another restored and delivered up to him, and of the validity of the fugitive slave law, enacted for this purpose, together with a declaration impairing or defeating this right, are violations of the Constitution, and are consequently null and void.[2]

Sir, this is the plan of the Executive. It is comprehensive at least. Besides, it has the virtue of being explicit. The President has not been deterred by words. I commend him in this respect. Other gentlemen, whose plans are before us, might well have imitated his example. Again, the President may be commended in the fact that he has proposed the proper mode by which an amendment may be originated. That is, by Congress or the Legislatures of the States. In this he differs from the Senator from Kentucky, whose plan is wholly outside and independent of the Constitution. Beyond this, sir, there is nothing in the plan of the President I can approve. I know of no contingency which would compel me to its support. Of what value would be the Union itself, with all its unnumbered blessings, after such an abandonment and sacrifice of principle? Sir, in my opinion, it would be worthless. Adopt it, and where, on all this American continent, could there be a nook or corner where liberty could fly for refuge or hide her divine form?

But I will not detain the House with the plan of the President. It is a subversion of the principles of civil liberty; it is despotism. But, we may congratulate ourselves upon one thing; that while history shall record that the President of the United States—perhaps the last President of the United States—was so unworthy of his high position as to offer and earnestly press such an adjustment of the question which has disturbed and revolutionized the country, still it will at the same time record the fact, that the representatives of twenty million people rejected the proposition, and refused it sanction in any form.

I proceed to the consideration of the plan of the distinguished Senator from Kentucky. I say distinguished. Sir, the Senator from Kentucky stands without a peer. He is the last of that race of statesmen who have shed undying luster upon the American name. In public and private life; in the councils of the nation, or upon its battlefields; his long career has been without spot or blemish. Sir, not only all Kentucky, but all America, venerates his name.

Here is the danger in the resolutions of the Senator. I am afraid that the influence of his great name may persuade the people of the United States to commit an irreparable wrong. I am afraid that the affection which the people everywhere bear for that Senator will control their judgment and shape their action.

But what are the propositions of the Senator from Kentucky? What is his plan? At the very outset we are struck with a remarkable fact. That is, that the proposition of the honorable Senator is a violation of the Constitution itself. The Constitution prescribes the mode, and the only mode, by which amendments may be made. Does it prescribe the mode of the Senator from Kentucky? It does not. I will read it:

"*Resolved by the Senate and House of Representatives of the United States of America in Congress assembled*, That provision ought to be made by law, without delay, for taking the sense of the people, and submitting to their vote the following resolutions as the basis for the final and permanent settlement of those disputes that now disturb the peace of the country, and threaten the existence of the Union."

It is an unauthorized procedure. How can the Constitution be amended? There are two modes. First, Congress, whenever two thirds of both Houses shall deem it necessary, shall propose amendments; or, second, on the application of the Legislatures of two thirds of the States, Congress shall call a convention for proposing amendments, which, in either case, shall be valid as part of the Constitution, when ratified by the Legislatures of three fourths of the States, or by the conventions in three fourths of the States, as may be determined by Congress.[3] Does the Senator from Kentucky propose either of these modes? Sir, he proposes an appeal to the judgment of the people. The judgment of the people has been recently heard, in one respect. That judgment must first be respected and obeyed before I shall invoke it again, Then {*sic*} will be the time to consider this proposition, if it should be considered at all. Why submit these resolutions to the people? There is no authority to do so. Because it is said there is great emergency? Well, sir, the Constitution has provided for all emergencies. I then insist upon the constitutional remedy. Are amendments needed to the Constitution? Let two thirds of both Houses of Congress propose them. Will Congress refuse to do so? Then, sir, let two thirds of the States, through their Legislatures, apply to Congress to call a national convention to propose amendments. Will the Legislatures of the States refuse to do so? Then the whole matter is at an end.

But again: I beg gentlemen to consider one moment. If amendments are to be dictated by the popular judgment, can gentlemen hope that such amendments, so unconstitutionally obtained, and thrust into the Constitution in accordance and by virtue of its result, would be final and permanent? If the opinion and judgment of the people is proper now to obtain constitutional provisions in favor of slavery, may not hereafter a similar appeal be made and justified to overthrow every vestige of slavery? Would gentlemen admit then that the judgment of the people should be appealed to and implicitly obeyed? I think not. Sir, it is a dangerous precedent. Besides, if the character of the Constitution of the United States is to be determined by a popular vote whenever appealed to, then its stability is gone. Instead of a permanent and stable character of rights, the Constitution would become a mere patchwork of whatever the passions and prejudices of the people determined it to be in a popular vote. But it may be said that neither Congress nor the conventions of the States, are compelled to carry out the judgment of the people in their vote. The proposition of the Senator from Kentucky means that it shall be an instruction not to be set aside, or it means nothing, and is useless. It means that if the popular vote of the people of the United States shall be in favor of the amendments, they shall be incorporated into the Constitution. That is just what the proposition does mean, and, therefore, violates and overthrows the Constitution in its attempt to preserve and maintain it. The Constitution of the United States was never intended to be placed in the hands of the people for their revision by a popular vote. I do not intend to place it there now. I suppose if the joint resolutions of the Senator from Kentucky should pass, I would have a right to vote upon them on their submission. I do not want the right; I do not intend that any other person shall have the right. It is an unconstitutional right; it should by voted down, and I believe it will.

But if there was nothing in the mode proposed by the honorable Senator, still I cannot support the propositions; and therefore will not consent to their submission in the manner prescribed. I do not believe there is any necessity to incorporate such amendments in the Constitution. What are they? Seven amendments in favor of slavery; seven everlasting and irreversible amendments to perpetuate slavery. Look at them: protection to slavery in all the territory now held or that shall hereafter be acquired south of the line 36°30'; protection to slavery in all the public property of the United States situate within the limits of a slave State; protection to slavery in the District of Columbia; protection to slavery in the transportation of slaves from one State to another or to a Territory in which slaves by law are held; protection to slavery in the Treasury of the United States, in the payment of the value of a rescued slave; protection to slavery in the rendition of persons held to service; protection to slavery in the right of representation, and protection to slavery in all the slave States. Sir, these amendments are to be unchangeable—irreversible. No future amendments, under any circumstances, nor at any time, nor by all the millions which shall come hereafter, shall affect them in any way. Sir, can this be done in America? Can this be written in the Constitution of the United States? If so, lift not to the dome of the Capitol the statue of Liberty, with her robe of stars. Place not another stone on the rising monument to the peerless Washington. Let them stand as they are now, uncrowned and unfinished, forever.

But, sir, I wish to examine these amendments more in detail. The first proposed amendment is as to the condition of the Territories. As to the territorial question, three propositions are advanced:

1. The right of future acquisition.
2. The idea of property in man in the Territories recognized in the Constitution.
3. The duty of protecting such property by all the departments of the territorial government.

In my opinion, all of these propositions are unwise, dangerous, and fruitful only of evil.

{Here Wilson argued that the acquisition of territories from Louisiana to Texas to New Mexico have only created "great disquiet and disturbance," and that the real possibility exists that Cuba and even more of Mexico could be acquired, which would create "an empire of slavery, such as the world has never before witnessed."}

I will not detain the House much longer with the consideration of the resolutions of the Senator from Kentucky. They are all to the same end; their object is unmistakable. The power of Congress is to be denied wherever it might affect the slightest interests of slavery. In the dockyards and arsenals, in all the public property of the United States within the limits of a slave State, in the District of Columbia, in the transportation of slaves into States or Territories, everywhere where slavery now exists, where it may hereafter exist, the Congress of the United States, even though it have absolute jurisdiction, is to be forever silent; add to this a solemn approval of the fugitive slave law in all of its parts; add to this an approval of its constitutionality in all its parts; add to this, the repeal of all State laws which the several States have deemed necessary for the protection of their citizens, and then you have, in all its proportions, the plan of conciliation of the Senator from Kentucky. Sir, it is a plan for perpetuating slavery. It bristles all over with "devilish enginery" to guard every outpost and protect every advance of slavery. In every word, line, and period, it is a protest against liberty. I cannot congratulate the Senator on such a close of his long, useful, and patriotic public life.

{Here Wilson stated his opposition to the proposed constitutional amendment by the House of Representatives Committee of Thirty-Three, which would prohibit Congress from interfering with slavery in the states where it already exists. The amendment, proposed by Charles Francis Adams of Massachusetts, would have required any amendment to the Constitution regarding slavery to be ratified by all the states instead of three-fourths of the states. Wilson objected for that reason and because the Constitution, as written, did not allow Congress to interfere with slavery in the states. "I do not know of any person anywhere," he lectured, "who have claimed the power under the Constitution to abolish slavery in the slave States." He also opposed the entry of the New Mexico Territory as a state because the inhabitants there "are almost entirely of the Mexican race . . . and not Americans, as we understand the term American." "The great mass are not fit to form a State government and be admitted into this Union on an equality with the other States of the Union." It was due to racist sentiments such as those expressed by Representative Wilson that New Mexico did not attain statehood until 1912.}

Mr. Speaker, I have now considered all the plans of adjustment before Congress. No one of them can bring permanent and lasting peace to the country. I admit the Union is in peril. But the plan of the President cannot save the Union; the plan of the Senator from Kentucky cannot save the Union; the plan of the committee of thirty-three cannot save the Union. I do not believe that there is any possibility that this Congress can do anything to effect a settlement—we differ too widely and radically. I say to you, and I say to my constituents, that if I believed we ought to concede, I would not offer the half made-up compromise of the committee of thirty-three. No, sir, it is a sham; and I believe with Carlyle,[4] that whenever you meet a sham, smite it and smite it—in God's name, smite it until it dies or you die. But I see nothing to compromise, nothing to concede, and therefore I will give none whatever.

What then can be done? Sir, in the shadows which have fallen so thick around us, I can see but one path—it is the path of duty. We have a Union. For eighty years it has been the admiration of the world. We have a Constitution, the most perfect ever conceived. We have laws, the wisest and best, with all their faults, it has been the fortune of any people to enjoy. Let them all be preserved—all; every one in all its parts. But if this cannot be done; if treason has become stronger than the Union and the Constitution and the laws; if America has fallen from her high position and become the laughter of the world; if this is the only Government of all those which have existed, or which now exist, that cannot protect itself, then I would vote for the following resolution:

Resolved by the Senate and the House of Representatives of the United States of America in Congress assembled, That it be, and is hereby, recommended to the several States of the Union that they, through their respective Legislatures, request the Congress of the United States to call a convention of all the States, in accordance with article five of the Constitution, for the purpose of amending said Constitution in such manner and with regard to such subjects as will more adequately respond to the wants, and afford more sufficient guarantees to the diversified and growing interests of the Government and of the people composing the same.

Sir, it is possible that a convention of all the States could adjust all our national differences. Such a national convention is constitutional. It may be both wise and proper at this time; and if it should fail to continue us as one people, it can at last, when all else fails, provide for a peaceful and constitutional separation of the States of the Union, not for reconstruction, but for the formation of independent republics. In that event, I know where my allegiance will be. It will be to the North; that North which to-day, as well as two hundred years ago, when the first foot stepped from the Mayflower upon her soil, reveres religion and law and civil liberty; and they cannot be extinguished in all the fires of dissolution. To that North in which I think will be realized the vision of John Milton, when he exclaimed, I see in my mind a noble and puissant nation rousing herself like a strong man after sleep, and shaking her invincible locks; methinks I see her as an eagle muing {*sic*} her mighty youth, and kindling her undazzled eyes at the full mid-day beam, and purging her long-abused sight at the fountain itself of heavenly radiance; to that empire of liberty upon whose soil no slave now stands, and no slave will ever stand, I give all my allegiance.[5] But, until that hour of separation shall come, (which may He who guides the destinies of nations avert,) until that hour, although the sun in the heavens be darkened, and the vail of the temple of liberty be rent in twain, still will I stand amid its falling columns, and maintain with all my power the sacred cause of human rights.

Mr. Speaker, I will compromise no longer with slavery.

Source: *Congressional Globe*, 36th Cong., 2nd Sess., February 1, 1861, Appendix, 131–33.

Representative John Hutchins (Republican)

US House of Representatives
February 9, 1861

John Hutchins (1812–1891) was a native Ohioan who practiced law in Warren, Ohio. He served in the Ohio House of Representatives (1849–1850), as mayor of Warren, and was elected to the Thirty-Sixth and Thirty-Seventh Congresses. In 1862, he failed to be re-elected and returned to his law practice in Warren.

Representative Hutchins began his speech by examining the "alleged" causes for secession and expressing his belief that they did not justify disunion. He further objected to the remedies proposed by the House of Representatives Committee of Thirty-Three. Hutchins specifically addressed the committee's proposed constitutional amendment prohibiting Congress from interfering with slavery in the states. "I affirm that I never heard a Republican any where claim the right to interfere, by an act of Congress, with the institution of slavery as it exists in the several States of this Union. I object to this amendment, as being against the spirit of the age."

I will next refer to what is called the Crittenden proposition. There have been presented to us many petitions for the adoption of these propositions as an amendment to the Constitution, and I have no doubt that many signatures have been obtained on the supposition that these propositions are identical with the Missouri compromise, which was repealed in 1854. They are, in form and substance, materially different. The Missouri compromise simply prohibited slavery in all the Louisiana Territory, not included in the State of Missouri, north of 36°30', and left its existence south of that line an open question.

The Crittenden propositions provide:

1. That in all the Territory of the United States, now held or *hereafter acquired*, south of latitude 36°30', slavery of the African race is *hereby recognized as existing, and shall not be interfered with by Congress; but shall be protected* as property, by all the departments of the territorial government, during its continuance.

2. "That Congress shall have no power to abolish slavery in places under its exclusive jurisdiction, and situated within the limits of States that permit the holding of slaves."

3. That Congress shall have no power to abolish slavery in the District of Columbia, so long as it exists in the States of Maryland and Virginia, nor without the consent of the inhabitants, nor without just compensation.

4. That Congress shall not interfere with the transportation of slaves from one State to another, or to a Territory, in which slaves are permitted to be held, whether that transportation be by sea, by land, or by navigable rivers.

5. That the United States shall pay the owner, who shall apply for it, the full value of his fugitive slave, in all cases when the marshal or other officer, whose duty it was to arrest a fugitive, was prevented from arresting by violence or intimidation, or when, after arrest, the fugitive was rescued by force. And that the United States shall have power to reimburse themselves by imposing and collecting a tax on the county or city in which the violence, intimidation, or rescue was committed, equal in amount to the sum paid, with interest and the costs of collection. And the county or city may sue the persons who prevented the arrest or committed the rescue, and recover the amount paid.

6. That no future amendment shall affect the five proceeding propositions, nor the third paragraph of the second section of the first article of the Constitution; nor the third paragraph of the second section of the fourth article

of the Constitution; and no amendment shall be made to the Constitution which shall give power to Congress to abolish slavery in the States.

7. That the elective franchise and the right to hold office, whether Federal, State, territorial, or municipal, shall not be exercised by persons who are, in whole or in part, of the African race.

8. That the United States shall have power to acquire, from time to time, districts of country in Africa or South America, for the colonization, at the expense of the Federal Treasury, of such free negroes and mulattoes as the several States may wish to have removed from their limits, and from the District of Columbia.

I cannot examine these atrocious propositions in detail. A more carefully guarded plan for the perpetuation of slavery in this country could not well be devised. Every imaginable security is here provided for. It gives a constitutional recognition of slavery in all territory now owned and *hereafter to be acquired* south of latitude 36°30'. It proposes an irrepealable constitutional slave code for the Territories south of 36°30'; and the recent Democratic convention in Ohio adopted it, and other Democratic conventions in free States have proposed to adopt the Crittenden plan of compromise.

Why did the Democrats object to a legislative slave code, at Charleston and Baltimore, if they are so ready now to adopt a constitutional one? They feared to go before the people on that issue. This is the plan of compromise which Republicans, day after day, are eloquently appealed to to adopt; and they are charged with criminal partisan obstinacy, because they will not adopt this plan to placate the slave power, now intent on destroying the Government. Mr. Speaker, I believe the people of the free States, when they fairly understand these propositions, will spurn them as an insult. Now, sir, what are the circumstances under which these amendments to the Constitution and other propositions of compromise are proposed? Abraham Lincoln and Hannibal Hamlin have been lawfully elected President and Vice President, upon a platform opposed to many if not all of these propositions of compromise. Other parties went into the canvas with their candidates and platforms, and the verdict of the people was invoked in relation to them. The verdict has been rendered fairly, without fraud, and without connivance, in favor of the principle that our Territories are forever to remain free. What is the proposition? Before that verdict is rendered into a judgment, a proposition comes up for a new trial to set it aside.

We find Republican lawyers standing here to advocate the rights of their clients, willing to set aside that verdict before it is rendered into judgment. Why must it be done? Because it is said, if that verdict is rendered into judgment, then a certain number of the slaveholding States will break up this Government. Does not every one see, if we grant them what they desire, it will sap the very foundation of the Government? It will invite similar rebellion in relation to any interest that may feel disturbed by the result of an election. There are other interests in this country, besides those of slavery, which may feel aggrieved at the result of an election; and if we encourage the idea that the verdict of the people may be set aside, we cannot fix where it shall terminate. We are entitled to our judgment, and we intend to have it, by the help of Almighty God, and the strong arms of the people of all sections.

We are appealed to, sir, as partisans. It is said that we are indifferent to the actual condition of the country. My colleague from Ohio [Mr. COX][6] made a very able argument against the right of a State to secede; but, like other northern Democrats, he is opposed to secession, but objects to coercion in order to prevent it. They are like the man who, when asked whether he approved the Maine liquor law, said that he did, but he was very much opposed to its execution. [Laughter.][7]

Mr COX. Will the gentleman yield to me?

Mr. HUTCHINS. I cannot just now.

Mr. COX. The gentleman misrepresents me.

Mr. HUTCHINS. The Democratic party, Mr. Speaker, are attempting to make capital out of this controversy. I have no doubt my colleague from the Columbus district [Mr. COX] is in favor of this Union, provided he can preserve it and destroy the Republican party. I am not quite sure he is heartily in favor of it, if the Republican party is to remain in power. Why do I judge him thus? I find him upon every occasion active and instant, in season and out of season, in hunting facts and furnishing southern men with material to prejudice the already excited public mind of the South. He appears to have implicit faith in compromises. He said, in his speech the other day, that "sacrifice and compromise are words of honorable import; the one gave us Calvary, the other the Constitution."[8] The gentleman's rhetoric is well; but in its practical application to the subject in controversy it is meaningless. Patriotism and statesmanship gave us the Constitution, slightly marred by compromise; but let it stand. The word compromise has been too much desecrated, of late, in our political history, to be talismanic now to save the Union.

I am not surprised that the gentleman should use the word sacrifice as connected with compromise, after his announcement that he was willing to vote for the Crittenden proposition, because it involved a *sacrifice* of his political professions.

Before the election he was for popular sovereignty, and objected to even a legislative slave code for the Territories; but now he declares his readiness to vote for a constitutional slave code. It is not, therefore, strange that he should regard sacrifice as a better word to use, in connection with these propositions, than compromise; and I think, Mr. Speaker, that "*sacrifice*" accurately defines most of these propositions which go under the nomenclature of compromise; and the question really is, shall the people of the free States sacrifice principles which, in their judgment, are essential to the welfare of the Republic, to placate those who are plotting its overthrow? Others *may*, but I will NEVER knowingly do it.

Mr. Speaker, the Crittenden plan—which is misnamed compromise—would no more be a final settlement of the slavery question, than the different compromises heretofore adopted have been. What slaveholders demand, is supremacy in the Government; nothing short of this will satisfy them. What most alarms them, at this time, is the growing power of the free States, as shown by the recent census. If my colleague from the Columbus district wishes at once to reach the root of the difficulty, he must sacrifice still further his political principles; and, as he appears to be in a sacrificing mood, I would suggest what, for a time at least, would restore peace to the country and coax the cotton States to lay down the weapons of their rebellion. The power of the free States, he will remember, is the chief difficulty. Let him, then, destroy their free-school system; put down free speech; silence the press and pulpit; put a censorship upon their literature; dry up the source of their power; paralyze the energies of their prosperity; destroy the emblems of their civilization; eradicate from the breasts of their people the love of justice and the hatred of oppression; and he will have brought about a final settlement of the slavery question. This would out-Crittenden Crittenden.

{Hutchins continued to condemn the "conspiracy to destroy the government" by arguing, "The question is not now whether the Government should coerce a State, but whether the people of a State shall coerce the Government."}

I believe that a large majority in the slave States are yet loyal to the Constitution, and that there is a Union feeling in the States which have passed ordinances of secession that will yet put down rebellion there. It is, for the time being, overborne by the terrorism which prevails. I think the reaction has already commenced. Well, it is said we must do something to aid this reaction, and at least save the border slave States. Sir, is not the Constitution as it is, broad enough for all Union men to stand upon? It is not proposed to take from the people of the slave States one single constitutional guarantee which they now have.

At the commencement of this session, I was opposed to all measures which held out plans of compromise; and I firmly believe that the position of the Union men in the border slave States would have been stronger to-day, if a majority of this House had given them the firm platform of the Constitution to stand on, instead of throwing to them rotten planks of compromise, which must ultimately give way before the surging waves of the disunion fanaticism that is sweeping over those States. I know their position is embarrassing; and if they can stand at all, they must stand upon the declaration of General Jackson, that *"the Union must be preserved."*[9]

I am willing to unite with all men who are for the integrity of the Union. I do not thereby adopt their views upon the slavery question, or other questions, nor do they adopt mine. If the people of any State desire the Constitution amended, they can submit propositions of amendment; and they would be entitled to a respectful consideration, if not coupled with a threat to break up the Government, if not granted.

I hope, sir, that the Constitution will *never* be so amended as to give any additional guarantees to slavery. All who vote for such amendments are guilty of its criminality and injustice. All the elements of agitation are now at work to bring about such amendments; but I trust they will signally fail. The people are still true to their convictions, and, whatever their representatives may do, they will *never*, I trust, in the eloquent language of Dr. Channing, "give countenance to the doctrine which all tyrants hold, that material power, physical pain, is mightier than the convictions of reason, than the principle of duty, than the love of God and mankind."[10] They will, if necessary, with warm hearts and strong arms, rally to the support of a *just* Government; and let us, their Representatives, stand FIRM to our convictions, leaving the result in the hands of that Providence that has never forsaken us in the darkest hour of our history.

Source: *Congressional Globe*, 36th Cong., 2nd Sess., Appendix, 202–3.

Representative Daniel Wheelwright Gooch (Republican)

US House of Representatives
February 23, 1861

Daniel W. Gooch (1820–1891) graduated from Dartmouth College in 1843, was admitted to the bar three years later, and began his practice in Boston. He was elected to the Massachusetts House of Representatives in 1852 and then to the United States House of Representatives in which he served from 1857 until 1865.

On the same day that the people of Texas voted 3 to 1 in favor of secession, Representative Gooch attempted to dissuade southern Democrats that Republicans had any interest in interfering with slavery in the states. In this speech titled "Any Compromise a Surrender," he argued that Crittenden's plan of prohibiting slavery north of the 36°30' line gave the North nothing, since climate had already determined it would never flourish there. He further spoke out against Crittenden's seventh article that would have prohibited persons "of the African race" from voting or holding public office. Gooch argued that the right to determine citizenship and voter eligibility was a "cherished" state right that no state would willingly surrender. He condemned the racism that undergirded the notion by arguing that it would deprive African American citizens of Massachusetts "whose fathers fought in the [American] Revolution" of rights "which they and their ancestors have enjoyed from the foundation of the Government." The core problem between the North and the South, Gooch lectured, was that southerners misunderstood northern interests and concerns because they were ill informed. "No northern newspaper, representing the political sentiments of the North, is permitted to enter or be read in your States. . . . Freedom of speech and the press is everywhere in the South denied."

The House having under consideration the report from the select committee of thirty-three—

Mr. GOOCH said:

Mr. SPEAKER: Why is it that the people of six or seven States are today arrayed in open rebellion against this Government, and the people of as many more doubting whether they shall remain loyal or join in the rebellion?

Why is it that almost one half of this nation, the most prosperous and happy the world has ever known, speaking the same language, living under the same laws, enjoying the same political institutions, having the same common Government, participating in the same glorious recollections of the past and bright hopes for the future, bound together by every tie that interest, long and pleasant association, consanguinity, a common origin and destiny can throw around a people to unite and make them forever one, is to-day looking upon the other half as enemies, and ready to take up arms against them? This is the question we must answer before we can prescribe the remedy for existing evils. It is not enough that we know the fact that these evils exist; we must also know the causes which produced them. The nature and cause of the disease in the body-politic, as well as in the physical body, must be ascertained before the remedy is applied.

Two systems of labor, free labor and slave labor, exist in the land; one in the North, the other in the South. They have existed since the beginning of the Government precisely as they exist to-day; and the conflict between them is no more irrepressible now than it has been for the last half century.

No reason for severing the Union of these States can be given to-day which could not with equal justice and propriety have been given at any day since the Union was formed. It was seen and known from the beginning that free labor, and free labor alone, would be employed in the North; and while it was hoped and believed by the founders of the Government that slavery would not be perpetual, it was fully understood that slave labor would continue to be employed in the South long after it had been abolished by the States of the North.

No right or power was conferred by the people upon the Federal Government to legislate in relation to, or to interfere with, any system of labor in a State, whether free or slave. This Government has no more right or power to legislate in relation to, or interfere with, the system of slave labor in South Carolina, than it has to legislate in relation to, or interfere with, the system of free labor in Massachusetts; no more right or power to abolish slavery in the one than to establish it in the other. And no State, or people of a State, have the right or power to interfere with the system of labor in another State. Each can control its own; not another's.

I think scarcely a man can be found in the whole North who will deny these propositions. We have always so understood the Constitution and the powers and relations of the States; and we ask for and desire no change of the Constitution in this respect, and no alteration or change of the Constitution in any respect. The Constitution which our fathers made, and under which we have lived, we will obey, preserve, protect, and defend under all circumstances. I know that there are a few men in the North, some of them eminent for their ability and virtues in private life, who are not satisfied with the Constitution as it is, and desire to see it annulled and the existing Government overthrown, in order that a new Constitution may be made, and the Government reconstructed with power to abolish and prohibit slavery in every State. These men are few in number, belong to no political party, take no political action, refuse even to vote, and look upon the Republican party as the obstacle in the way of the accomplishment of their object; because that party, representing, as it does, the opinions and sentiments of the North in relation to slavery, is pledged to support the Constitution as it is, maintain the Union, and give to every section of the country all its rights.[11]

These men are so few in the North that they exert no considerable influence or power over the people to control political action; and could not, if they should unite with any existing political organization. They hold the same relation to the Federal Constitution and Government that the disunionists of the South do. Both desire their overthrow and destruction, that another and a different Constitution and Government may take their places. They differ in this: the disunionists of the North wish a Constitution and Government with power to abolish and prohibit slavery everywhere; the disunionists of the South desire a Constitution and Government with power to establish and protect slavery everywhere. Both wish to give to this Government greater powers; the one that it may abolish and prohibit slavery everywhere in all the States; the other that it may establish and protect slavery everywhere in all the States. The one wishes that the power of the Federal Government shall extend into the slave States to free all slaves; the other that it shall extend into all free States to protect the master in the possession of his slaves, whenever he may choose to take them into a free State. Neither is content with the Constitution as it is; neither is willing to obey the Constitution, and live under the Government which our fathers made. Both think that they can make a wiser and better Constitution and Government; and, to try the experiment, are willing to peril all the prosperity, security, happiness, and peace, which thirty million people enjoy under the Constitution and Government as it is.

Shall we permit either to try the experiment? Shall we, at this time, recommend to the people to so alter or amend the Constitution as to satisfy men who demand the alteration of the Constitution or the overthrow of the Government? These alterations are not proposed because experience has shown that the Constitution needed amendment. No man dreamed of amending the Constitution before the result of the late election was known; and had the section of country which now asks these alterations elected to office their candidates, no man would have heard of any alteration or amendment to the Constitution. Mr. Speaker, a Constitution which is good enough with the Democratic party in power, is, in my opinion, good enough with the Republican party in power. A Constitution which is good enough with the administration of the Government in the hands of men who think that all the influence and power of this Government should be used to extend slavery into free territory, is also good enough with the administration in the hands of men who think that the free Territories of the United States should remain free.

I have said that the number of these men in the North is small, and that, although they embrace men of the highest order of intellect and attainment, they exert no considerable influence over the mass of the northern people. But we find a few disunionists at the South now exerting a controlling influence over the people, molding and directing the popular will at pleasure, arraying whole communities of men against the best Government on earth, from which they have received nothing but the richest benefits a benign Government can bestow upon its subjects. It is not at all strange that men should be found in both sections of the country advocating radical changes in the Constitution and laws. But it is strange that in the one section of the country they should lead and control the whole mass of the people, while in the other they are wholly unable to exert any influence over the people; that in one section they should be able to organize open rebellion against the Government, while in the other they can scarcely disturb the loyalty of any citizen to the Government, or excite the least hostility towards the people of the other section of the country. Why this difference? The people of the North know and understand everything that pertains to the South. Your newspapers are found in all our villages, and are read by all classes of men. Southern men speak freely their opinions at the North, both in public and private. Freedom of speech and the press, liberty of thought and action, are everywhere protected. We ask no safeguard against error, but truth. Not so in the South. Your people do not understand the feeling, principles, and motives of the people of the North. No northern man, who correctly represents the sentiments of the North, is permitted to speak to your people. No northern newspaper, representing the political sentiments of the North, is permitted to enter or be read in your States. All that your people know of the principles and intentions of the Republican party they have learned from our political opponents. The more of that kind of knowledge they have the less they know of us. Freedom of speech and the press is everywhere in the South denied, and the passions of your people are so constantly inflamed against the people of the North that a northern man, when in one of your States, is under the same surveillance and restraint that he would be in an enemy's country. Any expression of thought or opinion not satisfactory to your people exposes him to indignity, and sometimes to death.

If freedom of speech and the press had never been denied by you, the disunionists in the South would be no more numerous or powerful to-day than they are in the North. They would not now be an appreciable quantity among the political forces of the country. Here, I think, we find the origin and cause of the evils which are now upon us. Had freedom of speech and the press been maintained with you as with us, it would have been as impossible to make the people of South Carolina revolt against this Government as it would the people of the most loyal State in the North. The principles and intentions of the men of the Republican party would then have been understood by your people; and although there probably would have been a difference of opinion in some respects as to what the action of this Government should be in relation to slavery, still that difference would never have led the people of the South into rebellion against the Government.

All your people would have known, as you, their Representatives, know, that we claim not the right, and have not the wish, or intent, to interfere with slavery or any other institution in your States.

{Representative Gooch continued here to comment on the lack of freedom of the press and speech in the South, lecturing southern Democrats, "If you have permitted your people to be deceived in relation to the principles, intentions, and wishes of the Republican party, you must go home and undeceive them."}

The questions which now present themselves to us must be met, not avoided. They involve the integrity, if not the existence, of the Government. In determining how these questions shall be settled, we must consider, not merely what settlement will show the best balances on ledgers at the end of

1861, but what settlement will give most security and stability to the Government, and conduce most to the peace and happiness of the millions who shall come after us.

We see, Mr. Speaker, that slavery has driven six States into open rebellion against this Government, and the indications now are that it may compel still other States to follow their example. And this it has done, not because slavery has not received all that it has wished from the Government. Oh! no; it has controlled the Government almost all the time for the last half century. What slavery has willed the Government has executed. And during all this debate I do not remember that the first grievance received by any State from this Government has been alleged, or the first complaint against it made. Six States are in open rebellion, without being able to bring the first accusation against the Government or any of its officers; and that, too, while a President elected to office by these very States is still at the head of the Government, a majority of the Senate their especial friends, the Republican party in a minority in the House of Representatives, and the Supreme Court making decrees and giving opinions especially acceptable to the South.

The only reason that can be assigned for this rebellion at this time, is the fact that the people have elected a President who will not use the influence and power of his office in favor of the extension of slavery into the Territories, and because slaveholders know that they will no longer have the absolute control of the Government. The personal liberty laws, of which we hear so much, are no new enactments, they have been on the statute-books of the States for years. In some States they have been recently repealed; in others modified. The doctrines of the Republican party in relation to slavery in the Territories are not new. They have been before the people of the country for a long time. In 1856 you joined issue with us on these same doctrines, and we were defeated. We acquiesced in the decision of the people, as we had always done before, and always intended to do. In 1860, you again joined issue with us on the same doctrines, and you were defeated. Each of us, by going before the people and asking for votes, pledged ourselves to abide by the decision of the people. If we had been defeated, we should have acquiesced in that decision. You would have answered us with scorn and contempt if we had come here and demanded that the principles which we had advocated, and the people had rejected, should be incorporated into the Constitution. Yet this is exactly what is now asked of us. The amendments of the

Constitution proposed by the distinguished Senator from Kentucky, [Mr. CRITTENDEN,] in behalf of slavery, include all that was asked for slavery in the Breckinridge platform, and even more. These propositions the people refused to accept as the basis of the administration of the Government for four years, and now the demand is made that we shall recommend to the people to insert them into the Constitution, and that they shall forever be a part of the fundamental law of the land, without the possibility of alteration or repeal. The amendments proposed by the gentleman from Maryland, [Mr. HARRIS,][12] commonly called the border-State propositions, although they do not propose to strike a fatal blow at the rights of all the free colored men in our country, as does one of the propositions of the Senator from Kentucky, [Mr. CRITTENDEN,] are still liable to the same general objection. The doctrine of the North is that slavery is a moral and social evil, and ought not to be extended into the Territories of the United States. We believe that every citizen of all the States has a voice and a responsibility in determining what shall be the laws and institutions of the Territories; and if we permit slavery to go into and exist in the Territories, then we of the free States are as much responsible for its existence there as is any citizen of a slave State responsible for slavery in his State. And for this reason we will not consent that slavery shall be established in any of the Territories, either by law or by constitutional amendment, if it is in our power to prevent it.

The obligations which the Constitution, as it is, imposes upon us, we will perform, but we are under no obligation to amend the Constitution for the benefit of slavery. The first amendment[13] of the Senator from Kentucky [Mr. CRITTENDEN] excludes slavery north of 36°30', and fastens it upon all territory south of that line; so that neither Congress nor the people of the Territory can ever abolish or prohibit it, but requires that it shall be protected by all the departments of the territorial government.

Now, sir, the prohibition north of 36°30' is worthless to the North and to freedom. After the experience in Kansas, I think the attempt will not again be made to fasten slavery upon territory north of that line. This amendment is, in substance, that slavery shall be protected in all the territory of the United States where the climate and soil will permit it to exist; and it would have been no more objectionable, but much more fair and honest towards the people of the North, if it provided in express terms that slavery should be protected everywhere in the Territories where it is possible for it to exist.

It would then have deceived nobody. The South agreed with the North, forty years ago, that slavery should be excluded from all the territory we then had north of that line, and Missouri came into the Union as a slave State.

The law excluding slavery continued unrepealed more than thirty years, and until it was thought that slavery might be introduced into Kansas; and then it was repealed by the South, in violation of the compact with the North. The attempt was made to force slavery into Kansas, and a slave constitution upon the people.[14] To accomplish this object, all the powers of slavery, and all the powers of the Federal Government, were employed. And the action of the highest officers of the Government in relation to this matter furnishes the most disgraceful chapter in American history. The attempt failed ignominiously, and covered with shame and disgrace all who participated in it. The experiment demonstrated that slavery could not be planted above that line; and now, the South, satisfied of that fact, proposes to prohibit slavery north of that line, where it knows, by actual experiment, it can never go. And, in return for this, slavery is to be established and protected in all the territory south of that line, by all the powers of every department of the Government. And now, all the advantage being on the side of the South, without the possibility of change, the contract is to be made a part of the Constitution, and irrepealable.

Mr. Speaker, since the repeal of the Missouri compromise, any proposition from the South to the North to adjust this question on the line of 36°30', or any other line, is a simple insult. If slavery is right in itself, or has the right under the Constitution to go into the Territories of the United States, let it go into all the Territories where climate and soil will permit it to go. We are not responsible for it. If it is wrong in itself, and has no right under the Constitution to go into the Territories of the United States, let us exclude it from all the Territories. If slavery is wrong north of 36°30', it is not right south of 36°30'. I am not willing that the North shall be a second time cheated in this matter, and will not vote into the Constitution any new powers for slavery. I can never vote to give further powers or constitutional guarantees to an institution which has controlled this Government up to this time, and now, when one department of the Government is about to be beyond its control, threatens to destroy the Government itself. It seems to me that this is the most fatal remedy for existing evils that can be devised by man.

I should like, Mr. Speaker, to examine each of these propositions at length, but time will not permit me to do so. They are all designed and intended to give new and further constitutional powers and guarantees to slavery. The words *slave* and *slavery*, which our fathers would not permit to be in that instrument, are now to be written on the forefront of the Constitution, in characters so indelible that all the people who shall ever come after us can never erase them, and slavery is to be fastened as a national badge forever upon this capital. We are asked to provide that, while all things else may be changed, amended, or repealed, the provisions for the benefit of slavery shall be eternal.

Mr. Speaker, before passing from this subject, I must ask the attention of the House to article seven of the amendments proposed by the Senator from Kentucky, [Mr. CRITTENDEN.] It is in these words:

> ARTICLE VII.
>
> SEC. 1. The elective franchise and the right to hold office, whether Federal, State, territorial, or municipal, shall not be exercised by persons who are, in whole or in part, of the African race.

Now, sir, what the object or purpose of such an amendment is, I am at a loss to understand. Under the pretense of securing State rights, it strikes one of the most fatal blows ever aimed at the rights of a State. The right of each State to determine who of her people shall be citizens of the State, who shall exercise the elective franchise, and who shall be eligible to office in the State, is one which I supposed had always been among the cherished rights which no State would willingly surrender. I find that those men who have always claimed to be the especial guardians of State rights, value them only as they make in favor of slavery; and while they claim the power to extend them over all the territory of the United States for its protection, are willing to strike them down in every State in obedience to its demands. This proposed amendment deprives every State of the power to determine for itself who of her citizens shall have the elective franchise, and who shall be eligible to even State and municipal offices; and, at the same time, deprives a class of men, whose fathers fought in the Revolution and voted for the adoption of the Constitution under which we now live, of rights which they and their ancestors have enjoyed from the foundation of the Government.

In his opinion in the Dred Scott case, Mr. Justice {Benjamin R.} Curtis says: "At the time of the ratification of the Articles of Confederation, all free native born inhabitants of the States of New Hampshire, Massachusetts, New York, New Jersey, and North Carolina, though descended from African slaves, were not only citizens of those States, but such of them as had the other necessary qualifications possessed the franchise of electors on equal terms with other citizens."

And again, in the same opinion, in speaking of the political rights which colored men have enjoyed in Massachusetts, under the Constitution adopted in 1780, he says: "It is true, beyond all controversy, that persons of color, descended from African slaves, were by that Constitution made citizens of the State; and such of them as have had the necessary qualifications, have held and exercised the elective franchise, as citizens, from that time to the present."

The only reason that can be given for this proposed amendment is, that slavery, to justify itself, feels bound to degrade the colored man wherever he can be found. Shall we recommend to the people of this country to alter their Constitution for such a reason?

{Here Gooch expressed his objection to the recommendations of the House of Representatives Committee of Thirty-Three, especially the Corwin amendment and the admission of New Mexico as a state.}

All these propositions are offered as concessions or compromises; and what is the consideration which the North is to receive? Mr. Lincoln is to be President of the United States.

Have the people of the free States fallen so low that they are willing, after a President has been duly elected according to the Constitution and the laws, to buy the right for him to administer the Government? Are they willing to change and alter the fundamental law of the land, in obedience to the demands of traitors and rebels, with threats in their mouths, and weapons in their hands?

{Gooch expressed his conviction that compromise with and concessions to the South would neither bring the seceded states back nor appease slave states that have not yet seceded. "Will the slave States that have not seceded agree to remain? Not unless we are willing to give them the absolute control of the Government."}

Mr. Speaker, I have still other objections to all these compromises and concessions at this time. If we buy the right for men elected to office by a constitutional majority of the people to administer the Government, no matter what we pay for it, we strike a fatal blow at republican liberty and republican Government.

Hereafter, an election by the people will determine nothing, not even who are to hold the offices. Hereafter, the man who is to be President must not only be elected by the people, but he must be able to make terms with the defeated party; and his power to administer the Government will be as dependent upon the one as the other. Hereafter, the defeated party will demand, as the terms of acquiescence in the election, that its favorite political doctrines shall be made a part of the Constitution; and that instrument will soon become a piece of political patchwork, made up of party platforms which have been rejected by the people.

{Representative Gooch ended his speech by expressing his opposition to the idea of secession and his strong belief in the perpetuity of the Union.}

Source: *Congressional Globe*, 36th Cong., 2nd Sess., Appendix, 261–63.

Representative Luther Cullen Carter (Republican)

US House of Representatives
February 27, 1861

Luther C. Carter (1805–1875), a native of Maine, moved to New York City to engage in business pursuits. He served as a member of the New York City Board of Education in 1853 before being elected to the United States House of Representatives where he served one term.

Representative Carter represented many in the Republican Party who opposed any change in the Constitution that would "extend the area of slavery." He attempted in this speech to use Senator Crittenden's words against him in arguing against the Kentuckian's amendments.

The house having under consideration the report from the select committee of thirty-three—

Mr. CARTER said:

Mr. SPEAKER: I know there are many questions more or less connected with the subject now under discussion before this House; but as they all ostensibly grow out of the offense taken by the South at the election of a Republican as chief executive officer of the nation, for the next four years, I propose to first say a few words on this subject, before proceeding to investigate those more immediately named as matters of dispute.

{Representative Carter here devoted a great deal of time analyzing the cause "of all this turmoil and disturbance and defection." Listing the issues of fugitive slaves, northern personal liberty laws, inequality in the western territories, and the southern need for guarantees "that the North will not assail its rights and its property," Carter dismissed all as being insufficient to justify secession.}

But, Mr. Speaker, we are told that it matters not by which party, or which section, the troubles were got up; they exist, and they must be healed, and that without considering their source and origin. I confess that, to a certain extent, this may be true; but I think I perceive in it the presence of a policy which would secure for a particular political party (of which even patient men have grown weary) a new and perpetual lease of power, by snatching from hurry, panic, and incaution, advantages that could not be wrung from cool judgment and right reason.

But, sir, I forego all objection on that score, and am willing to do what I can and ought towards repairing the mischiefs that have been so wickedly inflicted on the public weal. I am willing to vote for any measures calculated to remove the causes of reasonable dissatisfaction, if any such exist; but, sir, I am not going either to speak against, or to vote away, the Constitution as a bribe to any State or section of this country for staying in the Union. If South Carolina, or Mississippi, or Virginia, does not esteem and love the Union sufficiently to remain in it, without being bribed by a surrender of that Constitution which their noble fathers made as well as mine, then I, for one, will offer no bribe to their acceptance. If the people of the southern States, who felt themselves aggrieved, or thought that their constitutional rights were not respected, had specified their grievances, and proposed remedies for the same, I have been ready at all times since I have been a member of this House, and am still, to vote for the adoption of such remedies; provided it comes within our constitutional power to apply them. And, if they asked for anything which involved a change of the Constitution, and desired to submit such proposed alteration to a convention of the people of the nation, that *they* might consider and decide upon the propriety of such alterations, I have been ready, and am still, to vote with them to accomplish that end; provided that, in the mean time, they acknowledge the imperative duty of the executive Administration to enforce, and of all the people to obey, the Constitution and the laws of the United States. At the same time, I should, individually, be opposed to any alteration of the Constitution which would extend the area of slavery.

But, sir, what are we asked for, as the consideration we are to pay for the boon of continued union? Why, sir, it is useless to conceal it, the "Crittenden resolutions" have been all the cry. No matter who might speak, however moderate and temperate the gentlemen of the South, or the Democrats of the North, it has been all "the Crittenden resolutions," "the Crittenden resolutions!" But what do these resolutions involve? They involve a fundamental perversion of the Constitution; they demand a change, which Mr. CRITTENDEN and his followers, both here and in the other House virtually resisted and denied during the late campaign. Hear what Mr. CRITTENDEN himself said on the 2d August, 1860, in a speech at Louisville, (referring to the disaffection at the South):

> Why are they for a dissolution of the Union? What harm has this Union done? Wrongs may have been done individuals—they may have received wrongs of this sort; but, is the Union the author of these wrongs? What is the remedy which must be sought? It is to turn out of their places, in the proper constitutional mode, those who have misadministered the Government. The Government has done no wrong—the Constitution and the Union have done no wrong. They command equal justice to every man and every State and every section. Their agents may have disobeyed their injunctions, and everything may have been done wrong through individuals; but individuals are amenable. What remedy would the destruction of the Constitution afford? Could they get out of its ruins indemnity for the wrongs on account of which they would tear it down? Could it give any satisfaction? Could it make any atonement? No; and yet, by some strange perversity or other, their minds have been brought to look upon disunion as a remedy for political wrongs.

It has caused none of them—the destruction of it would be a remedy for none—but the greatest of all evils to the people of the United States.

In speaking of conventions, he said: "You know not whether these conventions, to whose rod you humbly submit yourselves, were composed of patriots, pondering the good of the Commonwealth, or of knaves, consulting the best policy of robbing it. When we forget our country, and disobey our Constitution, we listen to the summons of party."

And again, on the presidential question, he thus expressed himself: "I want a President elected upon the Constitution—a bold man, who will not fear to perform his duty; a man who cannot be scared; a man who loves the Union, the whole Union, and will stand by it, and consider it his sacred duty to protect or perish with it."

One other extract on the subject of the Constitution reads as follows: "The Constitution is platform enough for me. The Constitution, and a man to represent the people, is all the platform that will ever avail us. This question about which the Democratic party is quarreling is one of the most minute and unimportant questions that can well be imagined."

Such was the language of Mr. CRITTENDEN as the honored advocate of the constitutional party, claiming the Constitution as their platform, in August, 1860. He said at that time that "individuals were amenable" for any wrong which they had committed, or might commit. Would he have us understand by this that they were amenable, but could not be punished? Strange paradox! Yet it would seem that he must have had some such intention, for punishment implies coercion; and certainly they must not be coerced, especially in any matter involving national rights; for, according to southern doctrine at this day, such a course would be altogether impolitic, and decidedly wrong. It is possible that some difference of opinion may exist on this subject in other latitudes. However, I will not discuss it further just now, but proceed with my inquiries.

And now, sir, I ask, would the bold and patriotic, and, I am proud to say, "the unterrified" gentleman from Tennessee, [Mr. ETHERIDGE,][15] or the eloquent gentleman from Maryland, [Mr. HARRIS,][16] have voted for the Crittenden resolutions had they been presented to either of them on the morning of the 6th of last November? Can it be possible that we are now called upon by any of these gentlemen to change the Constitution in order to compromise with secession, which I conceive to be the greatest of felonies? *It is rebellion!* Are we now asked to change the Constitution that we may compromise with treason? There can be no such thing as rightful secession from the national Government. If rightful secession be admitted, it at once destroys the foundation of the Government, and the whole fabric of our free institutions will be scattered to the winds.

{Carter continued here to assail Crittenden's proposal by declaring, in part, "I say, sir, it is a misnomer to call the proposition to amend the Constitution, so as to nationalize slavery, by the specious title of a 'compromise.' No, sir; it is no compromise, but it is an audacious intrusion—an impudent invasion of a province never yet yielded, and which never ought to be yielded, to the grim spirit of political power."}

When I first spoke in this House, on the 14th December, 1859, I said that the people would elect the next President; and when elected, they would require him to administer the Government in accordance with the true intent and meaning of its framers. They have done so; they have elected the man of their choice; and they now require at his hands an honest and faithful discharge of the duties of his high office. Yes, sir, in a few days at longest, he will have assumed the reins of office; and we have good reason to believe that he will not disappoint us; that the sacred trust we have committed to his keeping shall be faithfully guarded, and every duty fearlessly performed. The wise men of the nation should rally around him and strengthen his hands; not for war, but that he may win back the hearts of the people of his country to the true principles of the Government, which protects every State in its sovereignty and every individual in his independent manhood. But, if any portion of the people of this country will not respect themselves, nor the rights of others, then the strong arm of the Government ought to protect itself, and all those who are loyal to it. In this, there should be but one voice throughout the nation.

More especially, while the public mind is under such extreme excitement, should we guard the Constitution, as the ark of our liberty, from the hands of designing politicians or aspiring demagogues. If it must be changed—if the people so will it—then may calm deliberation mark the action of every man who takes share in the weighty task! If sound reason and judgment be not exercised in the adoption of every change, even the slightest, in that time-honored charter of our liberties, the true source of our national greatness and prosperity, then we shall have great reason to fear that all will be lost, and we become a byword and a reproach among the nations of the earth.

May the God of our fathers avert such calamity!

Source: *Congressional Globe*, 36th Cong., 2nd Sess., Appendix, 276–80.

CHAPTER FIVE

Exchange between Senators Charles Sumner and John J. Crittenden

US Senate
February 12, 1861

Charles Sumner (1811–1874) was, by 1861, a Harvard University and Harvard Law School graduate, an established attorney in Boston, one of the founders of the Free Soil Party in 1848, and a member of Congress since 1851. He led the radical wing of the Republican Party that advocated for immediate abolition. On May 22, 1856, he was severely beaten, while sitting at his Senate desk, by South Carolina representative Preston Brooks in retaliation for a speech Sumner had given a few days before attacking slavery and slave owners. In "The Crime Against Kansas," Sumner accused slave owners of being in bed with the "harlot" slavery, and singled out Brooks's cousin, South Carolina senator Andrew Butler, as being a pimp for slavery. After the beating, Brooks promptly resigned his House seat and was immediately reelected, but died the following year from a throat infection. Sumner did not return to his Senate seat until December 1859.

In this exchange with Senator Crittenden, Sumner accused Crittenden of attempting to "foist into the Constitution of the United States constitutional guarantees of slavery which the framers of that instrument never gave." The Massachusetts statesman argued that Crittenden's resolutions offered greater protections for slavery than the southern Democratic platform of 1860 which had been "solemnly condemned by the American people." Sumner found the "hereafter acquired" clause to be especially offensive. Throughout the debate, Crittenden more than held his own with Sumner.

STATE OF THE UNION.

Mr. CRITTENDEN. I feel no ordinary satisfaction, Mr. President, in presenting to you the petition which lies before me, on my desk, from people of the State of Massachusetts.[1] This petition is from one hundred and eighty-two of the cities and towns of Massachusetts, and signed by twenty-two thousand three hundred and thirteen citizens of that State. These signatures were obtained during four secular days, under great disadvantages. In some instances the petition remained only twelve hours in the town from which it was sent; and in almost every case, when the petition was returned, it was returned with the remark, "if we had only had time to present it to the voters of the town, the number of signatures could have been doubled;" or, "if there had been time to see them, a majority of the voters of the town would have been glad to sign it." The little town of Natick sends the signatures of two hundred and fifty-nine of her citizens. What the number of voters of that town is, I do not know; it is the residence of the Senator from Massachusetts, [Mr. WILSON,][2] who will know best.

Mr. WILSON. Twelve hundred.

{Here Senator Crittenden listed the towns in Massachusetts whose citizens signed a petition stating that Crittenden's amendment should be adopted.}

Mr. CRITTENDEN. Mr. President, I wish to make a single remark. The fact that my name is mentioned in this petition creates not the least degree of vanity or selfish feeling on my part. No, sir; I honor this petition and these petitioners. I am cheered by such a voice, coming up from Massachusetts in favor of the Union of the people of this country. I consider it simply as an evidence of their attachment to the Union; and it is in that light that I think it is to be estimated, and that all the country, I hope, will hear the voice of twenty-two thousand of the voters of Massachusetts in one petition. We have had more than fourteen thousand petitioners from the city of Boston, containing only nineteen thousand votes. Sir, this speaks largely and loudly for the sentiment of that State—her patriotic sentiment. It must be accepted as such by all. However wrong they may be in their opinions and in their judgment, it shows hearts devoted to the Union; hearts that are devoted to that Constitution and that Union which their ancestors so much contributed to establish. Sir, I feel peculiar and especial satisfaction in presenting it; and will no longer trouble the Senate with any remarks on the subject. I move that it be laid on the table.

The PRESIDING OFFICER, (Mr. FOSTER[3] in the chair.) The petition will be laid on the table.

Mr. SUMNER. As I desire to say a few words on that petition, I move that it be printed.

These petitioners, as I understand, ask you to adopt what are familiarly known as the Crittenden propositions. Their best apology, sir, for that petition, is their ignorance of the character of those propositions. Had they known what they are, I feel sure that they never would have put their names to that paper.

Those propositions go beyond the Breckinridge platform, which has already been solemnly condemned by the American people. If adopted, they foist into the Constitution of the United States constitutional guarantees of slavery which the framers of that instrument never gave; which Washington, Jefferson, Franklin, Patrick Henry, and John Jay, if we may credit the testimony of their lives and opinions, would have scorned to give. Had any such propositions been made the condition of Union, this Union never could have been formed.

Mr. Madison told us in the convention that it was wrong to admit into the Constitution the idea of property in man; but these propositions propose to interpolate that idea; and, practically carrying it out, they run a black line at latitude of 36°30', and give a constitutional protection to slavery in all territory now belonging to the Republic south of that line; and to make the case still more offensive, and more impossible to be received at the North, they make it applicable to all territory hereafter acquired; so that the flag of the Republic, as it moves southward, shall always be the flag of slavery, and every future acquisition in that direction shall be Africanized; and all this by virtue of the Constitution of the United States. This is bad enough in an age of civilization; but it is not all. Still further: they insist upon giving constitutional guarantees to slavery in the national capital, and in other places within exclusive Federal jurisdiction. Nor is this all. As if to do something repugnant to just principles, and especially offensive to the people of Massachusetts, they propose to despoil our colored fellow-citizens there of political franchises long time secured to them by the institutions of the honored Commonwealth.

Sir, it is for these things that these petitioners now pray; and they insist that they shall be interpolated into the Constitution of the United States. I have an infinite respect for the right of petition, and I desire always to promote the interests and to carry forward the just and proper desires of my fellow-citizens; but I must express my regret that these gentlemen have missed the opportunity, when uniting in such numbers, of calling plainly and unequivocally, as lovers of the Union of their fathers, for two things—two things all-sufficient for the present crisis—with regard to which, I should expect the sympathies of the Senator from Kentucky. First, that the Constitution of the United States, as administered by George Washington, to be preserved intact and blameless in its text, without any tinkering for the sake of slavery; and secondly, the verdict of the people last November, by which Abraham Lincoln was elected President of the United States, be enforced without price or condition. Here is ground on which every patriot and loyal citizen of the land can take his stand, and have over him the flag of the Union. How much better this than any scheme, device, juggle, hocus-pocus of compromise. On such a ground, all men who really love the Union of their fathers, without an *if* or a *but*, can plant themselves.

I remember, sir, that on the night of the passage of the Nebraska bill—it was at midnight—I made the declaration in the debate that then went on, that the time for compromise had passed. The events taking place all verify this truth. It is obvious that existing difficulties can now be arranged only on permanent principles of justice, freedom, and humanity. Any seeming settlement founded on an abandonment of principles, will be but a miserable patchwork, which cannot succeed. It is only a short time ago, you will remember, that the whole country was filled with shame and dismay, as the reports came to us of the surrender of the southern forts; and when it was known that Fort Sumter, too, was about to be given up, there was a cry that went forth from the hearts of the people, by which that fortress was saved, at least for the present. Propositions are made and brought forward by the Senator from Kentucky, and now enforced by petitions from constituents of my own State, calling upon the North to surrender its principles—to surrender those impregnable principles of human rights which constitute our northern forts. It is even proposed, sir, to surrender the principle of freedom in the Territories—the Fort Sumter of the North. I trust, sir, that they will all yet be saved; and as their safety depends upon the people, and not upon a President, I hope that a cry will go forth from the people like that which, only a few days ago, saved that other Fort Sumter when it was menaced. For myself, if I stand with many, or with few, or alone, I have but one thing to say: "No surrender of the Fort Sumter of the North; no surrender of any of our northern forts. No, sir; not of one of them."

But the bankers and the merchants of New York and Boston tell us that the Government shall not have money if we do not surrender our principles. Then again, sir, do I appeal to the people. I believe that the American people are not less patriotic than the French people, and that they only want the opportunity to come forward and supply the necessities of the Government, as the French people, only recently, at the hint of Louis Napoleon, came forward with their loan, all composed of small sums, in order to conduct that war which ended in the liberation of Italy. Our Government stands on the aggregate virtue and intelligence of the people. It only remains, now, that we should make an appeal to the *aggregate* wealth of the people. The farmer, the mechanic, the laborer—every man who truly loves his country, will contribute out of his earnings to uphold the Constitution and the national flag. Out of these small sums, inspired by a generous patriotism, we shall have a full Treasury, even if the bankers and the merchants stand aloof.

There is but one thing, now, for the North to do. It is, to stand firm in their position. They may be guided by the testimony of one of the greatest benefactors of our country. I mean LaFayette;[4] who, in his old age, when his experience had been ripened by time; when he saw the old French revolution as a surviving actor and a surviving sufferer, from his seat in the Chamber of Deputies, while recognizing the unutterable calamities of that revolution, said that it was his solemn duty to declare that, in his opinion, they were to be referred, not so much to the bad passions of men as to those timid counsels that sought to substitute *Compromise* for *Principle.* Lafayette may well speak to his American fellow-citizens, now, and inspire them to stand firm against any timid counsels that would substitute compromise for principle.

{A short procedural discussion ensued here resulting in the decision by the presiding officer that Senator Crittenden had the floor.}

Mr. CRITTENDEN. Mr. President, it might seem to be a little ungracious in me to step between the honorable Senator and his constituents who have sent this petition here. He charges them with ignorance. He is better acquainted with them than I am; but it has been a boast long made, and I have thought it a well-founded boast, that education at the North was more universal than in any other part of the Union; that the Commonwealth of Massachusetts especially took the most parental care of her people, and that they were generally more enlightened, and a more reading and writing people, than the population of any other State of the Union. I had supposed that this was the case. I have no particular acquaintance with these gentlemen. The tie that is between us is that of our common citizenship. Another tie that is between us is the coincidence of our opinions and our attachment in favor of this Union, and the honor they have done me in confiding the presentation of this petition to my hands.

The gentleman says they have signed it out of ignorance. In presenting it, I supposed I might appeal to the Senate to give additional force and effect to this petition, because of the intelligence of the people by whom it had been sent. The gentleman supposes they have signed it without understanding it; and for the purpose of showing that they do not understand it, he has characterized my resolutions so as to render it, as he supposes, impossible that an intelligent person could sign the petition. They would have spurned it, I understand him, instead of signing it, if they had understood it. It calls upon the North to abandon her settled and impregnable principles, he says. What principles? To permit slavery, is all that is asked, in our present Territory. All that is asked is, that the condition of slavery shall remain in the Territory of New Mexico as it now is. That is the substance. When I first offered these resolutions, I presented them as a mere basis upon which to establish some measure of compromise. I invited gentlemen of all sides to suggest amendments and alterations, and particularly I called their attention to that provision which embraced in these resolutions territory to be hereafter acquired. I stated that my principal inducement to it was that it might prevent, and would be calculated to prevent, the future acquisition of territory.

The North, the ruling power of the country, apprehensive that if southern territory was acquired slavery would be established there, would, of course, oppose such acquisitions. The South would oppose northern acquisitions in the same way, for the same reason. But I said at the same time, and I say now, that if this is not acceptable as a comprehensive settlement, which is to settle now, and prevent hereafter, all controversy on this subject, it shall not be with me an indispensable condition. What right has the gentleman to complain, when he was invited to make amendments. These resolutions have been before us since the 18th day of December, and he has made no proposition to amend or alter them? None. Here is the great measure of pacification. Every Senator is bound, as far as he can, to contribute to the settlement of our great national troubles. If the propositions I offered, and which I offered with diffidence, are not adequate to the purpose, if they ask too much, why have not gentlemen moved to amend? Why has the honorable Senator sat here for one month and more, and proposed no amendment to the propositions which he now rises to condemn his constituents for approving?

Mr. SUMNER. Will the Senator allow me to say, that every time I could get an opportunity, I have voted against his propositions? I have missed no opportunity, direct or indirect, of voting against his propositions, from beginning to end, every line and every word of them.

Mr. CRITTENDEN. I do not controvert that, Mr. President; it may be so; but that is not what I am asking of the gentleman. It is: that if he desired union and conciliation at all, why did he not move to amend the propositions which he now condemns?

Mr. SUMNER. I will answer the Senator. Because I thought there could be no basis of peace on the Senator's propositions. The Senator's propositions were wrong in every respect, in every line, in every word. That is what I thought. I was for the Constitution of the United States—the Constitution of our fathers, as administered by George Washington.

Mr. CRITTENDEN. If that was all true, and the gentleman desired an amicable settlement of the difficulties which now threaten the country, had he no proposition whatever to make?

Mr. SUMNER. Certainly; the proposition which I have already made, that the Constitution, as administered by George Washington, should be preserved pure and free from any amendment for the sake of slavery.

Mr. CRITTENDEN. Why did he not move that? Why did he sit sullen and silent here for one month or more, with his breast full of resentment? [Applause in the galleries.]

The PRESIDING OFFICER. Order will be preserved in the galleries, or they will be cleared immediately.

Mr. CRITTENDEN. With such a spirit of opposition to, and thinking as he did of, these resolutions, why did he not propose to strike them all out?

Mr. SUMNER. Will the Senator let me answer?

Mr. CRITTENDEN. Yes; I will.

Mr. SUMNER. I did vote for the proposition of the Senator from New

Hampshire, [Mr. CLARK.][5] I voted for it as soon as it could come to a vote; and that expresses precisely my ideas. That displaced the Senator's proposition entirely.

{Senator Clark's resolution read as follows: "*Resolved*, That the provisions of the Constitution are ample for the preservation of the Union, and the protection of all the material interests of the country; that it needs to be obeyed rather than amended; and that an extrication from the present dangers is to be looked for in strenuous efforts to preserve the peace, protect the public property, and enforce the laws, rather than in new guarantees for particular interests, compromises for particular difficulties, or concessions to unreasonable demands.

Resolved, That all attempts to dissolve the present Union, or overthrow or abandon the present Constitution, with the hope or expectation of constructing a new one, are dangerous, illusory, and destructive; that, in the opinion of the Senate of the United States, no such reconstruction is practicable, and therefore, to the maintenance of the existing Union and Constitution should be directed all the energies of all the departments of the Government, and the efforts of all good citizens."[6]}

Mr. CRITTENDEN. All that I say remains true. The Senator now has particularized some three or four instances in which he considered these resolutions particularly condemnable, and now denounces the ignorance of his constituents, as evidenced by their signing this petition. What are they? We want a guarantee for slavery, he says. Sir, the gentleman only half speaks the truth. He states as though we had risen up here in a time of peace and quiet, to ask an alteration of the Constitution, simply for the purpose of extending slavery. That is not the case. Of the territory acquired from Mexico by the common blood and the common treasure, all has been appropriated according to the wishes of the North, and the slaveholding States excluded. Here remains one arid, sterile Territory alone—New Mexico—.

{A short procedural discussion ensued here prompted by a motion to curtail Crittenden's remarks. By a vote of 23 to 21, he was allowed to continue.}

Mr. CRITTENDEN. I am not surprised that Senators manifest such an anxiety to do what is called the business of the session, and to proceed to that. I take no exception to it, no offense at it whatever. It is but little that I have to say, and it would have been said in less time than has been occupied in determining this question. I thought the gentleman was not exactly correct in stating the effect of the resolutions introduced by me; and I wish to say a word in reference to those points which he has selected.

He says we ask guarantees in the Constitution for the protection of slavery in the Territories. By those resolutions, in all the territory north of the line designated, slavery is prohibited; all south of it, which, in reference to our present territory, is nothing more than the Territory of New Mexico, the most sterile and worthless of its extent upon this whole continent, is reserved for the South; and how, sir? That slavery, as it now exists there, as a matter of fact, shall be recognized as existing; and that it shall continue until the population of the Territory warrants its admission into the Union as a State. The people are then to decide for themselves, as they please, whether they will have slavery or not. That is the proposition, and that only. What principle does this conflict with? All California—that vast and rich territory—has been already converted into a free State, and New Mexico is all that remains of our conquest from Mexico. From all the rest, the South—the slaveholding portion of the community—are excluded. We do not ask you here to initiate slavery; we do not ask you to introduce slavery; we ask you simply to admit the fact that slavery does now exist by law in the Territory of New Mexico, and simply to agree that it shall continue so to exist until it becomes a State; that is all.

This, the gentleman says, would violate principle. What principle? Any principle of equity or justice as between the several States of the Union? Is there any constitutional principle to be violated? It may violate notions and opinions which gentlemen entertain outside of the Constitution; it may violate anti-slavery notions; but it does not violate the Constitution; nor, so far as I have heretofore understood it, does it violate even the notions of the Republican party. They go against the extension of slavery. I thought their doctrine was to let it rest where it existed, but not to extend it; and now here a question comes up, whether you will recognize it as it in point of fact exists, and as you know it to exist, and allow it to remain until the people, by coming into the Union as a State, have the right to decide it for themselves.

That is the whole substance of the proposition, when you exclude from it after-acquired territory. Where is the principle of the Constitution that this violates? Nowhere. As a mere question of equity between equal partners in the Commonwealth, is it too great a concession? Is it more than an equal, or a ratable, or an equitable proportion? Certainly, I think, it cannot be said to be. It violates nothing but some dogma that has been sometimes asserted by extreme members of the Republican party, that no slavery shall be allowed to exist in any Territory, and that no future slave State shall be admitted into the Union. It may violate that dogma; but, sir, does not this occasion call upon us to make sacrifices, if they are necessary, for the preservation of peace and union in the country? That is a question submitted to the people of the United States; that is a question submitted to us.

Your platform, gentlemen, [addressing the Republican Senators,] is a little thing of but a hands-breath, manufactured by a few politicians. You are governing a great nation. Are you to look to that platform, or to look to the nation which you have been called, in the course of Providence, to govern? Is it a fitting measure by which to govern a nation? Although every principle announced in the platform may be dear to your hearts, would you not sacrifice it rather than see secession and revolution go on, and this country be necessarily dismembered? You are pledged by every principle of the Constitution, by every principle of morality, by your own platform, to preserve the Union of this country. You obtained confidence from the country by that pledge! Devotion to the Union was assumed by you as a peculiar principle and a peculiar duty of your party. That is forgotten. When you cannot carry out all your notions and preserve the Union, is it better to let the Union go, and preserve every little peculiarity of doctrine, of opinion, which you may entertain, not of the essence of the Constitution, not belonging to the Constitution; but which, according to your fancy and notions of morality, you may desire to see carried into effect? Will you carry all these into effect, and let the Union go down and be destroyed? That is the question. These twenty-two thousand patriotic citizens of Massachusetts have said, let the Union be preserved; and so, gentlemen, I persuade myself that you yourselves will say.

{Crittenden here lectured his Republican colleagues on the general subject of compromise.}

Mr. SUMNER. I have no desire to prolong this debate, or to occupy the time of the Senate. I will make two remarks. The Senator from Kentucky is not aware of his own popularity in Massachusetts, of the extent to which his name is there an authority, of the willingness of the people of that State to adopt anything that bears his respectable name. I do not think that distinguished Senator is aware of that fact; consequently he is not aware how easily the people of Massachusetts may be seduced to adopt a proposition bearing the name which they so much respect; when, if they examined that proposition, they would at once reject it. Now, all that I would suggest in regard to these petitioners is that, under the lead of that distinguished Senator, they put their names to a paper which, I think, they did not, in all respects, in all its bearings, in all its obligations, in all its propositions, fully understand. I will do them the justice to believe that, if they did know all the bearings of those propositions, they would not put their name to any such paper.

That is all I have to say on that point; but I wish to make one other remark on another. The Senator intimated, if I understood him aright, that his propositions, at least in his own mind, were not applicable to territory hereafter acquired.

Mr. CRITTENDEN. No; I do not mean to be understood as saying that.

Mr. SUMNER. I understood the Senator so.

Mr. CRITTENDEN. I said I did not consider that proposition as an essential part of mine; that I did not intend to insist upon it, if I found it would not be acceptable. I did not intend that that should be any obstacle to an adjournment, and I would propose to strike it out, if necessary.

Mr. SUMNER. The Senator did not consider that proposition an essential part; and yet in the Journal of the Senate, which is now before me, in the yeas and nays, I find his name recorded in the affirmative on introducing those words, "now held or hereafter to be acquired" into the proposition. There is the record; the name of the Senator from Kentucky answering yes, when we were all asked to answer yea or nay on that proposition.

Mr. CLARK. I was one of those who voted against continuing this discussion to-day—

Mr. CRITTENDEN. Will the gentleman allow me a single moment?

Mr. CLARK. Certainly.

Mr. CRITTENDEN. I did, upon the motion of my colleague, vote for his amendment, and would be content with it; but subsequent reflection, and the objections made to it here and elsewhere, have satisfied me that I ought not to adhere to it, if it was to become an obstacle to prevent the passage of these resolutions. That is the explanation.

{After some procedural discussion, the Senate agreed to postpone consideration of Crittenden's proposals for several days.}

Source: *Congressional Globe*, 36th Cong., 2nd Sess., 862–65.

CHAPTER SIX

Constitutional Amendments Proposed by Kentuckians

Between December 3, 1860, and April 13, 1861, the elected officials of the country proposed sixty-eight compromise amendments to the United States Constitution as an alternative to disunion. Kentuckians offered six in Congress, the general assembly, and the Washington Peace Conference. Those propositions reflected the national aggregate as they were designed to protect slavery in the territories, the District of Columbia, and federal installations in the South; and ensure the return of fugitive slaves and the safe transit of slaves traveling with their owners. Some of these articles would have prohibited free blacks from voting or holding office and prohibited Congress from interfering with the interstate slave trade or with the institution of slavery in the states. One would have nationalized slavery. All six had the intent of shifting the protection of slavery from the state level to the federal. John J. Crittenden's amendment appears in chapter 2.

While Kentucky's amendments are similar to other compromise suggestions proposed over Secession Winter, certain details are worthy of mention. James Clay, for example, simply reiterated Crittenden's original amendment, but specifically included his January 3 additions which would have prohibited African Americans from voting or holding office, and would have allowed the United States to acquire land in Africa and South America for the colonization of "free negroes and mulattoes as the several States may wish to have removed from their limits." Benjamin Cissell introduced an amendment covering all of Crittenden's articles (except the one dealing with the elective franchise), but included an article that explicitly identified slaves as property everywhere in the country except in the non-slave states. As an Oppositionist and later

Unionist, Robert Mallory's compromise included a prohibition on Congress from interfering with the interstate slave trade or with slavery in the District of Columbia or federal installations in slave-owning states. Governor Magoffin was the only Kentuckian to propose an amendment to guarantee the free navigation of the Mississippi. He also displayed his concern for the future of the South's peculiar institution by suggesting that the Constitution be altered "so as to give the South the power, say in the United States Senate, to protect itself from unconstitutional and oppressive legislation upon the subject of slavery."

Senator Lazarus Whitehead Powell (Democrat)

December 6, 1860

Lazarus W. Powell (1812–1867) served as Kentucky's governor from 1851 to 1855, and a Democratic senator from 1859 to 1865. After leaving Congress, he resumed his law practice in Henderson.

Mr. POWELL. In pursuance of the notice I gave yesterday to the Senate, I desire to introduce the following resolution:

Resolved, That so much of the President's message as relates to the present agitated and distracted condition of the country, and the grievances between the slaveholding and the non-slaveholding States, be referred to a special committee of thirteen members; and that said committee be instructed to inquire whether any additional legislation within the sphere of Federal authority be necessary for the protection and security of property in the States and Territories of the United States; and if so, that they report by bill. And that said committee be also instructed to consider and report upon the expediency of proposing such an amendment or amendments to the Constitution of the United States as may be necessary to give certain, prompt, and full protection to the rights of property of the citizens of every State and Territory of the United States, and ensure the equality of the States, and the equal rights of all the citizens aforesaid, under the Federal Constitution.

Source: *Congressional Globe*, 36th Cong., 2nd Sess., 19.

Governor Beriah Magoffin (Democrat)

December 9, 1860

COMMONWEALTH OF KENTUCKY
Executive Department
Frankfort, December 9, 1860.

To his Excellency, the Governor of the State of[1]

Entertaining the opinion that some movement should be instituted at the earliest possible moment, to arrest the progress of events which seem to be rapidly hurrying the Government of the Union to dismemberment, as an initiatory step, I have, with great diffidence, concluded to submit to the Governors of the slave States a series of propositions, and ask their counsel and co-operation in bringing about a settlement upon them as a basis. Should the propositions be approved, they can be submitted to the assembling Legislatures and Conventions of the slave States, and a Convention of all of said States, or of those only approving, be called to pass upon them, and ask a general Convention of all the States of the Union that may be disposed to meet us on this basis for a full conference. The present good to be accomplished would be to arrest the secession movement, until the question as to whether the Union can be preserved upon fair and honorable terms, can be fully tested. If there be a basis for the adjustment of our difficulties within the Union, nothing should be left undone in order to its development. To this end, it seems to me there should be a conference of the States in some form, and it appears to me the form above suggested would be the most effective. I, therefore, as the Governor of a State having as deep a stake in the perpetuity of the Union, and at the same time as much solicitude for the maintenance of the institution of slavery as any other, would respectfully beg leave to submit for your consideration the following outline of propositions:

1st. Repeal, by an amendment of the Constitution of the United States, all laws in the free States in any degree nullifying or obstructing the execution of the fugitive slave law.

2d. Amendments to said law to enforce its thorough execution in all the free States, providing compensation to the owner of the slave from the State which fails to deliver him up under the requirements of the law, or throws obstructions in the way of his recovery.

3d. The passage of a law by Congress, compelling the Governors of the free States to return fugitives from justice, indicted by a grand jury in another State, for stealing or enticing away a slave.

4th. To amend the Constitution so as to divide all the Territories now belonging to the United States, or hereafter to be acquired, between the free and the slave States, say upon the line of the 37th degree of north latitude—all north of that line to come into the Union with requisite population as free States, and all south of the same to come in as slave States.[2]

5th. To amend the Constitution so as to guarantee forever to all the States the free navigation of the Mississippi river.

6th. To alter the Constitution so as to give the South the power, say in the United States Senate, to protect itself from unconstitutional and oppressive legislation upon the subject of slavery.

Respectfully, your obedient servant,
B. MAGOFFIN.

Source: *Journal of the Called Session of the House of Representatives of the Commonwealth of Kentucky, Begun and Held in the Town of Frankfort, on Thursday the Seventeenth Day of January, in the Year of Our Lord 1861, and of the Commonwealth the Sixty-Ninth* (Frankfort: Printed at the Kentucky Yeoman Office, John B. Major, State Printer, 1861), 19.

Representative Robert Mallory (Oppositionist)

December 12, 1860

Robert Mallory (1815–1885) graduated from the University of Virginia in 1827, practiced law in New Castle, Kentucky, and served as an Opposition, and later Unionist, member of the US House of Representatives from 1859 to 1865.

By Mr. MALLORY:

Resolved, That the special committee of thirty-three be instructed to report amendments to the Constitution of the United States, so that in all the Territories of the United States north of the line 36°30' north latitude, slavery or involuntary servitude, except for crime, be prohibited; that in all territory south of that line, the institution of African slavery, as it exists at this time in the slave States of this Union, may exist, and shall be protected by the Government of the United States. That when any Territory shall have attained a population sufficient to entitle it to at least one Representative in Congress, and not until then, it shall be authorized to form a State government, and, provided its form of government be republican, be admitted into the Union on a perfect equality with the several States, with or without slavery, as its constitution may provide; that Congress shall be prohibited from abolishing or interfering with the inter-State slave trade; from abolishing slavery in the District of Columbia, in the arsenals and dock-yards of the United States, and wherever it may have the power of exclusive legislation.

Source: *Congressional Globe*, 36th Cong., 2nd Sess., 78.

State Senator Benjamin P. Cissell

January 25, 1861

Benjamin P. Cissell (1823–?) was an attorney who represented Union County.[3]

Mr. Cissell read and laid upon the table the following joint resolution, viz:

Resolved by the General Assembly of the Commonwealth of Kentucky, That a convention of delegates from all the slaveholding States should assemble at Nashville, Tennessee, or such other place as a majority of the States co-operating may designate, on the 4th day of February, 1861, to digest and define the basis upon which, if possible, the Federal Union and the constitutional rights of the slave States may be perpetuated and preserved.

Resolved, That the General Assembly of Kentucky appoint a number of delegates to said convention of our ablest and wisest men, equal to our whole delegation in Congress, to be appointed in the following manner, to-wit: one from each of the Congressional districts in the State, by the joint vote of the Senators and Representatives from said districts, and the other two by the Governor, all of whom shall be by him commissioned to represent the State of Kentucky in said convention; and that the Governor of Kentucky immediately furnish copies of these resolutions to the Governors of the slaveholding States, and urge the participation of such States in said convention.

Resolved, That in the opinion of this General Assembly, such plan of adjustment should embrace the following propositions as amendments to the constitution of the United States:

First. A declaratory amendment that African slaves, as held under the institutions of the slaveholding States, shall be recognized as property, and entitled to the *status* of other property in the States where slavery exists; in all places within the exclusive jurisdiction of Congress within the slave States; in all the territories south of 36 degrees 30 minutes; in the District of Columbia; in transit and whilst temporarily sojourning with the owner in the non-slaveholding States and territories north of 36 degrees 30 minutes; and when fugitives from the owner in the several places above named, as well as in all places in the exclusive jurisdiction of Congress in the non-slaveholding States.

Second. That in all the territory now owned, or which may be hereafter acquired by the United States, south of the parallel of 36 degrees 30 minutes, African slavery shall be recognized as existing, and be protected by all the departments of the Federal and Territorial Governments; and in all north of that line, now owned or to be acquired, it shall not be recognized as existing; and whenever States formed out of any of said territory south of said line, having a population equal to that of a Congressional district, shall apply for admission into the Union, the same shall be admitted as slave States; whilst States north of the line, formed out of said territory, and having a population equal to a Congressional district, shall be admitted without slavery; but the States formed out of said territory, North and South, having been admitted as members of the Union, shall have all the powers over the institution of slavery possessed by the other States of the Union.

Third. Congress shall have no power to abolish slavery in places under its exclusive jurisdiction, and situate within the limits of States that permit the holding of slaves.

Fourth. Congress shall have no power to abolish slavery within the District of Columbia, as long as it exists in the adjoining States of Virginia and Maryland, or either, nor without the consent of the inhabitants, nor without just compensation made to such owners of slaves as do not consent to such abolishment. Nor shall Congress, at any time, prohibit officers of the Federal Government, or members of Congress whose duties require them to be in said District, from bringing with them their slaves, and holding them as such, during the time their duties may require them to remain there, and afterwards take them from the District.

Fifth. Congress shall have no power to prohibit or hinder the transportation of slaves from one State to another, or to a territory in which slaves are by law permitted to be held, whether that transportation be by land, navigable rivers, or by the sea.

Sixth. In addition to the fugitive slave clause, provide that when a slave has been demanded of the executive authority of the State to which he has fled, if he is not delivered, and the owner permitted to carry him out of the State in peace, that the State so failing, shall pay to the owner the value of such slave, and such damages as he may have sustained in attempting to reclaim his slave, and secure his right of action in the Supreme Court of the United States, with execution against the property of such State and of the individuals thereof.

Seventh. No future amendment of the constitution shall affect the six preceding articles, nor the third paragraph of the second section of the first article of the constitution, nor the third paragraph of the second section of the fourth article of said constitution, and no amendments shall be made to the constitution which will authorize or give to Congress any power to abolish or interfere with slavery in any of the States by whose laws it is or may be allowed or permitted.

Eighth. That slave property shall be rendered secure in transit through, or whilst temporarily sojourning, in non-slaveholding States or Territories, or in the District of Columbia.

Ninth. An amendment to the effect that all fugitives are to be deemed those offending the laws within the jurisdiction of the State, and who escape therefrom to other States; and that it is the duty of each State to suppress armed invasions of another State.

Source: *Journal of the Called Session of the Senate of the Commonwealth of Kentucky Begun and Held in the Town of Frankfort, on Thursday the Seventeenth Day of January, in the Year of Our Lord 1861, and of the Commonwealth the Sixty-Ninth* (Frankfort: Kentucky Yeoman Office, 1861), 83–85.

Delegate James Brown Clay (Democrat)

February 26, 1861

James B. Clay (1817–1864), son of Kentucky senator Henry Clay, studied law at Lexington Law School, practiced law with his father in Lexington, appointed by President Zachary Taylor as *chargé d'affaires* to Portugal and served from August 1, 1849, to July 19, 1850, elected as a Democrat to the Thirty-Fifth Congress (1857–1859), and served as a delegate to the Washington Peace Conference.

Clay's reintroduction of John J. Crittenden's amendment from December 18 included the Article 7 that Crittenden had added on January 3. Crittenden acknowledged borrowing both sections of Article 7 from Senator Stephen Douglas's amendment that he had proposed to the Senate's Committee of Thirty-Three on December 24, 1860.

Mr. CLAY:—I gave notice some days ago that I should offer as a substitute the CRITTENDEN resolutions—pure and undefiled—without the crossing of a "t" or the dotting of an "i." I now offer them as follows, and demand a vote by States:

WHEREAS, the Union is in danger; and owing to the unhappy divisions existing in Congress, it would be difficult, if not impossible, for that body to concur, in both its branches, by the requisite majority, so as to enable it either to adopt such measures of legislation, or to recommend to the State such amendments to the Constitution as are deemed necessary and proper to avert that danger; and whereas, in so great an emergency, the opinion and judgment of the people ought to be heard, and would be the best and surest guide to their representatives: Therefore,

Resolved, That provision ought to be made by law, without delay, for taking the sense of the people, and submitting to their vote the following resolutions as the basis for the final and permanent settlement of those disputes that now disturb the peace of the country and threaten the existence of the Union.

And that whereas serious and alarming dissensions have arisen between the Northern and Southern States, concerning the rights and security of the rights of the slaveholding States, and especially their rights in the common territory of the United States; and whereas, it is eminently desirable and proper that those dissensions, which now threaten the very existence of this Union, should be permanently quieted and settled by constitutional provisions, which shall do equal justice to all sections, and thereby restore to the people that peace and good will which ought to prevail between all the citizens of the United States: Therefore,

Resolved, That the following articles be, and hereby are, proposed and submitted as amendments to the Constitution of the United States, which shall be valid to all intents and purposes as part of said Constitution, when ratified by conventions of three-fourths of the several States:

ARTICLE 1. In all the territory of the United States now held or hereafter acquired, situate north of latitude 36°30', slavery or involuntary servitude, except as a punishment for crime, is prohibited, while such territory shall remain under territorial government. In all the territory south of said line of latitude, slavery of the African race is hereby recognized as existing, and shall not be interfered with by Congress; but shall be protected as property by all the departments of the territorial government during its continuance; and when any Territory, north or south of said line, within such boundaries as Congress may prescribe, shall contain the population requisite for a member of Congress, according to the then Federal ratio of representation of the people of the United States, it shall, if its form of government be republican, be admitted into the Union on an equal footing with the original States, with or without slavery, as the constitution of such new States may provide.

ARTICLE 2. Congress shall have no power to abolish slavery in places under its exclusive jurisdiction, and situate within the limits of States that permit the holding of slaves.

ARTICLE 3. Congress shall have no power to abolish slavery within the District of Columbia, so long as it exists in the adjoining States of Virginia and Maryland, or either, nor without the consent of the inhabitants, nor without just compensation first made to such owners of slaves as do not consent to such abolishment. Nor shall Congress at any time prohibit officers of the Federal Government or members of Congress, whose duties require them to be in said District, from bringing with them their slaves, and holding them, as such, during the time their duties may require them to remain there, and afterwards taking them from the District.

ARTICLE 4. Congress shall have no power to prohibit or hinder the transportation of slaves from one State to another, or to a Territory in which slaves are by law permitted to be held, whether that transportation be by land, navigable rivers, or by the sea; and the right of transit by the owners with their slaves in passing to or from one slaveholding State or Territory to another, between and through the non-slaveholding States and Territories, shall be protected.

ARTICLE 5. That, in addition to the provisions of the third paragraph of the second section of the fourth article of the Constitution of the United States, Congress shall have power to provide by law, and it shall be its duty so to provide, that the United States shall pay to the owner who shall apply for it, the full value of his fugitive slave in all cases, when the marshal or other officer whose duty it was to arrest said fugitive was prevented from so doing by violence or intimidation, or when, after arrest, said fugitive was rescued by force, and the owner thereby prevented and obstructed in the pursuit of his remedy for the recovery of his fugitive slave, under the said clause of the Constitution and the laws made in pursuance thereof. And in all such cases, when the United States shall pay for such fugitive, they shall have the power to reimburse themselves by imposing and collecting a tax on the county or city in which said violence, intimidation, or rescue was committed, equal in amount to the sum paid by them, with the addition of interest and the costs of collection; and the said county or city, after it has paid said amount to the United States, may, for its indemnity, sue and recover from the wrong-doers, or rescuers, by whom the owner was prevented from the recovery of his fugitive slave, in like manner as the owner himself might have sued and recovered.

ARTICLE 6. No future amendment of the Constitution shall affect the five preceding articles, nor the third paragraph of the second section of the first article of the Constitution, nor the third paragraph of the second section of the fourth article of said Constitution; and no amendment shall be made to the Constitution which will authorize or give to Congress any power to abolish or interfere with slavery in any of the States by whose laws it is or may be allowed or permitted.

ARTICLE 7. SEC. 1. The elective franchise, and the right to hold office, whether federal, State, territorial, or municipal, shall not be exercised by persons who are, in whole or in part, of the African race.

SEC. 2. The United States shall have the power to acquire, from time to time, districts of country in Africa and South America, for the colonization, at expense of the Federal Treasury, of such free negroes and mulattoes as the several States may wish to have removed from their limits and from the District of Columbia, and such other places as may be under the jurisdiction of Congress.

And whereas, also, besides those causes of dissension embraced in the foregoing amendments proposed to the Constitution of the United States, there are others which come within the jurisdiction of Congress, and may be remedied by its legitimate power: and whereas it is the desire of this Convention, as far as its influence may extend, to remove all just cause for the popular discontent and agitation which now disturb the peace of the country, and threaten the stability of its institutions: Therefore,

{Clay included here the four resolutions that Senator Crittenden attached to the end of his December 18 proposal to amend the Constitution.}

The question on agreeing to said amendment resulted in the following vote:

AYES.—Kentucky, Missouri, North Carolina, Tennessee, and Virginia—5.

NOES.—Connecticut, Delaware, Illinois, Indiana, Maine, Massachusetts, Maryland, New Jersey, New York, New Hampshire, Ohio, Pennsylvania, Rhode Island, and Vermont—14.

So the amendment was not agreed to.

Source: Lucius E. Chittenden, *A Report of the Debates and Proceedings in the Secret Sessions of the Conference Convention, for Proposing Amendments to the Constitution of the United States, Held at Washington, D.C., in February, A.D. 1861* (New York: D. Appleton & Company, 1864), 421–24.

CHAPTER SEVEN

Selected Memorials, Petitions, and Resolutions to the Second Session of the Thirty-Sixth Congress

January–March 1861

Beginning on January 3, 1861, memorials and petitions in support of, and against, Crittenden's proposed amendment began to appear in the *Congressional Globe*. Most of those in favor of Crittenden's resolutions came from the border states, north and south, where lay the greatest interest in compromise, although some originated in cities and towns in New England. Others urged Congress to preserve the Union "by upholding the Constitution as it is," and implored Congress "not consent to any compromise by which slavery shall be established or extended into territory of the United States." One from Illinois professed its opposition to all "compromise with traitors," while another from Minnesota prayed for "the adoption of the compromise measures proposed by Hon. Mr. Crittenden."

A petition from LaPorte County, Indiana, reported that petitions were being circulated there to "procure false representation of the sentiments of the people." To make their position clear, the petitioners emphatically stated that they were "opposed to any compromise with parties who are in hostility to the Government." Another from Bordentown, New Jersey, echoed the sentiments reflected in chapter 4 that the Republican Party had won the election of 1860 by constitutional means and that it would be "not only incompatible with honor and patriotism, but cowardly and base, for Republicans to surrender, under the pressure of secession and secession threats." At one point, Senator John C.

Ten Eyck,[1] having grown weary of the introduction of various petitions and memorials, caustically proposed an amendment that would have prohibited no state to secede "save and alone the State of South Carolina, who may be allowed to come in and go out whenever she pleases."

Petitions and Memorials

January 3, 1861

Mr. BIGLER.[2] Mr. President, I present two memorials of like import, numerously signed by citizens of the city of Philadelphia, setting forth that they "earnestly pray your honorable bodies to pass the resolutions introduced by Hon. Mr. CRITTENDEN, of Kentucky, a copy of which is hereunto annexed," or any other resolutions embodying the same principles and measures. They believe this course will be acceptable to our constituents in all sections of the country, and will have the effect of allaying the present excitement. These memorials purport to be signed by men of all political parties. I move that they be laid on the table.

The motion was agreed to.

Mr. BIGLER. I also present the proceedings of a public meeting held at Harrisburg, the seat of government of my State, called to take into consideration the present imminent condition of the country. Also the proceedings of a meeting at Carlisle, Pennsylvania, on the same subject. I will remark in this connection, Mr. President, with the indulgence of the Senate, that meetings of a similar character have been held in different parts of that great State, and I believe in every instance their proceedings have breathed a spirit of loyal devotion to the whole country, and fidelity to the institutions of the country, to the Constitution, and the Union as they now stand. They further manifest the utmost disposition on the part of the people of that State to avoid even an appearance of evil, for the purpose of producing harmony and peace in this great Confederacy. Furthermore, they indicate very distinctly a desire to adopt promptly the measures of adjustment suggested by the Senator from Kentucky; and I will venture to repeat what I have said before, that if the Congress of the United States will give the people an opportunity to act, they will embrace any reasonable measure of adjustment. Our friends in the South will discover that the people are prepared and willing to meet their complaints in the spirit of kindness and generosity, and respond favorably to any demand which the States complaining may make.

Source: *Congressional Globe*, 36th Cong., 2nd Sess., 237.

Petitions and Memorials

January 10, 1861

Mr. SUMNER.[3] I offer the memorial of the synod of the Reformed Presbyterian Church, now in session in Alleghany {*sic*} city, Pennsylvania, asking that Congress will take measures for the amendment of the Constitution, so that it may contain, first, an express acknowledgment of the being and authority of God; secondly, an acknowledgment and submission to the authority of Christ; thirdly, a recognition of the paramount obligation of God's law; and, fourthly, that it be rendered in all its principles and provisions clearly and unmistakably adverse to the existence of any form of slavery within the national limits. This is testified by their moderator and the clerk of the Synod.

Source: *Congressional Globe*, 36th Cong., 2nd Sess., 304.

State of the Union

January 19, 1861

Mr. LEACH,[4] of North Carolina, asked and obtained unanimous consent to present to the House the proceedings and action of a very large meeting, irrespective of party, held in the town of Lexington, North Carolina, upon the present alarming crisis. The series of resolutions passed at that meeting, with the view and hope of leading to a settlement of our national troubles, were based upon the Crittenden propositions of adjustment, with some slight modifications, and he believed they reflected the sentiments of nine tenths of the people of North Carolina, who were patriotic, Union-loving men, but who desired a final settlement of the issues now agitating the public mind. He invoked members to read, and give a respectful consideration to said resolutions, with the hope that the voice of North Carolina might be, in some degree, instrumental in effecting an adjustment of our difficulties.

Source: *Congressional Globe*, 36th Cong., 2nd Sess., 476.

Petitions and Memorials

January 28, 1861

Mr. WILSON.[5] I present the petition of Moses Davenport and others, citizens of Newburyport, Massachusetts, asking for the passage of the compromise resolutions of Mr. CRITTENDEN. I understand that these petitioners ask for an amendment to the Constitution of the United States recognizing and protecting slavery south of 36°30' in existing territory, and in territory not yet purchased, conquered, or stolen. They ask that the Constitution may be amended so as to prevent the General Government from abolishing slavery in the District of Columbia while it exists in Virginia; and to have the Constitution amended so that the citizens of Massachusetts of the African race, who have had the right of suffrage since 1780, shall be denied that right; and the consideration, I believe, is the equalization of the fees of the commissioners under the fugitive slave law.

Source: *Congressional Globe*, 36th Cong., 2nd Sess., 586.

Union Resolution

January 28, 1861

Mr. BOTELER.[6] I desire to present to the House a resolution adopted at a meeting of the conservative Union men of Jefferson county, Virginia, held at Charlestown, on Monday last. The resolution is as follows:

Resolved, That, in the opinion of this meeting of delegates, the present condition of this country is such as requires the pending difficulties between the slave and free States to be permanently settled, and that the convention of the people of this State should not finally adjourn before such permanent settlement is had; and further, that the convention, before taking any such action as would separate this State from the existing Federal Government, should use every exertion to preserve the Union upon a basis of justice to all the sections—such, for instance, as that known as the Crittenden resolutions.

Source: *Congressional Globe*, 36th Cong., 2nd Sess., 599.

Compromise Memorials

February 2, 1861

Mr. NOELL.[7] I desire to present three memorials from my constituents in reference to existing difficulties; one from citizens of Dent county, and another from citizens from Phelps county, Missouri, both signed by the farmers and workingmen of those counties, asking Congress to adopt the Crittenden propositions. The third memorial is from Lucy A. James and thirty-five other ladies of Phelps county. They come here not in the spirit of dictation, but as the descendants of those honored women who showed their devotion to the country in the days of the Revolution, asking this House to take such measures as may avert the calamities which now threaten the country, and in which those nearest and dearest to them will be involved.

Source: *Congressional Globe*, 36th Cong., 2nd Sess., 710.

Resolutions of New Jersey

February 7, 1861

Mr. THOMSON.[8] Mr. President, I ask leave to present the resolutions of the Legislature of the State of New Jersey in reference to the present distracted condition of our country, and setting forth, among other things, that the resolutions and propositions submitted to the Senate of the United States by Hon. JOHN J. CRITTENDEN, of Kentucky, for the compromise of the questions in dispute between the people of the northern and of the southern States, *or any other constitutional method* that will permanently settle the question of slavery, will be acceptable to the people of the State of New Jersey; and the Senators and Representatives in Congress from New

Jersey be requested and earnestly urged to support those resolutions and propositions.

Source: *Congressional Globe*, 36th Cong., 2nd Sess., 778.

Petitions, Memorials, and Reports

February 18, 1861

Mr. KING.[9] I desire to present a memorial from the German Republican central committee of the city of New York, praying for the preservation of the integrity of the Union. They have presented their views at considerable length, and adopted certain resolutions, in which they declare that, in their judgment, the Union, as designed and made by the fathers, can only be preserved inviolate by upholding the Constitution as it is, and by executing and enforcing the Federal laws. The memorial is signed by delegates from each of the twenty-two wards of the city of New York. I move that it be laid on the table.

It was so ordered.

Mr. BIGLER[10] presented a petition of citizens of Bradford County, Pennsylvania, praying for the adoption of the compromise measures proposed by Hon. Mr. CRITTENDEN; which was ordered to lie on the table.

He also presented a petition of citizens of Safe Harbor, Lancaster County, Pennsylvania, praying for the adoption of the compromise measures proposed by Hon. Mr. CRITTENDEN; which was ordered to lie on the table.

{Several other petitions were introduced here unrelated to the sectional crisis.}

Mr. SUMNER. I present a memorial of citizens and voters of the town of Hopkinton, Massachusetts, on the state of the country. This memorial is signed by comparatively few persons, but it speaks the true and prevailing sentiment of Massachusetts. Three things in it are declared. First, that slavery is repugnant to the principles of the founders of our Constitution; secondly, that it is repugnant to the genius of our Constitution; and thirdly, that it is repugnant to that righteousness that exalteth a nation; wherefore, these petitioners pray that Congress will not consent to any compromise by which slavery shall be established or extended into territory of the United States. Any other petitioners from Massachusetts speak a sentiment which is alien to the principles of that Commonwealth. It is a sentiment which may be found on the pavements of cities; for it is only when you get off those pavements, away from the paving stones, that you find the true sentiment of Massachusetts. I offer the memorial, and ask that it lie on the table.

It was so ordered.

Mr. SUMNER. I present also, a memorial of citizens of Philadelphia, Pennsylvania, remonstrating against the passage of any act of Congress or of any amendment to the Constitution of the United States, which shall extend human servitude or give it new guarantees: "what our forefathers would not grant to their companions and fellow-sufferers in the Revolution, we hope their sons will not grant to the present holders of slaves." I ask that this petition also lie on the table.

It was so ordered.

Mr. SUMNER also presented a memorial of citizens of Philadelphia, praying Congress to stand firm for the Union, the Constitution, as it is, and the enforcement of all the laws; which was ordered to lie on the table.

Source: *Congressional Globe*, 36th Cong., 2nd Sess., 984–85.

State of the Union

February 18, 1861

The SPEAKER,[11] by unanimous consent, and in compliance with the request of the Common Council of the city of Boston, Massachusetts, presented resolutions of that body, expressive of their unalterable devotion to the Union, asking the immediate adoption of such measures of a pacific and conciliatory character as will effectually check the spirit of disunion, and tend to consolidate the fraternal bonds of our national brotherhood, and recognizing the proposition of Mr. CRITTENDEN, of Kentucky, as a satisfactory basis of adjustment.

Source: *Congressional Globe*, 36th Cong., 2nd Sess., 999.

Petitions and Memorials

February 19, 1861

Mr. RICE[12] also presented a memorial of citizens of St. Anthony, Minnesota, praying for the adjustment of the sectional difficulties on the principles contained in the resolutions of Mr. CRITTENDEN, or that of Mr. RICE; which was ordered to lie on the table.

He also presented a petition of citizens of St. Cloud, Minnesota, praying for the adjustment of the sectional difficulties on the principles contained in the resolutions of Mr. CRITTENDEN, or that of Mr. RICE; which was ordered to lie on the table.

He also presented a memorial of citizens of Stillwater, Minnesota, praying for the adjustment of the sectional difficulties on the principles contained in the resolutions of Mr. CRITTENDEN, or that of Mr. RICE; which was ordered to lie on the table.

{Senator Bigler of Pennsylvania presented a petition from the "pure-minded and patriotic ladies in my State" supporting constitutional amendments so that "peace will again be restored" to the country.}

Mr. JOHNSON,[13] of Arkansas I hope there are no more petitions.

The VICE PRESIDENT,[14] There are evidently a good many more.

Mr. TEN EYCK. I have one.

Mr. JOHNSON, of Arkansas. If I have the right to object to the explaining and reading of petitions, I do so. You might as well sing psalms to a dead horse [laughter] as to get up and read these petitions, and consume all the little time left of the morning hour, but about fifteen minutes. It is too bad; and it is so every morning, and it will continue to be so until the end of the session, unless it is arrested in some way or another.

Mr. TEN EYCK. By the leave of the Senator, I should like to present a petition, without any remark. I have a petition of more than six hundred citizens of Jersey City praying Congress to stand by the Constitution as it is, and to enforce a wholesome respect for the Federal laws. I move that the petition lie on the table.

The motion was agreed to.

Mr. CRITTENDEN. I present a petition of legal voters of Machias, Maine, and its vicinity, without distinction to party, praying Congress to adopt the measures of conciliation and compromise submitted by me, or any similar plan which will insure tranquility and the peaceful perpetuity of the present American Union. I have no speech to make; but I may say that these petitions are about the best speeches I hear on this floor on the subject.

The memorial was ordered to lie on the table.

Mr. SEWARD[15] presented a petition of citizens of school district No. 10, in Bethany, Genesee county, New York, without distinction to party, requesting Congress to stand firm for the Union, the Constitution as it is, and the enforcement of the laws; which was ordered to lie on the table.

He also presented a petition of citizens of Brooklyn, New York, praying Congress to stand firm for the Constitution and the Government, and to make no compromise whatever;

Source: *Congressional Globe*, 36th Cong., 2nd Sess., 1011.

Petitions and Memorials

February 21, 1861

Mr. DOOLITTLE[16] presented the petition of H. W. Drake and six hundred others, citizens of the United States, and residents of the city of Milwaukee, Wisconsin, without respect to party, representing that they are firmly and irrevocably attached to the Constitution and laws of the United States as they are, and opposed to all compromises with traitors, and with all men who are directly or indirectly plotting the overthrow of the Government; and praying Congress at once to adopt such measures as may be necessary to hold and to protect the property of the Government, to maintain the honor of our flag, and the integrity of the Union; which was ordered to lie on the table.

He also presented the petition of R. P. Eaton, and one hundred and fifty others, citizens of the State of Wisconsin, setting forth that they believe that the Constitution and laws, as they now exist, furnish the slaveholders all the security and protection which, in good faith, the free States ought to furnish, and that humanity and the spirit of the age can tolerate; and asking the President of the United States to enforce all the laws of the United States, and to see that the ship of State suffers no harm while the helm is in his hands; and also asking of their delegation in Congress to look well and carefully to the interests and good of the whole Union, and if any acts of Congress now in existence are found to conflict with the provisions of the Constitution, then, that they see to it that those laws are so altered, amended, or repealed, as the cause of justice and humanity may require; which was ordered to lie on the table.

Mr. POWELL[17] presented a petition of citizens of Superior City, Wisconsin, praying for the adoption of the compromise measures proposed by Hon. Mr. CRITTENDEN; which was ordered to lie on the table.

Mr. ANTHONY[18] presented a memorial of citizens of Newport, Rhode Island, approving of the compromise measures proposed by the Representatives of the border States; which was ordered to lie on the table.

{Several petitions were introduced here encouraging Congress to approve the Crittenden amendment. Connecticut senator Lafayette S. Foster presented one from the "inhabitants of Mystic, Connecticut, opposed to any compromise for the extension of slavery."}

Mr. FESSENDEN[19] presented the petition of Samuel Garland and others, inhabitants and legal voters of Windham, Maine, representing that there has come to be an irreconcilable difference of views on the subject of slavery, its morality and expediency, between the free States and some or all of the slave States, which must be a perpetual and consistently increasing source of irritation and discord; and praying Congress to take such measures as its wisdom may devise to refer to a vote of the people of the United States a proposition that any slave State which, by a fair vote of its citizens, shall so decide, shall be released from any legal obligations to the Constitution and Federal Union; which was ordered to lie on the table.

Mr. CRITTENDEN presented a petition of five hundred and seventy-five citizens of Jefferson county, Illinois, praying for the adoption of the compromise measures proposed by him; which was ordered to lie on the table.

{Senator Crittenden here presented a petition "praying that pensions may be granted to the soldiers of the war of 1812."}

He also presented a petition of citizens of Liberty Corner, New Jersey, praying for the adoption of the compromise measures proposed by him; which was ordered to lie on the table.

He also presented a memorial of citizens of Michigan, in favor of the adoption of the Crittenden propositions as modified by the committee of the border States; which was ordered to lie on the table.

Source: *Congressional Globe*, 36th Cong., 2nd Sess., 1076.

Petitions and Memorials

February 22, 1861

Mr. THOMSON.[20] I present the petition of thirteen hundred and forty-five citizens of Jersey City, New Jersey, three hundred of whom voted for Mr. Lincoln at the late election for President, in favor of the Crittenden resolutions, or any other mode of settlement by which peace and amity may be restored to the country.

I also present a petition of the same character, signed by a large number of citizens of the city of New Brunswick, New Jersey, at the head of which is the venerable name of Theodore Frelinghuysen.[21] I move that they lie on the table.

It was so ordered.

Mr. KING presented resolutions unanimously adopted at the annual town meeting of Stockholm, New York, disapproving of compromises, or concessions to the slave power now in open rebellion against the Constitution and Government of the United States; protesting against altering the Constitution, and praying Congress to abide by their oath to support the Constitution and Government of the United States; and to put down, with a firm hand, all insurrection, treason, or rebellion, and subdue or drive all traitors out of the Union; which was ordered to lie on the table.

He also presented the memorial of Isaac McGay and one hundred others, of the city of New York, deploring any attempt to defeat the will of the people, as expressed at the ballot-box, and petitioning Congress to be firm in maintaining the Union, the Constitution, and the laws; which was ordered to lie on the table.

Mr. TRUMBULL[22] presented the petition of James Irvine, and other residents and legal voters in the town of Savannah, county of Carroll, State of Illinois, representing that they are firmly and irrevocably attached to the

Constitution and laws of the United States as they are; that they are opposed to all compromise with traitors, and with all men who are, directly or indirectly, plotting the overthrow of the Government; and praying Congress at once to adopt such measures as may be necessary to hold and to protect the property of the Government, to maintain the honor of our flag, and the integrity of the Union; which was ordered to lie on the table.

Mr. RICE presented a petition of citizens of St. Paul, Minnesota, in favor of a settlement of the sectional difficulties on the plan of compromise proposed by the resolutions of Hon. Mr. CRITTENDEN or Hon. Mr RICE; which was ordered to lie on the table.

Mr. WADE[23] presented a petition of citizens of Kingsville, Ohio, praying Congress to stand firm for the Union of the States, the Constitution as it is, and the execution of the laws, and against all compromise with armed rebels, or those who sympathize with them; which was ordered to lie on the table.

Source: *Congressional Globe*, 36th Cong., 2nd Sess., 1108.

Petitions and Memorials

January 25, 1861

Mr. TEN EYCK presented a petition of citizens of Bordentown, New Jersey, without distinction of party, praying Congress to stand firm for the Union, the Constitution as it is, and the enforcement of all the laws; which was ordered to lie on the table.

He also presented a petition of citizens of New Market, New Jersey, setting forth that it is not only incompatible with honor and patriotism, but cowardly and base, for Republicans to surrender, under the pressure of secession and secession threats; that they have done no wrong, but have in the last election succeeded, by constitutional means, by addressing the enlightened reason and conscience of the people, in view of long years of misrule and rapacity of a corrupt party and Administration; and that it is incumbent upon all good citizens to maintain the supremacy of the Constitution and the laws. They recommend to their Senators and Representatives in Congress, and all others in authority, to stand by the Constitution as it is and the Government of the country, and to make no compromise whatever. The petition was ordered to lie on the table.

Mr. GREEN[24] presented a memorial of inhabitants of Dakota, praying Congress to grant them such a territorial organization as will, without embodying the contested provisions of the Wilmot proviso,[25] enable them to enjoy in peace the fruits of their labor, and to feel the protecting hand of authority; which was ordered to lie on the table.

Mr. TRUMBULL. I have a petition of six hundred and fifty-two legal voters in the county of Laporte, in the State of Indiana, representing that strenuous efforts have been made in that county to procure false representation of the sentiments of the people by circulating petitions favorable to what is generally known as the Crittenden propositions. These petitioners, six hundred and fifty-two in number, legal voters, represent that they are attached to the Constitution and the Union, and are willing to redeem all the pledges of American citizens for the enforcement of the laws, and opposed to any compromise with parties who are in hostility to the Government. I move that the petition be laid on the table.

The motion was agreed to.

Source: *Congressional Globe*, 36th Cong. 2nd Sess., 1158.

Petitions and Memorials

February 27, 1861

Mr. CRITTENDEN. I present a petition of citizens of Iowa, praying for the settlement of our national difficulties by the adoption of resolutions submitted by me, or those of the Representatives of the border States, or the substitute of Mr. Douglas.[26] I will only read the first two lines: "The Union, now and forever, one and inseparable."

I also present a petition, to the same purpose, from the citizens of Muhlenburg county, Kentucky. I ask that the petitions lie on the table.

It was so ordered.

Mr. TRUMBULL presented a petition of residents and legal voters of the town of Tuscola, county of Douglas, State of Illinois, representing that they are firmly and irrevocably attached to the Constitution and laws of the United States as they are, and that, they are opposed to all compromises with traitors and with men who are directly or indirectly plotting the overthrow of the Government, and praying Congress at once to adopt such measures as may be necessary to hold and to protect the property of the Government; to maintain the honor of our flag and the integrity of the Union; which was ordered to lie on the table.

Mr. TEN EYCK. In obedience to what I consider the right of petition, I present the following:

> We the undersigned, citizens of the United States, in view of the alarming and distracted state of the country, and the well-founded apprehensions of civil war, beg your honorable bodies to embrace any just and equitable compromise that may be proposed, in the hope that our national difficulties may be speedily settled.
>
> To this end, among any amendments that may be offered to the Constitution, we beg leave respectfully to propose, that hereafter, no State may be permitted to secede from the Union without the consent of all the other States, save and alone the State of South Carolina, who may be allowed to come in and go out whenever she pleases. [Laughter.]
>
> I move that the memorial lie on the table.
>
> The motion was agreed to.

Source: *Congressional Globe*, 36th Cong., 2nd Sess., 1243.

Petitions and Memorials

February 28, 1861

Mr. KING. I have also a petition in the form of resolutions, which I will read:

We, the undersigned, have the honor to present to your honorable body the following resolutions of the German adopted citizens of Albany:

Whereas it is the duty of every citizen to express himself about the present political condition of the country, in order to enable the legislative and administrative authorities—whose power reposes in the majority—to form an accurate knowledge of the wishes of the people; we therefore pronounce it as our convictions—

That the Constitution of the United States as it is can satisfy all just demands of all parts of the Union, and does not need any alteration, additional or otherwise.

That the executive officers ought immediately to make use of all and any means for executing the existing laws.

That any receding from the constitutional basis, and any conceding to the treasonable insurrection of southern States, would be utterly dishonorable, and must inevitably lead to complete disunion.

We declare ourselves ready at any time to prove the sincerity of our convictions, and offer ourselves unconditionally to the disposal of Government.

Source: *Congressional Globe*, 36th Cong., 2nd Sess., 1265.

Petitions and Memorials

March 1, 1861

Mr. WILKINSON.[27] I present the petition of a number of citizens of Preston, Fillmore county, Minnesota, who state that they have learned that several States of this Union have rebelled against the Government of the United States; have captured forts, arsenals, cannon, small arms, and other property of the United States to the amount and value of several million dollars; that within those States citizens of the free States who have gone thither for health, pleasure, or business, relying upon the guarantee of our national Constitution, that "the citizens of each State shall be entitled to all privileges and immunities of citizens in the several States," are, by the score and hundred, tarred and feathered, banished, and even murdered by lawless mobs without judge or jury, indictment or trial, and their property confiscated without any process of law; that the authorities of the States wherein these crimes are perpetuated take no measures to prevent or punish them, but rather encourage and approve them; that among those who have been so maltreated are citizens of Minnesota; that within said rebellious States the Constitution and laws of the United States are a dead letter, and the authority of the General Government defied; that an American vessel bearing the flag of the United States, and in Government employ, has been by rebels and traitors fired upon, and by force prevented from entering a port of the United States;[28] that the channels leading into some of the ports of the United States have been by the authority of the rebellious States aforesaid, blocked up and obstructed; that conspiracies have been set on foot to take possession of the capital of the United States by an armed foe in open rebellion against the Government; that the navigation of the Mississippi river has been, and is, impeded and prevented by means of a battery or batteries planted on its shores by authority of one of the rebellious States; and that they cannot learn that the constituted authorities of the Government have taken, or are taking, efficient measures to put a stop to or punish such proceedings, or to prevent their repetition and indefinite extension. They state also that they learn that certain measures have been urged upon Congress having mainly in view the extension and perpetuation of slavery as a means of buying off the perpetrators of the above-stated outrages from continuing and aggravating them. They are convinced that such measures will not have the desired effect; and that it is due to the integrity of our Government, as well as to the law-abiding citizens who claim its protection, that the laws should be enforced, "and that the Federal Constitution, the rights of the States, and the Union of the States, shall be preserved;" and they pray Congress to place at the disposal of the President of the United States such means in men and money as may be necessary for the purpose, and call upon him to enforce the laws; to reinforce the forts threatened by rebels; to recapture (if not peaceably delivered up on demand), the forts and munitions of war of which the Government has been robbed; to take measures to bring traitors to trial and punishment; and generally to see to it that the Republic receives no detriment at the hands of rebels and traitors. They protest against the consideration by Congress of any proposition for amending the Constitution, with a view to conciliate States which are in open rebellion, or which threaten rebellion if their demands be not complied with, until such States shall have returned to their allegiance and have withdrawn their threats of rebellion; and especially protesting against the enactment of any law, or the adoption of any proposition for amending the Constitution, which has in view the extension of human slavery. I move that the petition lie on the table.

It was so ordered.

Source: *Congressional Globe*, 36th Cong., 2nd Sess., 1300–1301.

CHAPTER EIGHT

Washington Peace Conference

The Washington Peace Conference met at the Willard Hotel in Washington, DC, from February 4 through February 27, 1861. Twenty-one states sent 131 representatives who elected former president John Tyler of Virginia as presiding officer. Virginia's general assembly had requested the gathering to resolve the "unhappy controversy which now divides the States of this Confederacy." Virginia supported John J. Crittenden's proposed constitutional amendment as the basis of compromise and noted that, slightly modified, it "would be accepted by the people of this commonwealth." The general assembly specifically wanted the protection of slavery below the 36°30' line to apply to all territory "now held or hereafter acquired" in the hopes that Cuba and even additional parts of Mexico might eventually be annexed. Virginia's other stipulation was that Crittenden's fourth article be so written that it "shall secure to the owners of slaves the right of transit with their slaves between and through the nonslaveholding States and territories." Virginia was particularly sensitive to this issue due to the recent decision in the Lemmon Slave Case.[1]

By the time the Conference delegates gathered in Washington, an astute observer could have predicted that agreement on the issues of the day would be highly unlikely. Border state representatives were divided between Democrats and Oppositionists just as some northern state contingents presented a mix of Republicans and Democrats. The seven slave states that had seceded, or were in the process of seceding, did not send representatives, nor did Arkansas which was seriously pondering secession. California and Oregon declined to send delegates, as did the pro-Lincoln states of Minnesota, Michigan, and Wisconsin. For reasons mentioned earlier, Republicans were not inclined to compromise on any issue and certainly not on the primary point of disagreement—the protection of slavery in the territories. They had won the presidency on a campaign platform that opposed the extension of slavery, but not the existence of it. Voting for an amendment that would permit slavery anywhere in the territories would be tantamount to negating the primary issue upon which Lincoln was elected.

When it came time to vote on the final amendment, some states were so divided they abstained and others recorded dissenting opinions. Delegations from Iowa and Maine (dominated by hard-core Republicans) voted against all seven articles while delegates from Vermont registered "no" votes on all except article 5 prohibiting the foreign slave trade. The slaveholding states of North Carolina and Virginia voted against the slave trade article because it would have prevented the exchange of slaves between those states and their southern neighbors which had just seceded. Kentucky, Tennessee, Delaware, Maryland, Pennsylvania, New Jersey, Rhode Island, and Ohio voted in favor of all seven articles.

The conference's final amendment reflected neither of Virginia's original stipulations. Republicans were not willing to place limits on a state's right to restrict the transit of slaves into their political domain. Neither were they willing to unilaterally protect slavery in any future territories acquired by the United States. Kentucky, Delaware, Maryland, and Tennessee approved the territorial clause (Article 1); Virginia and North Carolina opposed the first article securing slavery throughout the New Mexico Territory because the article did not contain the phrase "now held or hereafter acquired." The subtle distinctions in the various positions held by the delegates are evident in the majority and minority reports of Kentucky's commissioners.

Virginia's Call for a National Convention

January 19, 1861

Whereas, it is the deliberate opinion of the general assembly of Virginia, that unless the unhappy controversy which now divides the states of this confederacy, shall be satisfactorily adjusted, a permanent dissolution of the Union is inevitable; and the general assembly, representing the wishes of the people of the commonwealth, is desirous of employing every reasonable means to avert so dire a calamity, and determined to make a final effort to restore the Union and the constitution, in the spirit in which they were established by the fathers of the Republic: Therefore,

Resolved, that on behalf of the commonwealth of Virginia, an invitation is hereby extended to all such States, whether slaveholding or non-slaveholding, as are willing to unite with Virginia in an earnest effort to adjust the present unhappy controversies, in the spirit in which the constitution was originally formed, and consistently with its principles, so as to afford to the people of the slaveholding states adequate guarantees for the security of their rights, to appoint commissioners to meet on the 4th day of February next, in the city of Washington, similar commissioners appointed by Virginia, to consider, and if practicable, agree upon some suitable adjustment.

Resolved, that Ex-president John Tyler, William C. Rives, Judge John W. Brockenbrough, George W. Summers, and James A. Seddon, are hereby appointed commissioners, whose duty it shall be to repair to the city of Washington, on the day designated in the foregoing resolution, to meet such commissioners as may be appointed by any of said states, in accordance with the foregoing resolution.

Resolved, that if said commissioners, after full and free conference, shall agree upon any plan of adjustment requiring amendments to the federal constitution, for the further security of the rights of the people of the slaveholding states, they be requested to communicate the proposed amendments to congress, for the purpose of having the same submitted by that body, according to the forms of the constitution, to the several States for ratification.

Resolved, that if said commissioners cannot agree on such adjustment, or if agreeing, congress shall refuse to submit for ratification such amendments as may be proposed, then the commissioners of this state shall immediately communicate the result to the executive of this commonwealth, to be by him laid before the convention of the people of Virginia and the general assembly: provided, that the said commissioners be subject at all times to the control of the general assembly, or if in session, to that of the state convention.

Resolved, that in the opinion of the general assembly of Virginia, the propositions embraced in the resolutions presented to the senate of the United States by the Hon. John J. Crittenden, so modified as that the first article proposed as an amendment to the constitution of the United States, shall apply to all the territory of the United States now held or hereafter acquired south of the latitude thirty-six degrees and thirty minutes, and provide that slavery of the African race shall be effectually protected as property therein during the continuance of the territorial government, and the fourth article shall secure to the owners of slaves the right of transit with their slaves between and through the non-slaveholding states and territories, constitute the basis of such an adjustment of the unhappy controversy which now divides the states of this confederacy, as would be accepted by the people of this commonwealth.

Resolved, that Ex-president John Tyler is hereby appointed, by the concurrent vote of each branch of the general assembly, a commissioner to the president of the United States, and Judge John Robertson is hereby appointed, by a like vote, a commissioner to the state of South Carolina, and the other states that have seceded or shall secede, with instructions respectfully to request the president of the United States and authorities of such states to agree to abstain, pending the proceedings contemplated by the action of this general assembly, from any and all acts calculated to produce a collision of arms between the states and the government of the United States.

Resolved, that copies of the foregoing resolutions be forthwith telegraphed to the executives of the several states, and also to the president of the United States, and that the governor be requested to inform, without delay, the commissioners of their appointment by the foregoing resolutions.

Source: *Journal of the House of Delegates of the State of Virginia, for the Extra Session, 1861* (Richmond: William F. Ritchie, Public Printer, 1861), 65–66.

Kentucky Resolutions Appointing Commissioners

January 26, 1861

The Committee on Federal Relations, according to order of the Senate, made a report, which is as follows, viz:

WHEREAS, The General Assembly of Virginia, with a view to make an effort to preserve the Union and the Constitution in the spirit in which they were established by the fathers of the Republic, have, by resolution, invited all the States who are willing to unite with her in an earnest effort to adjust the present unhappy controversies, to appoint Commissioners to meet on the 4th of February next, to consider, and if practicable, agree upon some suitable adjustment:

Resolved, That we heartily accept the invitation of our Old Mother Virginia, and that the following five Commissioners, viz.: Wm. O. Butler, Jas. B. Clay, Joshua F. Bell, C. S. Morehead, and James Guthrie, be appointed to represent the State of Kentucky in the contemplated Convention, whose duty it shall be to repair to the city of Washington, on the day designated, to meet such Commissioners as may be appointed by any of the States, in accordance with the foregoing invitation.[2]

Resolved, That if said Commissioners shall agree upon any plan of adjustment requiring amendments to the Federal Constitution, they be requested to communicate the proposed amendments to Congress for the purpose of having the same submitted by that body, according to the forms of the Constitution, to the several States for ratification.

Resolved, That if said Commissioners cannot agree on an adjustment; or, if agreeing, Congress shall refuse to submit for ratification such amendments as may be proposed, the Commissioners of this State shall immediately communicate the result to the Executive of this Commonwealth, to be by him laid before this General Assembly.

Resolved, That in the opinion of the General Assembly the propositions embraced in the resolutions presented to the Senate of the United States by the Hon. John J. Crittenden, so construed as that the first article proposed as an amendment to the Constitution of the United States shall apply to all the territory of the United States now held or hereafter acquired, south of latitude thirty-six degrees and thirty minutes; and provided that slavery of the African race shall be effectually protected as property therein during the continuance of the Territorial government and the fourth article shall secure to the owners of slaves the right of transit with their slaves between and through the non-slaveholding States and Territories, constitute the basis of such an adjustment of the unhappy controversy which now divides the States of this Confederacy, as would be accepted by the people of this Commonwealth.

Resolved, That the Governor be, and he is hereby, requested to communicate information of the foregoing appointments to the Commissioners above named, at as early a day as practicable; and that he also communicate copies of the foregoing resolutions to the Executives of the respective States.

Source: *Journal of the Called Session of the Senate of the Commonwealth of Kentucky, Begun and Held in the Town of Frankfort on Thursday the Seventeenth of January, in the Year of Our Lord, 1861* (Frankfort: Printed at the Kentucky Yeoman Office, John B. Major, State Printer, 1861), 95–96.

Peace Conference's Proposed Constitutional Amendment

February 27, 1861

SECTION 1. In all the present territory of the United States, north of the parallel of 36°30' of north latitude, involuntary servitude, except in punishment of crime, is prohibited. In all the present territory south of that line, the status of persons held to involuntary service or labor, as it now exists, shall not be changed; nor shall any law be passed by Congress or the Territorial Legislature to hinder or prevent the taking of such persons from any of the States of this Union to said territory, nor to impair the rights arising from said relation; but the same shall be subject to judicial cognizance in the Federal courts, according to the course of the common law. When any Territory north or south of said line, within such boundary as Congress may prescribe, shall contain a population equal to that required for a member of Congress, it shall, if its form of government be republican, be admitted into the Union on an equal footing with the original States, with or without involuntary servitude, as the Constitution of such State may provide.

The vote upon said section resulted as follows:

AYES.—Delaware, Illinois, Kentucky, Maryland, New Jersey, Ohio, Pennsylvania, Rhode Island, and Tennessee—9.

NOES.—Connecticut, Iowa, Maine, Massachusetts, North Carolina, New Hampshire, Vermont, and Virginia—8.

So the section was adopted.

{A technical discussion on absentee voting followed, along with an enumeration of those delegates who dissented from the votes of their respective states.}

SECTION 2. No territory shall be acquired by the United States, except by discovery and for naval and commercial stations, depots, and transit routes, without the concurrence of a majority of all the Senators from States which allow involuntary servitude, and a majority of all the Senators from States which prohibit that relation; nor shall territory be acquired by treaty, unless the votes of a majority of the Senators from each class of States hereinbefore mentioned be cast as a part of the two-thirds majority necessary to the ratification of such treaty.

The vote on the adoption of section two was taken, and resulted as follows:

AYES.—Delaware, Indiana, Kentucky, Maryland, Missouri, New Jersey, Ohio, Pennsylvania, Rhode Island, Tennessee, and Virginia—11.

NOES.—Connecticut, Illinois, Iowa, Maine, Massachusetts, North Carolina, New Hampshire, and Vermont—8.

So the section was adopted.

{An enumeration of those delegates who dissented from the votes of their respective states followed.}

SECTION 3. Neither the Constitution nor any amendment thereof shall be construed to give Congress power to regulate, abolish, or control, within any State, the relation established or recognized by the laws thereof touching persons held to labor or involuntary service therein, nor to interfere with or abolish involuntary service in the District of Columbia without the consent of Maryland and without the consent of the owners, or making the owners who do not consent just compensation; nor the power to interfere with or prohibit representatives and others from bringing with them to the District of Columbia, retaining and taking away, persons so held to labor or service; nor the power to interfere with or abolish involuntary service in places under the exclusive jurisdiction of the United States within those States and Territories where the same is established or recognized; nor the power to prohibit the removal or transportation of persons held to labor or involuntary service in any State or Territory of the United States to any other State or Territory thereof, where it is established or recognized by law or usage; and the right during transportation, by sea or river, of touching at ports, shores, and landings, and of landing in case of distress, shall exist; but not the right of transit in or through any State or Territory, or of sale or traffic, against the laws thereof. Nor shall Congress have power to authorize any higher rate of taxation on persons held to labor or service than on land.

The bringing into the District of Columbia of persons held to labor or service for sale, or placing them in depots to be afterwards transferred to other places for sale as merchandise, is prohibited.

The question on the adoption of said section resulted in the following vote:

AYES.—Delaware, Illinois, Kentucky, Maryland, Missouri, New Jersey, North Carolina, Ohio, Pennsylvania, Rhode Island, Tennessee, and Virginia—12.

NOES.—Connecticut, Indiana, Iowa, Maine, Massachusetts, New Hampshire, and Vermont—7.

So the section was adopted.

{An enumeration of those delegates who dissented from the votes of their respective states followed.}

SECTION 4. The third paragraph of the second section of the fourth article of the Constitution shall not be construed to prevent any of the States, by appropriate legislation, and through the action of their judicial and ministerial officers, from enforcing the delivery of fugitives from labor to the person to whom such service or labor is due.

The question on the adoption of said section resulted in the following votes:

AYES.—Connecticut, Delaware, Illinois, Indiana, Kentucky, Maryland, Missouri, New Jersey, North Carolina, Ohio, Pennsylvania, Rhode Island, Tennessee, Vermont, and Virginia—15.

NOES.—Iowa, Maine, Massachusetts, and New Hampshire—4.

And the section was adopted.

{An enumeration of those delegates who dissented from the votes of their respective states followed.}

SECTION 5. The foreign slave-trade is hereby forever prohibited; and it shall be the duty of Congress to pass laws to prevent the importation of slaves, coolies, or persons held to service or labor, into the United States and the Territories from places beyond the limits thereof.[3]

The vote on the adoption of this section resulted as follows:

AYES.—Connecticut, Delaware, Illinois, Indiana, Kentucky, Maryland, Missouri, New Jersey, New York, New Hampshire, Ohio, Pennsylvania, Rhode Island, Tennessee, Vermont, and Kansas—16.

NOES.—Iowa, Maine, Massachusetts, North Carolina, and Virginia—5.

So this section was adopted.

{An enumeration of those delegates who dissented from the votes of their respective states followed.}

SECTION 6. The first, third, and fifth sections, together with this section of these amendments, and the third paragraph of the second section of the first article of the Constitution, and the third paragraph of the second section of the fourth article thereof, shall not be amended or abolished without the consent of all the States.

The vote on the adoption of this section stood as follows:

AYES.—Delaware, Illinois, Kentucky, Maryland, Missouri, New Jersey, Ohio, Pennsylvania, Rhode Island, Tennessee, and Kansas—11.

NOES.—Connecticut, Indiana, Iowa, Maine, Massachusetts, North Carolina, New Hampshire, Vermont, and Virginia—9.

{An enumeration of those delegates who dissented from the votes of their respective states followed.}

SECTION 7. Congress shall provide by law that the United States shall pay to the owner the full value of his fugitive from labor, in all cases where the marshal, or other officer, whose duty it was to arrest such fugitive, was prevented from so doing by violence or intimidation from mobs or riotous assemblages, or when, after arrest, such fugitive was rescued by like violence or intimidation, and the owner thereby deprived of the same; and the acceptance of such payment shall preclude the owner from further claim to such fugitive. Congress shall provide by law for securing to the citizens of each State the privileges and immunities of citizens in the several States.

The vote on the adoption of this section was as follows:

AYES.—Delaware, Illinois, Indiana, Kentucky, Maryland, New Jersey, New Hampshire, Ohio, Pennsylvania, Rhode Island, Tennessee, and Kansas—12.

NOES.—Connecticut, Iowa, Maine, Missouri, North Carolina, Vermont, and Virginia—7.

So this last section was also adopted.

{An enumeration of those delegates who dissented from the votes of their respective states followed.}

Source: Lucius E. Chittenden, *A Report of the Debates and Proceedings in the Secret Sessions of the Conference Convention, for Proposing Amendments to the Constitution of the United States, Held at Washington, D.C., in February, A.D. 1861* (New York: D. Appleton & Company, 1864), 440–45.

Kentucky Commissioners' Majority Report

February 28, 1861

WASHINGTON, February 28, 1861.

To His Excellency, Beriah Magoffin, Governor of Kentucky:

The undersigned, Commissioners appointed by a resolution of the General Assembly of the Commonwealth of Kentucky, to meet such Commissioners as might be appointed by the several States in accordance with the request of the State of Virginia, to confer together upon the present condition of our country, respectfully report.

That they assembled in the city of Washington on the 4th inst., twenty-one States being represented, and continued in session until the 27th inst., and finally agreed on the inclosed {*sic*} printed propositions as a basis of settlement and pacification. The journal of our proceedings, as soon as completed and printed, will be transmitted as part of this report.

Respectfully,
JAMES GUTHRIE,
C. S. MOREHEAD,
JOSHUA F. BELL,
C. A. WICKLIFFE.

P. S.—It is proper to remark, that before this report was written and signed, two of the Commissioners, Hon. J. B. Clay and Gen. Butler, had left the city.

{Here the commissioners inserted the conference's draft proposal to amend the Constitution of the United States.}

FRANKFORT, March 20th, 1861.

To His Excellency, B. MAGOFFIN, Governor of Kentucky:

The undersigned, having made a brief report to you as Commissioners from the State of Kentucky, to the Convention of States assembled at Washington City, on the 4th of February last, on the invitation of the State of Virginia, and not having it in their power at that time to transmit a journal of their proceedings, beg leave now to do so. It came to hand to-day, and we avail ourselves of the earliest moment to submit it to your Excellency, and through you to the Legislature.

From this document it will be perceived that the Crittenden propositions, as modified by the suggestions of Virginia, were offered and failed to be passed. The original propositions of Mr. Crittenden were afterwards offered and likewise failed. In both instances Kentucky voted as an unit in favor of the propositions. These having failed, the propositions heretofore transmitted to you were passed, and it may not be improper to give some explanations of the sections adopted.

The resolutions of Virginia suggested the amendments of the Constitution proposed by Mr. Crittenden, with additions proposed by that State, as the basis of the action of the Conference of States in their efforts to adopt some plan to restore harmony to a divided country and to preserve the Union. It will be proper here to state what were the leading provisions of Mr. Crittenden's proposed amendment, and also to state the amendment of the Constitution proposed by the Convention of States.

Upon the territorial question, the amendment of Mr. Crittenden provides, that "in all the territory now or hereafter to be acquired north of latitude 36 deg. 30 min., slavery or involuntary servitude, except as a punishment for crime, is prohibited; while in all territory south of that line slavery is hereby recognized as existing, and shall not be interfered with by Congress, but shall be protected as property by all the departments of the territorial government during its continuance; all the territory north or south of said line, within such boundaries as Congress may prescribe, when it contains a population necessary for a member of Congress, with a Republican form of government, shall be admitted into the Union on an equality with the original States, with or without slavery, as the Constitution of the State shall prescribe."

The corresponding section of the amendment proposed by the Conference of the States upon the same subject is as follows: "In all the present territory of the United States, north of the parallel of 36 deg. 30 min. north latitude, involuntary servitude, except as punishment of crimes, shall be prohibited. In all the present territories south of that line, the *status* of persons held to involuntary servitude or labor, as it now exists, shall not be changed; nor shall any law be passed by Congress or the territorial legislature to hinder or prevent the taking of such persons in the States of this Union to said territory, nor impair any rights arising from said relation; but the same shall be subject to the judicial cognizance of the Federal courts, according to the *course* of the common law;" the latter clause of which provides for the admission into the Union, in such convenient territory as Congress may provide, States with or without slavery, as their Constitution may provide, when the population shall be equal to the ratio of representation in Congress, shall be admitted into the Union. The only substantial difference between the two sections, that of Mr. Crittenden and the Convention of States, is, that the section of the Conference does not provide for a division of future acquired territory. This provision was objected to by many of the States represented, because they believed the present boundaries and territory of the United States were large enough; they did not wish to place in the Constitution a section which presented to the world that we were preparing our Government with power to make aggressions upon the territory of our neighbors.

It was believed that to insist upon this proposition, which may never be called into action, would prevent the harmonious settlement of the difficulties now existing between the two sections of the United States. We believe it would be regretted by every patriot if any honest and peaceful settlement of our present difficulties should be prevented, by insisting upon a provision dividing territory that the United States did not own, and may never acquire. With this exception, the proposition to divide the territory is the same in the amendment proposed by the Convention and by Mr. Crittenden's proposition. There is a difference of language, in some respects, between the two sections, but they both mean the same thing; that is, African slavery. The resolution of Mr. Crittenden declares that slavery or involuntary servitude shall not exist north of 36 deg. 30 min., while in all the territory south of that line, "slavery is hereby recognized as existing."

The section of the Conference employs the language of the present Constitution, the same language as is used in the ordinance of 1787 to express the same idea, which does mean, and has been held by the legislative, judicial, and executive departments of the Government to mean, African slavery and property in the same. The Representatives from the free States preferred the language employed in the Constitution, to which we could see no just objection; nor can there be any valid objection to the language employed in this section of the amendment.

The expressions used in Mr. Crittenden's section, "that slavery is hereby recognized as existing south of that line," was objected to by some, as it might be construed it meant to establish slavery in the territory by a constitutional provision. To obviate all difficulty, and remove all excuse for voting against this section of the Conference by those who manifested a desire to co-operate with the Southern States, the original proposition was amended in its language, and the section made to read, "that the *status* of persons held to involuntary service or labor, as it now exists, shall not be changed by any law of Congress or the territory."

It may be well here to state what is the *status* of persons held to involuntary service or labor in all the territory of the United States south of 36 deg. 30 min. By the law of New Mexico, which covers the whole of the territory south of that line, African slavery exists by territorial enactment, protected by the Constitution of the United States.[4] The laws of the Territory protect the right of the owner; provide remedies, civil and criminal, for injuries or violation of such right, as completely and as effectually as it is protected in the State of Kentucky. This right, as it now exists, and the right to take slaves into that territory, shall not be impaired or changed by Congress, or the laws of the territory. If, after the adoption of this clause as a part of the Constitution, the territorial legislature should repeal its laws, or there should be a change of the decision in the Dred Scott case, the right and interest of the master in his slave would not and could not be impaired.

It was thought by some that a territorial legislature might repeal the statutes furnishing the remedies now existing for the rights and protection of the owners of slaves, under the idea that it would not be a violation of the right or interest of the owner. The provision was added that the same—that is, the right in and to the slave, and for injuries—should be subject to the official cognizance of the Federal Courts, according to the course of the common law. It was believed that all intelligent minds, nay, any person of ordinary capacity, would comprehend the true meaning of this portion of the section. By some who are opposed to all adjustment of our present national difficulties, the meaning of this clause has been perverted. It is charged that the South has only secured to her such interest in African slavery as the common law recognizes; and as the common law does not recognize slavery in man, the provision is useless. Such objections do not discriminate between right and remedy. Slavery, as it now exists by law in New Mexico, is recognized, and is not to be impaired by law; and if the right be interfered with by others, if the territorial law has not furnished a remedy, the injured owner is remitted to that common law which provides an adequate remedy for every wrong committed upon person or property.

To charge that the section refers the master to the common law as giving or establishing his right to a slave, is an imputation upon the intelligence of the members of the Convention North and South, who voted for it. Take the clause as it stands, and the statute of New Mexico: if the clause were adopted as part of the Constitution, then we aver no owner of a slave in Kentucky is vested with a better right, or armed with a better remedy for the protection of that right and the redress of the injury committed upon his slave. The provision is better, it is more permanent for the protection of slave property in a territory, than the simple constitutional injunction, "that it shall be protected as property by all the departments of the territorial government."

The second section of the amendment proposed by the Conference is in these words: "No territory shall be acquired by the United States, except by discovery, and for naval and commercial stations, depots, and transit routes, without the concurrence of a majority of all the Senators, from the States which allow involuntary servitude, and from a majority of the Senators of the States which prohibit the relation. Nor shall territory be acquired by treaty, unless the votes of , {space in the original} of the Senators from each of the States hereinbefore mentioned be cast as a part of the two thirds majority necessary for the ratification of such treaty."

This section was proposed and insisted upon by Virginia, and was intended to qualify the treaty-making power of the United States, so as to secure each section against any improper annexation of territory; and if such majority be obtained, it will be upon an agreement for a fair division between the two sections for settlement and occupation.

The third section of the article agreed to by the Convention is as follows:

> Neither the Constitution, nor any amendment thereof, shall be construed to give Congress the power to regulate, abolish, or control, within any State or Territory of the United States, the relation established and recognized by the laws thereof touching persons held to labor or involuntary service therein, nor to interfere with or abolish involuntary service in the District of Columbia, without the consent of Maryland, or without the consent of the owners, or making the owners who do not consent, just compensation; nor the power to interfere with or prohibit

Representatives or others from bringing with them to the District of Columbia, retaining and taking away, persons so held to labor or service; nor the power to interfere with or abolish involuntary service in places under the exclusive jurisdiction of the United States, within those States and Territories where the same is established or recognized, nor the power to prohibit the removal or transportation of persons held to labor or involuntary service in any State or Territory of the United States, to any other State or Territory thereof, where it is established or recognized by law or usage; and the right during the transportation, by sea or river, of touching at ports, shores, landings, and landing in case of distress, shall exist; but not the right of transit in or through any State or Territory for sale or traffic against the laws thereof; nor shall Congress have power to authorize any higher rate of taxation on persons held to labor or service, than lands. The bringing into the District of Columbia persons held to labor or service for sale, or placing them in depots, to be afterwards transferred to other places for sale as merchandise, is prohibited.

This section embraces all of the 2d, 3d, and 4th sections of Mr. Crittenden's amendment, except the latter clause, which proposed to guarantee the right to take slaves through States where slavery does not exist. The amendment of the Convention does not embrace this clause; and the right to do so is left where it has always rested, to the comity of each State. Some of the States where slavery exists, have, by statutes prohibited the passage or importation of slaves as merchandise, in or through their territory. They have prohibited the importation of slaves by their own citizens, for their own use, from other States. It was deemed that such a provision would be an invasion upon the rights of the States, and, therefore, the amendment of the Convention left that question where it has rested ever since the Constitution was adopted. The right thus to transport any slaves through any State is not embraced by the amendment. This exception applies to all the States, slave as well as free. The 4th section is as follows: "The 3d paragraph of the 2d section of the 4th article of the Constitution shall not be construed to prevent any of the States, by appropriate legislation, and through the action of judicial and ministerial offices, from inforcing the delivery of fugitives from labor to persons to whom such labor is due."

It has been decided by the Supreme Court that any law of a State which provided means and furnished aid to the re-capture and return of fugitive slaves, was unconstitutional;[5] this section permits States to pass such laws. The 5th section is as follows: "The foreign slave trade is hereby forever prohibited, and it shall be the duty of Congress to pass laws to prevent the importation of slaves, coolies, or persons held to service or labor, into the United States and territories, from places beyond the limits thereof."

This section ought not to require any explanation; no one can object to it except such as may desire the re-opening of the African slave trade. We have heard it suggested by some who seem to favor the independence of the seceded States, that upon their becoming independent and alien States, this clause would prohibit the importation of such slaves from these seceded States into the United States. This should be so, else the United States might have their territory flooded by the African race, whenever the Southern Confederacy shall open the African slave trade.

The 6th section prohibits the repeal of any of the guarantees in the Constitution, or in this amendment, in relation to slave property, without the consent of all the States.

The 7th section is as follows: Congress shall provide by law that the United States shall pay the owner full value for a fugitive from labor, in all cases where the marshal or other officer, whose duty it was to arrest such fugitive, was prevented from so doing by violence, or intimidation, from mobs or riotous assemblages, or when, after arrest, such fugitive was rescued by like violence or intimidation, and the owner thereby deprived of the same; and the acceptance of such payment shall preclude the owner from further claim to such fugitive. Congress shall provide by law for securing to citizens of each State the privileges and immunities of citizens in the several States.

This article is substantially the same as Mr. Crittenden's amendment. It makes it the duty of Congress to pay the owner the value of the slave, where the marshal shall be prevented by force or intimidation from executing the law, and where the slave shall be wrested from the owner after he is delivered. It was not necessary to provide in this section that Congress should provide by law how the United States may be indemnified for such payment. Under this clause, and the section of the Constitution upon the subject of fugitives from labor, the power to pass such laws for the indemnity of the United States against such wrong-doers is plenary and full.

The second section of —— article of the Constitution of the United States now reads: "The citizens of each State shall enjoy the privileges and immunities of the citizens of the several States."[6] It gave Congress no right to legislate upon the subject; it operates as a prohibition to each State from discriminating against the citizens of other States, and would void all such legislation. The clause added to the 7th section of the article, that Congress shall provide by law for securing to the citizens of each State the privileges and immunities of citizens in the several States, cannot do more than to make such discriminating laws void, and is therefore harmless.

The section of Mr. Crittenden's amendment giving power to Congress to acquire territory in Africa, or South America, for the colonization of free negroes, was not acceptable to the majority of the States. They seem to prefer to leave that question to the Colonization Society,[7] as a subject better and cheaper managed than it would be under the Government of the United States. It is proper to state, that upon the 1st section of the amendment, the vote of the Commissioners of Kentucky was not unanimous, nor was it always so upon questions of amendments; but we claim for ourselves what we cheerfully accord to others, an honest and sincere purpose that some measure would be adopted that would give confidence, quiet, and security to the South; and we regret, that owing to the excited partisan state and condition of members of Congress, both North and South, the shortness of time permitted no fair test by a vote upon the amendment proposed.

Although the proposed amendment was not submitted to the States for adoption, the undersigned cannot hesitate to express a confident belief that the border free States would grant all the guarantees secured by the amendment, and they cannot believe that the remaining free States would refuse to do the same whenever the question shall be fairly presented to the people, which they hope may be done by the next Congress when it shall convene.

With great respect, yours, &c.,

C. A. WICKLIFFE,
JAMES GUTHRIE,
C. S. MOREHEAD,
JOSHUA F. BELL.

Source: *Report of the Kentucky Commissioners to the Late Peace Conference Held in Washington City, Made to the Legislature of Kentucky* (Frankfort: Printed at the Kentucky Yeoman Office, John B. Major, State Printer, 1861), 3–10.

Kentucky Commissioners' Minority Report

March 19, 1861

To His Excellency, Beriah Magoffin, Governor of Kentucky:

The undersigned, two of the Commissioners appointed by resolution of the General Assembly of the Commonwealth of Kentucky, to meet such Commissioners as might be appointed by other States, in accordance with the request of the State of Virginia, to confer upon the unfortunate condition of our country, not having had an opportunity to unite with their co-commissioners in the report which they understand they have made, although they remained in the city of Washington a full day after the adjournment of the Convention for the purpose of joining with them in a proper report to your Excellency, feel it due to themselves, and respectful as well as due to the General Assembly, that they shall make this their separate report.

The undersigned felt themselves bound, for the guidance of their action in the Convention, to regard in some degree the 4th resolution of the General Assembly which they beg here to quote:

Resolved, That in the opinion of the General Assembly of Kentucky, the propositions embraced in the resolutions presented to the Senate of the United States, by the Hon. John J. Crittenden, so construed that the first article proposed as an amendment to the Constitution of the United States shall apply to all the Territory of the United States now held or hereafter acquired south of the latitude 36 deg. and 30 min., and provide that slavery of the African race shall be effectually protected as property herein during the continuance of the territorial government; and the fourth article shall secure to the owners of slaves the right of transit with their slaves between and through the non-slaveholding States and Territories, constitute the basis of such an adjustment of the unhappy controversy which now divides the States of this Confederacy, as would be acceptable to the people of this Commonwealth.

They conceived that this resolution set forth clearly the opinion of the General Assembly, as to what adjustment would be acceptable to the people of Kentucky, and at the same time negatived the idea that the resolutions of Mr. Crittenden would be acceptable, unless construed in the manner set forth in the resolution. Whilst they did not consider it to give them positive instruction, they did not feel themselves to be at liberty to depart altogether from the wishes of the State, so solemnly announced by the representatives of its people.

The undersigned have delayed making their report until the present time, in the hope of being able to append to it, as a part thereof, the journal of the Convention, which would have shown every proposition made, with the vote by States upon such as were brought to a vote. They regret that although a committee was appointed for the express purpose of superintending the printing of said journal, they have not as yet received a copy of it, and that their report is more incomplete than they would have desired to have made it.

The Convention assembled in the city of Washington on the 4th of February, and continued its sessions until the 27th of that month, when it adjourned *sine die.*[8] Before the final adoption of the proposed amendments to the Constitution, twenty-one States were present by their delegates in Convention. A Committee on Resolutions, consisting of a member from each State, was appointed, to whom was referred various propositions of adjustment.[9] That committee finally reported, as the result of its deliberations, a proposition to amend the Constitution by a 13th article, consisting of 7 sections, a copy of which, marked A, is filed as a part hereof.[10]

Notice of various substitutes for the report of the committee was given, but it was claimed and conceded that before a vote upon any substitute could be taken, the report of the committee should be amended and perfected in convention.

Many amendments were proposed; upon some of them, the undersigned were so unfortunate as to differ from the opinion of the majority of their co-commissioners who cast the vote of the State. To one or two of the more important of them they would briefly call attention. A motion was made by Gov. Reid,[11] a delegate from North Carolina, to amend the 1st section of the series, by inserting at the end of the clause, "and in all the present territory south of said line," the words "*involuntary servitude is recognized, and property in those of the African race held to service or labor in any of the States of the Union, when removed to such territory, shall be protected and.*" This amendment received the votes of but three States—Virginia, North Carolina, and Missouri. Seventeen States voted against it, Kentucky being one of them. From this vote the undersigned caused their dissent to be recorded.

A motion was made by Mr. Seddon,[12] a delegate from Virginia, to amend the 3d section of the series, by inserting at the end of the clause, "and the right during transportation of touching at ports, shores, and landings, and of landing in case of distress, shall exist," the words, *"and if the transportation shall be by sea, the right to persons held to service or labor shall be protected by the Federal Government as other property."* This amendment was lost, Kentucky voting against it, from which vote the undersigned caused their dissent to be recorded.

The entire first section of the report of the committee was stricken out. In lieu thereof, a proposition made by Mr. Franklin,[13] a delegate from Pennsylvania, was adopted. This proposition is the first section upon the paper marked B.

One of the undersigned (Mr. Clay) proposed, as an additional section to the report of the committee, a proposition to construe the second paragraph of the second section of the fourth article of the Constitution, so that no State shall have the power to judge and determine what was treason, felony, or other crime, by the laws of another State, but that a person charged with treason, felony, or other crime in one State, who should flee from justice and be found in another State, should, on demand of the Executive authority of the State from which he fled, be delivered up, to be removed to the State having jurisdiction of the crime. This amendment was lost; a large majority voting against it.

Amendments too numerous to set forth in the limits of a report, were offered and voted upon. Finally, the report of the committee was perfected, and is filed herewith as a part hereof, marked B.

Substitutes for the report of the committee, as amended and perfected, being now in order: among others, Mr. Seddon, of Virginia, offered the amendments to the Constitution, known as the Crittenden resolutions, with such additions and amendments as were asked by Virginia, (in substance, the same as those set forth in the resolutions of the General Assembly of Kentucky.) This substitute was rejected by a large majority—receiving the votes of only a few States.

One of the undersigned (Mr. Clay) then offered as a substitute for the report of the committee, the amendments to the Constitution, known as the Crittenden resolutions, without the crossing a "t" or dotting an "i." This substitute was rejected—16 States voting against it, and only 5 States voting for it.

All substitutes having been rejected, the perfected report of the committee (B) came up in order. Upon it, the vote of the convention was taken by sections. On the first vote upon the first section, it was rejected by the votes of 11 States to 8. The convention adjourned until the next morning; when this vote was reconsidered.

The seven sections of the report were then passed by the convention.

Upon the first section, the vote stood, 9 States for, 8 States against. Four Southern States out of seven, and five Northern States out of fourteen, voting for it—Virginia and North Carolina both against it.

The second section was passed—11 States voting for it, 8 States against it.

The third section was passed—12 States voting for it, 7 States against it.

The fourth section was passed—15 States voting for it, 4 States against it.

The fifth section was passed—16 States voting for it, 5 States against it.

The sixth section was passed—11 States voting for it, 9 States against it.

The seventh section was passed—12 States voting for it, 7 States against it.

The vote of Kentucky was cast by the majority of her commissioners in favor of every section of the seven.

After the passage of the report by sections, a vote was demanded upon it as an entirety, but was ruled to be out of order.

The undersigned could not agree with their co-commissioners in casting the vote of Kentucky for the several sections of the proposed amendment to the Constitution, as adopted by the convention. They believed that the amendment, as a permanent settlement of the questions which have so unhappily divided the Northern and Southern sections of the United States, would prove wholly ineffectual, and that instead of providing securities and guarantees for the rights of the South, as they are believed now to exist under the Constitution and laws, involved a surrender of most important rights, and furnished adequate security to none. They propose to give briefly their reasons for this opinion.

The first section undertaken to settle the territorial question by dividing all the present territory of the United States by a line upon the parallel of 36 degrees 30 minutes, north latitude; and provides that north of that line involuntary servitude, except in punishment of crime, shall be prohibited; whilst south of that line the *status* of persons held to involuntary service or labor as it now exists, shall not be changed.

What is the present extent of the territory of the United States; and what is its *status* respecting persons held to involuntary service or labor?

The present territory of the United States, including 67,020 square miles held by the Cherokee Indians, under treaty grant, amounts to 1,287,277 square miles. By the southern construction of the decision of the Supreme Court, in the case of Dred Scott, into every foot of this vast territory persons held to involuntary service or labor may now be taken; and south of the line 36 degrees 30 minutes, the territorial law of New Mexico also permits it. The first section of the amendment proposes to take from the people of the South the right to carry persons held to involuntary service or labor into any of the territory north of 36 degrees 30 minutes; that is to say, forever to exclude such persons from 1,021,307 square miles of the territory of the United States; whilst it merely concedes the right, which they believe they already have as to the whole, to take such persons into the 265,970 square miles of the territory—about one fourth of the whole. Would this be concession to the South, or to the North?

But as to the *status* of the territory south of 36 degrees and 30 minutes, in respect to persons held to involuntary service or labor; what is it?

The right to take such persons into said territory rests, first, upon the decision of the Supreme Court in the Dred Scott case. Second, upon the territorial law of New Mexico, which territory embraces all south of 36 degrees and 30 minutes, except 50,290 square miles of the Cherokee treaty grant, where slavery now exists.

It is well known that a very large portion of the people of the North, as well as many of the South, maintain that the decision of the Supreme Court in the case of Dred Scott, so far as it relates to the question of slavery in the Territories, is no decision at all; simply *obiter dictu*,[14] which does not settle the law upon the subject. That such is the opinion of the present Chief Magistrate is clear from his late inaugural. It is also avowed by the dominant party, that it is their intention to remodel the Supreme Court, and to have that decision reversed. If, then, the Dred Scott decision does not correctly declare the law, or if it be reversed, in either case, so far as the *status* of the Territory rests upon it, it would be free and not slave.

The Dred Scott case no longer to be relied on as fixing a *status* of slavery, we should be thrown altogether upon the territorial law of New Mexico. But it is scarcely necessary to observe that a large portion of the American people believe that a Territorial Legislature has no power to pass laws either to introduce or to prohibit slavery in the Territories. Should the territorial law of New Mexico be hereafter decided to be void, the Dred Scott decision either no decision at all, or reversed, the *status* of even that small portion of the territory of the United States, 265,970 square miles out of 1,287,277 square miles, would be *free* and not slave.

What protection is proposed to be given to slave property south of the line 36 degrees and 30 minutes? The section merely provides, that neither Congress nor the Territorial Legislature shall pass any law to hinder or prevent the taking of persons held to involuntary service or labor to the Territory, nor to impair the rights arising from said relation; but the same (*the rights*) shall be subject to judicial cognizance in the Federal Courts, according to the course of the common law. What is the course of the common law in the remedies it affords to infringement upon the rights of property in slaves? Is it clear, unmistakable, not liable to misconstruction, especially when administered by judges unfriendly or adverse to the institution of slavery? Would the opinion, for example, of the distinguished Governor of New York,[15] who now holds so high a place in the Cabinet, that a slave, not being a free man, could not under the common law be kidnapped, and that, therefore, there is no common law remedy for kidnapping a slave, be followed? Is this such protection for the right of property in the territories as Kentucky seeks as further security and further guarantee? How vain! How delusive! The proposition was but a miserable attempt to withdraw from the institution of slavery in the territories the protection of the Constitution and the Federal laws, and to have its only security to depend upon the vague and uncertain remedies of the common law.

If there had been no other objection to it, the first section of the amendment proposed by the Peace Conference, which received only the votes of four slave States out of seven, and five free States out of fourteen, was too doubtful in meaning, too liable to misconstruction—different constructions having been given to it even in the convention which passed it—to allow the undersigned, in justice to Kentucky, to vote for it as a measure of final adjustment.

The undersigned objected to the second section, because, crippling present rights, it rendered the future acquisition of any territory whatever—Cuba, or any other, no matter how important and desirable—almost impossible.[16]

They objected to the third section because it failed to secure the right of transit, but left it in the power of any State or Territory to prevent the same. For example, placing it in the power of Illinois by Constitutional provision, if she chose to exercise it, to prevent the slaveholder of Kentucky from passing through that State with his slave property, on his way to Missouri or the South.

They objected to the 5th section, because, whether by constitutional right, or by revolutionary right, the so-called Southern Confederacy, being beyond the limits of the United States, or if not now beyond said limits, certainly to be so as soon as said Confederacy shall be recognized, it is made the duty of Congress, by the last clause of the section, to pass laws to prevent our friends and brothers, now residing within the limits of that Confederacy, from returning with their slaves to Kentucky; the passage of which laws would inevitably lead to retaliatory laws by the Southern Confederacy against the introduction of slaves from Kentucky into their territory.

They objected to the 6th section, because it proposed to make the 1st, 3d, and 5th sections, amendments to the Constitution virtually unalterable.

They objected to the 7th section, because it proposed that any citizen of a slave State, who should lose his fugitive slave, by reason of mob, riotous assemblage, or rescue after arrest, should himself pay a part of his own loss, whilst every other citizen of a slave State should pay a part thereof, thus offering a bonus to deprive the people of the South of their property, and in effect by providing that the fugitive, having been thus paid for, shall thereafter be free, to constitute the United States government a grand Emancipation Society.

The undersigned have felt it to be proper thus to set forth the reasons which caused them to oppose the amendment to the Constitution, which met the approval of the Peace Convention and of their co-Commissioners.

After the adoption of a preamble to the proposition of the Convention, the President was requested to cause the same to be presented to the two Houses of Congress, which was accordingly done, and its fate in that body is known to the country.

Before the final adjournment of the Convention, resolutions against the right of secession by a State from the Union, and in favor of such right, were proposed but not entertained. The following resolution was also proposed but not entertained by the Convention; its mover, however, asked and obtained leave to have it spread upon the journal:

Resolved, That while the adoption, by the States of South Carolina, Georgia, Florida, Alabama, Mississippi, Louisiana, and Texas, of ordinances declaring the dissolution of their relations with the Union, is an event deeply to be deplored, and while abstaining from any judgment on their conduct, we would express the earnest hope that they may soon see cause to resume their honored places in this Confederacy of States; yet to the end that such return may be facilitated, and from the conviction that the Union being formed by the assent of the people of the respective States, and being compatible only with freedom, and the republican institutions guaranteed to each, cannot and ought not to be maintained by force, we deprecate any effort by the Federal Government to coerce in any form the said States to reunion or submission, as tending to irreparable breach, and leading to incalculable ills; and we earnestly invoke the abstinence from all counsels or measures of compulsion towards them.

In conclusion, the undersigned will only add, that as Commissioners to the Convention at Washington, they were actuated, throughout its entire deliberations, by the single and sole desire of being in some degree instrumental to the restoration of confidence between the divided sections of the country, and of bringing about a reconstruction of that once happy Union bequeathed to us by our fathers. They regret most sincerely to have to say that they have returned home with abated confidence and diminished hope of satisfactory adjustment.

Should the journal of the Convention be hereafter received, it will be forwarded to your Excellency, to be laid before the General Assembly.

The undersigned have the honor to be, with great respect,

Your obedient servants,

WILLIAM O. BUTLER,
JAMES B. CLAY, Commissioners.
FRANKFORT, March 19th, 1861.

Source: *Report of the Kentucky Commissioners to the Late Peace Conference Held in Washington City, Made to the Legislature of Kentucky* (Frankfort: Printed at the Kentucky Yeoman Office, John B. Major, State Printer, 1861), 11–17.

CHAPTER NINE

Neutrality Proclaimed

Following the inauguration of Abraham Lincoln on March 4, 1861, Congress adjourned and the country waited to see how the new president would address the secession of the Deep South. While many southerners expected Lincoln to "coerce" the seceded states back into the Union, Lincoln played a waiting game believing latent southern Unionism would reverse, or at least mitigate, the disunion movement. The expected clash of arms came on April 12, but coercion came not from Washington, but from Montgomery. The Confederate attack on Fort Sumter and the surrender of United States forces there under the command of Kentuckian Major Robert Anderson prompted President Lincoln to issue a call for seventy-five thousand state militia troops to "suppress" the rebellion.

Magoffin immediately rejected the president's request for troops and called the General Assembly into special session. Believing that the people of Kentucky should decide which course the state should take, the governor recommended a convention of the voters; "a legal and orderly mode for a full, deliberate, and final disposition, by the people themselves, of their own destinies." To his mind, only in this manner could Kentucky properly and responsibly respond to the "frenzy of fanaticism" being displayed by the North which had resulted in "a violated Constitution, a subverted Government, and a broken Union." Buoyed by popular support, first the Kentucky senate and later the house affirmed Magoffin's refusal to supply troops. The General Assembly declined to support the convention desired by Magoffin, but declared instead that Kentucky should "occupy the position of strict neutrality" in the anticipated conflict. With the support of the state's elected officials, Magoffin then officially proclaimed Kentucky's neutrality on May 20, announcing the state's intention of "simply standing aloof from an unnatural, horrid, and lamentable strife."

Four days later, the General Assembly approved an act to arm the militia and the to-be-created Home Guards. The act specified that the allocated funds were to be spent "in protecting our soil from unlawful invasion." Concerned that the nation's upheaval might give the state's enslaved population aspirations of freedom, the act also directed that the arming of the Home Guards should display a preference for "those counties where servile insurrection is most to be apprehended."

Governor Beriah Magoffin's Address to the Kentucky General Assembly

May 7, 1861

A message in writing was received from the Governor, by the hands of Hon. Thos. B. Monroe, jr., Secretary of State, which is as follows, viz:

Gentlemen of the Senate and House of Representatives:

Since your recent adjournment events of the most startling character have followed in rapid succession. The comparative quiet in which the public mind was then lulled by the semi-official announcement of a pacific policy on the part of the Federal Administration has been broken, and the patriotic hope for a peaceful solution of our political complications, inspired by the proposed mediatorial interposition of the border slave States, has been disappointed by the sudden development of an evidently pre-determined purpose of the President and his supporters, the attempted execution of which has not only sealed the separation of the States, but has involved the country in civil war, and, if not successfully resisted, will prove fatal to the liberties of the people.

Powers not conferred by the Constitution have been usurped by the President of the United States; a standing army of gigantic proportions, gathered exclusively from one section, and mad with sectional hate, is being rapidly organized without authority of law; the Federal Capital is becoming a military camp, and martial law practically reigns in the District of Columbia; the Southern coast is blockaded by the armed vessels of the Federal navy, and the commerce of our western rivers is arrested by the interposition of military force; large bodies of armed men are collected in military posts along the line of our Northern frontier, impeding the lawful trade and menacing the safety of our peaceful citizens; in a word, the President of the United States has, without the advice or sanction of either branch of Congress,[1] declared a war of subjugation or extermination against the people of ten or more sovereign States; and is with extraordinary energy, gathering his strength for the unnatural conflict. You are now called upon, standing in the presence of a violated Constitution, a subverted Government, and a broken Union, to adopt such measures as, in your wisdom, may be demanded for the honor of the Commonwealth and the safety of the people.

Seven States of the late American Union, for causes unnecessary now to discuss, have severed their relations with the Government of the United States, and established a new Confederacy. That Government is now fully organized in all its departments, and seems to receive the cordial and undivided allegiance of the entire population within its limits. The State of Virginia has formally asserted her independence and entered into an allegiance with the "Confederate States," looking to an early admission to full and equal membership.[2] The States of North Carolina, Tennessee, and Arkansas will undoubtedly, at the earliest practicable moment, establish similar relations. In Missouri, Maryland, and Delaware, a strong public sentiment favors a like step, and the subject is now receiving the thoughtful attention of the people and authorities of those States. The deliberate action of ten sovereign States, moving in the capacity of political governments, and sustained by the approving voice of millions of American freemen, has been treated by the President as an insurrection of disorderly citizens, which he proposes to quell without the sanction or co-operation of the legislative branch of Government. He has, in the prosecution of that unholy purpose, called out the militia of the States, amounting in the aggregate to 158,000 men, to be enlisted for periods varying from three months to three years; and this gigantic army, exceeding in proportions any military force ever before organized upon this continent, is in rapid process of organization at a daily cost to the Government of over three quarters of a million dollars.[3]

A call was made upon me for four regiments of militia, the quota assigned to Kentucky of this army; I promptly responded to the Secretary of War, that Kentucky had no troops to furnish for the wicked purpose of subduing her sister Southern States. I have thus, as far as lay in my power, entered the public protest of Kentucky against this unnatural measure, and against her assumption of any part of the enormous debt now being contracted. Virginia, North Carolina, Tennessee, Arkansas, and Missouri have each emphatically refused to contribute any portion of the quota demanded of them. Maryland has not yet responded to the call by the tender of a single regiment. But the non-slaveholding States, without an exception, have, with unwonted alacrity, exceeding any zeal heretofore exhibited by them, responded to the call, and sent forth their troops. Moreover, an united public sentiment in the Northern States seems to sustain all these extraordinary usurpations of the President with a degree of enthusiasm amounting to the frenzy of fanaticism.

In view of these events, it is idle longer to refuse to recognize the fact that the late American Union is dissolved; that ten slaveholding States are now geographically united in a separate and independent government, and that war exists between those States so combined and the non-slaveholding States, acting under the United States Government. The avowed purpose of the United States Government is to compel the allegiance of the people of the seceded States, and enforce the supremacy of its jurisdiction throughout their limits. The achievement of this end involves the armed invasion of the seceded States, and the unlimited slaughter of their citizens. The sole object of the Confederate States, as authoritatively announced, is to maintain their independence and govern themselves. The condition of peace, as avowed by the President of the United States, is the overthrow of the Confederate State Government, and the reduction of the people of the South to unresisting submission to the United States Government, administered upon principles of the political platform adopted by the nominating convention in Chicago. The Confederate States make no other condition to the cessation of hostilities than "to be let alone."

What attitude shall Kentucky occupy in this deplorable conflict? Shall she continue her alliance with the Northern States, adhere to the United States Government, and assume her portion of the enormous war debt being incurred? Shall she declare her own independence, and prepare single-handed to maintain it? Shall she ally herself with the remaining slave States, and make common cause with them? I do not propose to discuss this subject. I recommend that these momentous questions, affecting so nearly and vitally the dearest rights, the liberties, the safety, and the honor of our people, be referred to their sovereign arbitrament. Both the Executive and Legislative departments of our State Government were constituted at a time when the public mind did not anticipate the grave issues now pressing for solution. We were elected two years ago at a time when no such subjects as those now under consideration were revolved in the public mind. Let us not attempt to employ our official power thus acquired to control this mighty question. Rather let us provide a legal and orderly mode for a full, deliberate, and final disposition, by the people themselves, of their own destinies. Not only does this plan of action commend itself to me as eminently just and right, but I verily believe it is the surest, if not the only mode, by which can be secured that unanimity of feeling and unity of action so necessary to enable Kentucky to move with the dignity and power answerable to her historic character. In view of the distracted condition of public sentiment in our State, the violent antagonism already excited, and daily becoming more embittered, the expressions of public opinion, through county meetings and private petitions, urging and demanding that opportunity be given to the people to pass upon this subject at the polls, and the manifest danger of internal commotion, I can see no other path of domestic peace and safety than through a reference of the question to the people. To their decision, expressed according to all the forms of law, every true and loyal Kentuckian will bow in loyal obedience. I cannot err when I say that unanimity of feeling among ourselves, and united action by our people, is not only the first desire of every patriot, but should be the very highest and controlling aim of your legislation. I appeal to you, therefore, as you hold dear the peace of the Commonwealth, not to ignore the feelings of the people in every locality of the State; but rather recognize the existing differences of opinion touching the duty of Kentucky, and secure the loyal acquiescence and willing allegiance of all the people by referring these mighty issues to that tribunal which alone can command the obedience of all. I would urge no hasty or inconsiderate action; would be far from advising any rash measures; but would greatly prefer that the action of the people in the premises be taken with all the thoughtful consideration and reflection which the subject demands. I renew the recommendation of a previous message for the passage of a law providing for the submission to the people of the question of a Convention and the election of delegates.

When last I had the honor of communicating with you touching the condition of our Federal affairs, I signified my ready purpose to co-operate with you in any proper measures looking first to the restoration of friendly relations between all the States, and failing in that, to their peaceful separation. But at the same time I did not conceal my apprehensions of the futility of all such efforts, and the early precipitation of the direful issues now upon us. I then urged active and energetic steps to place the State in an attitude of thorough military defense. I regret that I was unable at that time to impress upon you the impending necessity of such preparation. Allow me again to commend the subject to you, as one demanding immediate and energetic attention. The public necessity has been so clearly exhibited by the logic of events as to need no elaborate statement. We cannot conceal the fact that our State is comparatively defenseless. The very homes and firesides of our people are unprotected against invasion from without, or servile insurrection within. Every mail brings to me the most earnest appeals from the people, in all localities, for arms. Brave hearts and strong arms are now eager for the weapons of defense. Withhold them no longer.

The estimate of military appropriation demanded by the public necessity, as supplied by the Inspector General, a gentleman of known ability and thorough education, are herewith submitted. I recommend the adoption of the necessary measures to place the Commonwealth in a condition of military defence, and enable her to maintain whatever position her people, by authorized action, may determine to assume.

Realizing our exposed condition, when the clouds of civil war gathered thick and heavy over the land, I assumed the responsibility, even before your convocation, of appointing agents to purchase arms for the defense of the State. You will readily see that no time was to be lost, and that the step was justified by the necessity of the hour. Some of these agents were partially successful; but the limited means at my command defeated the more efficient negotiations I had instituted. In order to enable me to meet the contracts of these agents, I applied to the banks of issue of the State for temporary loans until provision could be made by the Legislature. The Southern Bank of Kentucky nobly responded to the application by placing to my official credit sixty thousand dollars. The Bank of Louisville and the Commonwealth Bank each furnished ten thousand dollars, and the President of the People's Bank notified me that that institution was ready to supply its quota. The other banks of the State declined my application, and I very much fear that opportunities have been lost of securing large supplies of effective guns and munitions of war. I have thus employed every resource at my command to supply the State with the necessary means of defense, and have now to recommend the adoption of measures to repay the loan to those banks which have so nobly and generously responded to the call upon them.

In order to secure the funds contemplated in your appropriation, I recommend provision for the issue of bonds of $1,000 each. Generous and wealthy citizens, impelled by a patriotic desire to come to the rescue of their State in an hour of danger, will find in them a safe investment. Provision should also be made by the imposition of an additional tax for the payment of an accruing interest on the bonds, and of the principal as it may fall due.

At your regular session of 1859–60 I recommended the passage of a militia law as a measure of the highest importance. The law was passed, but no appropriation for arms was made. By a timely arrangement with the then Secretary of War, the quota of arms due the State was commuted for repairs upon a large number of guns lying in our arsenal and regarded as worthless. By this means thousands of available guns have been secured, and a heavy expense to the State saved.

I am gratified to communicate that our existing militia law is proving itself a most complete and efficient system of military organization. No State can boast a more gallant corps than our "State Guard," composed, as it is, of the very best material in the State, and embracing men of all parties. The soldiers are gentlemen, and the officers men of the highest tone and character. All that is now needed is a proper supply of arms to swell its ranks and constitute the Guard a reliable army of defense for the State.

Pending the excitement occasioned by the extraordinary events of the past twenty days, my efforts have been constant and unrelaxed to maintain the friendly relations and commercial intercourse heretofore existing between the citizens of Kentucky and the people of the contiguous States on the North. I have endeavored by every means in my power, and every influence at my command, to restrain our own citizens from any acts which might have even the appearance of aggression upon the rights of the people of the neighboring States. In these efforts I have been, so far as I can learn, entirely successful. Our citizens have abstained with laudable forbearance not only from aggressions, but from any acts of retaliation, in the face of flagrant invasions of their rights. My especial attention has been directed to the continuance of commercial relations with the neighboring States, and to prevent any interruption of the usual and lawful trade of the States, regarding this character of intercourse as the very strongest bond of amity and peace.

I was much gratified to receive a commissioner from Governor Dennison, of Ohio, who called upon me to express the regret of the Executive of Ohio that any circumstance should interrupt the friendly relations and good understanding between the citizens of the two States, and his desire and readiness, at all times, to employ his official influence for the suppression of any acts of violence or aggression attempted to be practiced by citizens of Ohio towards the people of this State. I responded in the same spirit, and pledged my most earnest efforts to co-operate with the Governor of Ohio in this endeavor to maintain the peace along our border, and to continue free and open all the channels of trade. A similar understanding was effected with the Governor of Indiana; and, so far, I have no reason to doubt that either has failed to adhere in good faith to the amicable arrangement. I have labored to carry it out with our citizens, and have most happily succeeded.

I regret to say, however, that the Executives of Ohio and Indiana, though, no doubt, sustained by the mass of their own conservative people, have not been equally successful in their efforts to control some of their lawless citizens. Acts of aggression have been committed by citizens of those States upon the rights of our people. Private property belonging to citizens of this State in lawful transit has been stopped, the trade of our people is impeded by force, our commerce is interrupted, and citizens of Kentucky guilty of no act of pretended disloyalty to the State or Federal Governments, are now suffering serious and heavy losses by reason of these lawless acts. As yet, no act of retaliation has reached my notice. But you can readily understand that this condition of affairs cannot be long endured without collision. It will be impossible to restrain retaliatory measures, and prevent the early precipitation of armed collision along our whole border, unless effective measures are taken to remove the increasing provocation.

Encouraged by the manifestations of a desire for peace between the States, as exhibited by the Governors of Ohio and Indiana, I proposed to them to co-operate with me in a proposition to the General Government for a suspension of pending hostilities until the meeting of Congress, hoping that body might be able to point out a peaceful solution of our national troubles. The correspondence on that subject is hereto appended. In that mission, you will see that I met with no success.

I have directed all the power of the office to which a generous and confiding people elected me to the promotion of what I believed to be their highest interests. I have labored throughout the painful and trying ordeal of the day to save our people from dissensions at home, or unnecessary conflicts without. And now let me implore you, by all you hold sacred, to so shape your councils and actions as to secure unity of feeling and unity of action on the part of our people, as the first and highest object of patriotism. Let us lay aside all party feeling—expel from our minds all past jealousies, and unite our counsels as one man, in an earnest effort to maintain the peace, the honor, and the safety of those who have intrusted {*sic*} us with their dearest interests, invoking Almighty God for that wisdom which will lead us safely and successfully through the perils that surround us.

B. MAGOFFIN.

Source: *Journal of the Called Session of the Senate of the Commonwealth of Kentucky, Begun and Held in the Town of Frankfort, on Monday, the Sixth Day of May, in the Year of Our Lord 1861, and of the Commonwealth the Sixty-Ninth* (Frankfort: Kentucky Yeoman Office, 1861), 5–12.

General Assembly's Neutrality Resolution
May 16, 1861

The Committee on Federal Relations made the following report, viz:

A majority of your committee, consisting of Messrs. Hodge, Burnam, Wolfe, Carlisle, Lyne, Gowdy, Jacobs, and Buckner[4] recommend the passage of the following preamble and resolutions:

Considering the deplorable condition of the country, and for which the State of Kentucky is in no way responsible, and looking to the best means of preserving the internal peace, and securing the lives, liberty, and property of the citizens of the State; therefore,

Resolved by the House of Representatives, That this State and the citizens thereof should take no part in the civil war now being waged except as mediators and friends to the belligerent parties; and that Kentucky should, during the contest, occupy the position of strict neutrality; and your committee unanimously recommend the adoption of the following resolution.

Resolved, That the act of the Governor in refusing to furnish troops or military force upon the call of the executive authority of the United States, under existing circumstances is approved.

GEO. B. HODGE, Chairman.

Source: *Journal of the Called Session of the House of Representatives of the Commonwealth of Kentucky, Begun and Held in the Town of Frankfort, on Monday, the Sixth Day of May, in the Year of Our Lord 1861, and of the Commonwealth the Sixty-Ninth* (Frankfort: Printed at the Kentucky Yeoman Office, John. B. Major, State Printer, 1861), 91.

Governor Magoffin's Neutrality Proclamation

May 20, 1861

WHEREAS, Numerous applications have been made to me from many good citizens of this Commonwealth, praying to issue a proclamation forbidding the march of any forces of this or any other State or States, over our soil, to make an apprehended attack upon the Federal forces at Cairo in Illinois, or to disturb any otherwise the peaceful attitude of Kentucky with reference to the deplorable war now waging between the United States and the Confederate States; and whereas, numerous applications from like good citizens of this Commonwealth have also been made to me, praying me to issue a proclamation forbidding the occupation of any part or place, or the march over our sacred soil by any force of the United States for any purpose; and whereas, it is made fully evident, by every indication of public sentiment, that it is the determined purpose of the good people of Kentucky to maintain, with courageous firmness, the fixed position of self-defense, proposing or intending no invasion or aggression towards any other State or States, forbidding the quartering of troops upon her soil by either of the hostile sections, but simply standing aloof from an unnatural, horrid, and lamentable strife, for the existence of which Kentucky, neither by thought, word, nor act, is in any-wise responsible; and whereas, the policy thus recommended by so many of my fellow citizens of all political leanings, is, in my judgment, wise, peaceful, safe, and honorable, and the most likely to preserve peace and amity between the neighboring bordering States on both shores of the Ohio river and protect Kentucky, generally, from the ravages of a deplorable war; and whereas, the arms distributed to the "State Guard," composed as it is of gentlemen equally conscientious and honest, who entertain the opinions of both parties, are not to be used *against the Federal Government nor the Confederate States*, but to resist and prevent encroachments upon her soil, her rights, her honor, and her sovereignty by either of the belligerent parties, and to preserve the peace, safety, prosperity, and happiness and strict neutrality of her people in the hope she may soon have an opportunity to become a successful mediator between them; and in order to remove the unfounded distrust and suspicions of purposes to force Kentucky out of the Union, at the point of the bayonet—which may have been strongly and wickedly engendered in the public mind in regard to my own position and that of the "State Guard,"

Now, therefore, I, BERIAH MAGOFFIN, Governor of the Commonwealth of Kentucky, and Commander-in-Chief of all her military forces, on land or water, have issued this, my *proclamation*, hereby notifying and warning all other States, whether separate or united, and especially the "United States" and the "Confederate States," that I solemnly forbid any movement upon the soil of Kentucky or the occupation of any port, post, or place whatever within the lawful boundary and jurisdiction of this State, by any of the forces under the orders of the States aforesaid, for any purpose whatever, until authorized by invitation or permission of the Legislative and Executive authorities of this State previously granted. I also hereby especially and solemnly forbid all good citizens of this Commonwealth, whether incorporated in the "State Guard" or otherwise, making any warlike or hostile demonstrations whatever against any of the authorities aforesaid, earnestly requesting all citizens, civil and military, to be obedient hereto; to be obedient to the laws and lawful orders of both the civil and military authorities; to remain, when off military duty, quietly and peaceably at their homes, pursuing their wonted lawful avocations; to refrain from all words and acts likely to engender hot blood and provoke collision; to pursue such a line of wise conduct as will promote peace and tranquility, and a sense of safety and security, and thus keep far away from our beloved land and people the deplorable calamities of invasion; but at the same time earnestly counseling my fellow citizens of Kentucky to make prompt and efficient preparations to assume the armor and attitude prescribed by the paramount and supreme law of self-defense—and strictly of self-defense alone; praying Almighty God to have us evermore in His holy keeping and to preserve us in peace, prosperity, and security forever.

IN TESTIMONY WHEREOF, I have hereto set my name, and caused the seal of the Commonwealth to be affixed. Done at Frankfort this the 20th day of May, 1861, and in the 69th year of the Commonwealth.

B. MAGOFFIN

Source: Printed broadside in David M. Rubenstein Rare Book and Manuscript Library, Broadsides and Ephemera Collection, Folder KY2, Duke University. Original manuscript: Office of the Governor, Beriah Magoffin, May 28, 1861:

Governor's Official Correspondence File—Executive Journal, 1859–1862, Kentucky Department for Library and Archives, Frankfort, Kentucky.

General Assembly's Act Arming the State Militia

May 24, 1861

AN ACT for the regulation of the militia and to provide for the arming of the State.

WHEREAS, It is deemed necessary for the purpose of defense to arm the State; and to accomplish this object money will have to be borrowed; therefore,

Be it enacted by the General Assembly of the Commonwealth of Kentucky:

§ 1. That the following named persons, viz: Hon. B. Magoffin, Governor of the Commonwealth, Samuel Gill, Geo. T. Wood, Gen. Peter Dudley, and Dr. John B. Peyton,[5] are hereby constituted a Board of Commissioners, and authorized to borrow from the banks of issue in this State a sum not exceeding one million and sixty thousand dollars, for the term of ten years, and to execute to said banks, for and on behalf of the State of Kentucky, bonds for the amount borrowed from each of them, not to exceed in the aggregate the sum aforesaid, which bonds are to bear interest at the rate of six per centum per annum, payable semi-annually.

§ 2. Said Board of Commissioners are authorized, with the money so borrowed, to purchase arms and munitions of war; and in making said purchases shall ratify the contracts for the purchase of arms heretofore made by the Governor of the Commonwealth and pay for the same: *Provided*, Seven hundred and fifty thousand dollars only of said sum authorized to be borrowed shall be expended in the purchase of arms and accoutrements. Said arms, accoutrements, and munitions of war shall be equally distributed between the State Guard, the organization of which is now provided for by the military law, and such Home Guards as shall hereafter be organized in accordance with the provisions of this act. In making distribution of the arms and munitions of war among said Home Guards, due regard shall be had to the most exposed parts of the State, and to those counties where servile insurrection is most to be apprehended. A majority of said commissioners may exercise any of the powers hereby conferred on said board.

§ 3. The money borrowed under the provisions of this act shall be paid by the banks into the State treasury; and upon the requisition of said board, or a majority thereof, in writing, stating the purpose for which the money called for is applied, the Auditor of the State shall issue his warrant upon the Treasurer for the sum contained in such requisition: *Provided, however,* That the whole amount thus drawn from the treasury shall not exceed the sum borrowed from the banks and paid by them into the treasury.

§ 4. Said board shall have the power, if it shall be found necessary to exercise it, to have one or more mills for the manufacture of gunpowder erected and put into operation at convenient points within the State; and also to adopt and carry into effect such other measures as they may deem expedient to enable them to furnish the arms and munitions of war which they are authorized by this act to procure: *Provided,* That no mill or armory shall be erected, under the provisions of this act, in any border county.

§ 5. Companies of Home Guards may be organized for home and local defense exclusively, but the members of such companies shall not be exempt from the military duties to which they are subject under the present military laws of the State; nor shall such companies be considered as any part of the organized militia of the State, or be subject, as companies, to be called into the service of the State. They are, when organized, to be furnished with arms by said board, as provided for in the second section of this act, upon the following terms and conditions, viz: Application for arms for a company of Home Guards shall be made by the captain of the company, who must produce to the board a certificate from the county judge that a company has been organized in his county; that the applicant has been duly elected captain thereof, and that all the officers and members of the company have taken the oath now required by law to be taken by the officers of the State Guard. And to enable the county judge to make such a certificate, he is empowered to conduct the election for officers of the company, who are to be elected by the members thereof. Said applicant must also execute a bond, with good security, to the Commonwealth of Kentucky, containing a covenant that the arms shall be safely kept, and shall be returned to the State arsenal, at Frankfort, at the expiration of five years, or sooner if the company shall be previously dissolved; and the county judge must also certify that the person or persons offered as surety in the bond are good and sufficient to secure the performance of said covenant, or to answer for its breach.

§ 6. The arms and munitions of war which now belong to the State of Kentucky, and all that may be purchased or procured under the authority herein given, shall be subject to the control and disposition of said board under the provisions of this act. The State arsenal shall also be under its exclusive control and management.

§ 7. That a part of the money borrowed may be used for the purpose of having the Active Militia suitably trained, and the purchase of camp and other equipage necessary to the active service or troops: *Provided*, That no part of the seven hundred and fifty thousand dollars appropriated for the purchase of arms and accoutrements shall be used for this purpose.

§ 8. All persons receiving arms under the provisions of this act shall take the oath now required by law to be taken by the officers of the State Guard.

§ 9. The commissioners appointed by this act, before they enter upon the discharge of their duties, are required to take an oath, that they will faithfully execute the provisions of this act, to the best of their ability. Each of said commissioners who act under this appointment shall be paid, out of the money borrowed as aforesaid, the sum of five hundred dollars per annum, payable quarterly, as a compensation for their services. They may also appoint a secretary for the board, and allow him a reasonable compensation for his services out of the same fund, the amount of which allowance shall be certified by them to the Auditor of Public Accounts; and they are hereby authorized to act under this appointment for the term of two years, unless, in the meantime, their services shall be dispensed with by an act of the Legislature.

§ 10. Nothing contained in this act shall be so construed as to authorize said board, or any of the military organizations created by the militia law of this State, to use in any wise the arms and munitions of war herein authorized to be purchased, or those already belonging to the State, against the Government of the United States, nor against the Confederate States, unless in protecting our soil from unlawful invasion; it being the intention alone that said arms and munitions of war are to be used for the sole defense of the State of Kentucky.

§ 11. This act shall take effect from its passage.

Approved May 24, 1861

Source: *Acts of the General Assembly of the Commonwealth of Kentucky, Passed at the Called Session Which was Begun and Held in the City of Frankfort, on Monday, the 6th Day of May, 1861, and Ended on Friday, the 24th Day of May, 1861* (Frankfort: Jno. B. Major, State Printer, 1861), 4–6.

CHAPTER TEN

Border Slave State Convention

Kentucky's Border State Convention illustrates the state's persistence in finding a solution to the secession crisis short of war. When the general assembly called for the conference on April 3, 1861, seven states had already seceded, the Washington Peace Conference had concluded its deliberations over a month earlier without success, and tensions were increasing in Charleston Harbor. If a national gathering of twenty-one states could not broker a compromise, it was unlikely that a very small subset of slave states would be more successful. Nevertheless, Kentucky made the effort. A statewide election on May 4, resulted in overwhelming support for Union and neutrality and appointed Joshua Fry Bell (Danville), Francis Marion Bristow (Elkton), John Jordan Crittenden (Frankfort), Archibald Dixon (Henderson), George W. Dunlap (Lancaster), James Guthrie (Louisville), John B. Huston (Winchester), Charles Slaughter Morehead (Louisville), Robert Richardson (Covington), James F. Robinson (Georgetown), Charles Anderson Wickliffe (Bardstown), and R. K. Williams (Mayfield), as delegates. Bell, Guthrie, Morehead, and Wickliffe had also represented Kentucky at the Washington Peace Conference in February. John J. Crittenden was unanimously proclaimed president.

The small gathering which met for a week was decidedly proslavery and pro-Union. Unable to do more than express their desires for a peaceful future, the delegates developed two proclamations. In an "Address to the People of the United States," they declared that the assembled saw no justification in secession and expressed hope that some middle ground could yet be found. To that end, the delegates reiterated the wish that Congress could propose a constitutional amendment that would "secure to slaveholders their legal rights, and allay their apprehensions." Failing that, the address proposed the calling of a "voluntary convention," that would "develop measures of peaceable adjustment" and rescue the nation "from the continued horrors and calamities of civil war."

A second proclamation written by the Kentucky delegation titled, "Address to the People of Kentucky," endorsed the state's proclaimed position of neutrality "commended to her by every consideration of patriotism and by a proper regard for her own security." Hemmed in as Kentucky was by pro-slave states to the south and non-slave states to the north, her sense of "loyalty to the Union" demanded that she "insist on the integrity of the Union, its Constitution and the Government." Perceptively, the delegates anticipated that the war would bring about the abolition of slavery. If war cannot be avoided, they declared, "even the institution, to preserve or control which this wretched war was undertaken, will be exterminated in the general ruin."

Kentucky's Call for the Convention

Monday, May 27, 1861

In pursuance of an act passed by the Legislature of Kentucky, approved April 3rd, 1861, entitled "An act to provide for the election of Delegates to a Convention to be held at Frankfort," and which act is as follows:

AN ACT to provide for the election of Delegates to a Convention to be held at Frankfort,

§ 1. *Be it enacted by the General Assembly of the Commonwealth of Kentucky,* That an election shall be held, on the first Saturday in May next, at all the election precincts in this State, to elect twelve Delegates to a Convention of the Border Slave States, and such other slave States as have not passed ordinances of secession, to meet at Frankfort, Kentucky; and said Delegates shall be voted for and elected by the State at large, in the same manner that State officers are now elected; and the same laws which apply to and regulate the mode of the election of State officers by the qualified voters of the whole State, shall apply to and govern the election of said Delegates.

§ 2. That the persons who may be thus elected shall be commissioned by the Governor as Delegates to said Convention, and are empowered to meet the Delegates from the States aforesaid, in Convention, to consult on the critical condition of the country, and agree upon some plan of peaceable adjustment.

§ 3. The Convention shall be held on the 27th of May next, or at such other time as a majority of the Delegates elected in this State may appoint, to suit the convenience of the Delegates from the other States.

§ 4. That one of the Delegates to represent Kentucky in the Border Slave States Convention shall be required to reside in each Congressional district in this State.

§ 5. This act shall take effect from its passage.

Source: *Journal and Proceedings of the Convention of the Border Slave States, Begun and Held in the City of Frankfort, and State of Kentucky, on the 27th Day of May, 1861* (Frankfort: Printed at the Kentucky Yeoman Office, Jno. B. Major, State Printer, 1861), 3.

Convention's Address to the People of Kentucky

Monday, June 3, 1861

To the People of Kentucky

Having been elected by you as your Delegates to "A Convention of the Border Slave States, and such other slave States as have not passed ordinances of secession," with power to meet with Delegates from other States in Convention, "to consult on the critical condition of the country, and agree upon some plan of adjustment;" and having met in Frankfort, on the 27th of May, in pursuance of the act, we deem it proper to inform you, briefly, of what was done by us in the Convention.

It was a matter of regret to us that while the call for the Conference originated in Virginia, and had, apparently, the concurrence of all the Border Slave States, yet there were Delegates in attendance from Kentucky and Missouri only.[1] One representative[2] chosen by the counties of McMinn and Sevier, in Tennessee, appeared, and although not coming with such credentials as were necessary to constitute him a Delegate, he was invited to participate in our deliberations.

After a continuous session from day to day, during which the condition of the country and the various causes that led to it were maturely considered, it was resolved that the Convention should address an appeal to the people of the United States, and the Delegates from Kentucky determined to present to you a separate address in which the views of your members should be embodied. In the discharge of this duty we now attempt to address you.

Your State, on a deliberate consideration of her responsibilities—moral, political, and social—has determined that the proper course for her to pursue is, to take no part in the controversy between the Government and the seceded States but that of *mediator* and *intercessor*. She is unwilling to take up arms against her brethren residing either North or South of the geographical line by which they are unhappily divided into warring sections. This course was commended to her by every consideration of patriotism, and by a proper regard for her own security. It does not result from timidity; on the contrary, it could only have been adopted by a brave people—so brave that the least imputation on their courage would be branded as false by their written and traditional history.

Kentucky was right in taking this position—because, from the commencement of this deplorable controversy, her voice was for reconciliation, compromise, and peace. She had no cause of complaint against the General Government, and made none. The injury she sustained in her property from a failure to execute laws passed for its protection, in consequence of illegal interference by wicked and deluded citizens in the free States, she considered as wholly insufficient to justify a dismemberment of the Union. That, she regarded as no remedy for existing evils, but an aggravation of them all. She witnessed, it is true, with deep concern, the growth of a wild and frenzied fanaticism in one section, and a reckless and defiant spirit in another, both equally threatening destruction to the country; and tried earnestly to arrest them, but in vain. We will not stop to trace the causes of the unhappy condition in which we are now placed, or to criminate either of the sections to the dishonor of the other, but can say, that we believed both to have been wrong, and, in their madness and folly, to have inaugurated a war that the Christian World looks upon with amazement and sorrow; and that Liberty, Christianity, and Civilization stand appalled at the horrors to which it will give rise.

It is a proud and grand thing for Kentucky to stand up and say, as she can, truthfully, in the face of the world "we had no hand in this thing;" our skirts are clear. And, in looking at the *terrorism* that prevails elsewhere—beholding freedom of speech denied to American citizens, their homesteads subjected to lawless visitation, their property confiscated, and their persons liable to incarceration and search—how grandly does she not loom up, as she proclaims to the oppressed and miserable, we offer you a refuge! Here constitutional law and respect for individual rights still exist! Here is an asylum where loyalty to the name, nation, and Flag of the Union predominate; and here is the only place in this lately great Republic, where true freedom remains—that freedom for which our fathers fought—the citizen being free to speak, write, or publish any thing he may wish, responsible only to the laws, and not controlled by the violence of the mob.

Is this not an attitude worthy of a great people, and do not her position and safety require men to maintain it? If she deviates from it; if she suffers herself in a moment of excitement to be led off by sympathy with one side or the other—to ally herself with either section—inevitable and speedy ruin must fall upon her. What reason can be urged to incline her to such a fatal step? She is still, thank God, a member of the Union, owing constitutional allegiance to it—an allegiance voluntarily given, long maintained, and from which she has derived countless benefits. Can she, by her own act, forfeit this allegiance, and, by the exercise of any constitutional power, sever herself from that Government? In our opinion the statement of the proposition insures its rejection. It is of no more rational force than the argument of the suicide to commit self-slaughter. Secession is not a right. That the right of revolution exists, is as true in States as the right of self-defense is true of individuals. It does not exist by virtue of legal enactment or constitutional provision, but is founded in the nature of things—is inalienable and indestructible, and ought to be resorted to only when all peaceable remedies fail. Revolution is an extreme remedy, finds its justification alone in an escape from intolerable oppression, and hazards the consequences of failure, as success or defeat makes the movement one of rightful resistance or rebellion. It becomes the stern duty of Kentucky to look not only to the motives that might impel her to revolt, but to the probable results. She must contemplate her condition in a complex character—National and State—and see what must be her fate in the event of a separation.

Under the National Government, she has a right to the protection of thirty-three great States, and with them, thus protected, can defy the world in arms. Under it, she has become prosperous and happy. Deprived of it, she finds herself exposed to imminent danger. She has a border front on the

Ohio river of near seven hundred miles, with three powerful States on that border. She has four hundred miles on the South by which she is separated from Tennessee by a merely conventional line. Her eastern front is on Virginia, and part of her western on Missouri— thus making her antagonistic, in the event of collision, to Virginia, which is our mother, and to Missouri, which is our daughter. Hemmed in thus on every side by powers—each one of which is equal to her own—her situation, and her sense of loyalty to the Union, imperatively demand of her to insist on the integrity of the Union, its Constitution and Government. Peace is of vital consequence to her, and can only be secured to her by preserving the Union inviolate. Kentucky has no cause of quarrel with the Constitution, and no wish to quarrel with her neighbors; but abundant reason to love both. Of the great west she was the pioneer, and became the starting point of emigration to all around her. There is not a western or southwestern State in which Kentucky families are not settled, and she is bound to all by ties of interest and brotherhood. She has ever been loyal to the Government, answering to its requisitions, and sharing its burthens. At the command of that Government, when war was declared to protect the rights of *sailors*, although she had no vessels to float on the ocean, yet she offered up her blood freely in the common defense, from the lakes to the Gulf of Mexico.[3] Again, when war, growing out of territorial controversy, far from her own borders, was proclaimed, she was amongst the foremost in the fight, and Monterey and Buena Vista were made famous in history by the valor of Kentuckians.[4] Never has she faltered in her duty to the Union.

In declining to respond to a call made by the present administration of the Government, and one that we have reason to believe would not have been made if the administration had been fully advised of the circumstances by which we were surrounded, Kentucky did not put herself in factious opposition to her legitimate obligations. She did not choose to throw herself in hostile collision with the slave States of Missouri, Maryland, and Delaware, which have not seceded on the one hand, nor the slave States which have and are in process of secession on the other, and shed the blood of brethren and kindred at the very moment when she was striving to be an apostle of peace. Nature herself revolted at the thought, and her conduct in this matter had so much of love to God, and love to man, in it, that it will meet the sanction of an approving world. So far from being denounced for this action, it is everywhere looked upon as an act of purest patriotism, resulting from imperious necessity, and the highest instincts of self-preservation—respected by the very administration that alone could have complained of it, and will, we doubt not, be ratified by it—if not in terms, at least by its future action. That act did not take her out of the Union.

Kentucky, in so grave a matter as this, passes by mere legal technicalities and a discussion of theoretical difficulties of Government, poises herself upon her right to do what the necessities of her condition imperatively demanded of her, and relies upon the good sense and magnanimity of her sister States, seeing that there is no parallel in her condition and theirs, to do her justice.

In all things she is as loyal as ever to the constitutional administration of the Government. She will follow the stars and stripes to the utmost regions of the earth, and defend it from foreign insult. She refuses alliances with any one who would destroy the Union. All she asks is permission to keep out of this unnatural strife. When called to take part in it, she believes that there is more honor in the breach than in the observance of any supposed duty to perform it.

Feeling that she is clearly right in this, and has announced her intention to refrain from aggression upon others, she must protest against her soil being made the theater of military operations by any belligerent. The war must not be transferred, by the warring sections, from their own to her borders. Such unfriendly action cannot be viewed with indifference by Kentucky.

Having thus referred to this subject in its general aspects, we would invite your undivided attention to its direct bearings upon yourselves.

It is not now a question of party politics, although it may be the interest of some to make it so. The day of mere party platforms has, we trust, gone forever. It has passed from being a mere struggle for place that may gratify personal ambition, to one for the present and future welfare of a whole people, for the safety of homes and firesides. Whatever divisions have heretofore existed should now cease. In times past, in our elections, the questions which divided men related to mere party differences, and the members of all the parties rivaled each other in their expression of devotion to the Union, and were equally clamorous for their rights in the Union and not out of it. Now these party differences are passed away and forgotten. The direct question is Union or no Union—Government or no Government—Nationality or no Nationality. Before this grand and commanding question everything else gives way.

All can see that such a state of things cannot continue without a war, and that such a war was unnecessary. It resulted from the ambition of men, rather than from wrongs done to the people. There was a remedy for everything, already provided by the Constitution, which, with wise foresight, provided against the trials to which it might be subjected. There were countervailing powers to check encroachments, whether by a President or by Congress. And it so happened that at this dangerous crisis, when a sectional President had been elected, there was a majority in opposition to him in both houses of Congress, by which he could have been controlled, and the people protected. It was the duty of the opposition to have stood to their posts till the danger of encroachment had passed away. But Senators and Representatives, following the example of their States, vacated their seats and placed a President who would have been in a minority, at the head of a triumphant majority. It was a great wrong, for which they must answer to posterity. Kentucky remained true to herself, contending with all her might for what were considered to be the rights of the people, and although one after another of the States that should have been by her side, ungenerously deserted her, leaving her almost alone in the field, yet she did not surrender her rights under the Constitution, and never will surrender them. She will appear again in the Congress of the United States, not having conceded the least atom of power to the Government that had not heretofore been granted, and retaining every power she had reserved. She will insist upon her constitutional rights in the Union, and not out of it.

Kentucky is grieved to think that anything should have been done by her sister States that has made it necessary for her to assume the position she now occupies. It is not one of submission, as it has been insultingly called—it is one of the most exalted patriotism. But if she had no higher or holier motive; if she were not earnestly for Peace among her brethren; the great law of self-protection points out her course, and she has no alternative. Already one section declares that there will be no war at home, but that it shall be in Kentucky and Virginia. Already the cannon and bayonets of another section are visible on our most exposed border. Let those hostile armies meet on our soil, and it will matter but little to us which may succeed, for destruction to us will be the inevitable result. Our fields will be laid waste, our houses and cities will be burned, our people will be slain, and this goodly land will be re-baptized "the land of blood." And even the institution, to preserve or control which this wretched war was undertaken, will be exterminated in the general ruin. Such is the evil that others will bring upon us, no matter which side we take, if this is to be the battle-field.

But there is danger at home even more appalling than any that comes from beyond. People of Kentucky, look well to it that you do not get to fighting among yourselves, for then, indeed, you will find, that it is an ill fight where he that wins has the worst of it. Endeavor to be of one mind, and strive to keep the State steady in her present position. Hold fast to that sheet anchor of republican liberty, that the will of the majority, constitutionally and legally expressed, must govern. You have, in the election by which this Convention was chosen, displayed a unanimity unparalleled in your history. May you be as unanimous in the future; may your majorities be so decided that a refusal to obey may be justly called factious. Trust and love one another. Avoid angry strife. Frown upon the petty ambition of demagogues who would stir up bad passions among you. Consider as wise men, what is necessary for your own best interest, and in humble submission and trust look to that Almighty Being, who has heretofore so signally blessed us as a nation, for His guidance through the gloom and darkness of this hour.

J. J. CRITTENDEN, *President.*
JAMES GUTHRIE,
R. K. WILLIAMS,
ARCH'D DIXON,
F. M. BRISTOW,
JOSHUA F. BELL,
C. A. WICKLIFFE,
G. W. DUNLAP,
C. S. MOREHEAD,
J. F. ROBINSON,
JNO. B. HUSTON,
ROBT. RICHARDSON.

Source: *Journal and Proceedings of the Convention of the Border Slave States, Begun and Held in the City of Frankfort, and State of Kentucky, on the 27th Day of May, 1861* (Frankfort: Printed at the Kentucky Yeoman Office, Jno. B. Major, State Printer, 1861), 18–22.

APPENDIX.

TIMELINE FOR SECESSION WINTER

1860

November 6	Abraham Lincoln elected president of the United States
December 3	Second session of the Thirty-Sixth Congress convenes
December 17	South Carolina convenes secession convention
December 18	Senator John J. Crittenden introduces compromise amendment
December 20	South Carolina secedes

1861

January 3	Florida convenes secession convention
January 7	Mississippi convenes secession convention
January 7	Alabama convenes secession convention
January 9	Mississippi secedes
January 10	Florida secedes
January 11	Alabama secedes
January 16	Georgia convenes secession convention
January 17	Kentucky General Assembly convenes
January 19	Georgia secedes
January 23	Louisiana convenes secession convention
January 26	Louisiana secedes
January 28	Texas convenes secession convention
February 4	Secessionist convention convenes in Montgomery, Alabama
February 4	Washington Peace Convention convenes
February 8	Provisional Confederate States of America established
February 9	Jefferson Davis elected provisional president of the CSA
February 13	Virginia convenes secession convention
February 18	Jefferson Davis inaugurated president of the CSA
February 23	Texas secedes
February 27	Washington Peace Convention concludes
February 28	Missouri convenes secession convention
March 4	US Senate approves Thomas Corwin's compromise amendment
March 4	US Senate votes down Washington Peace Convention amendment
March 4	Abraham Lincoln inaugurated president of the US
March 4	Thirty-Sixth Congress adjourns
March 4	Arkansas convenes secession convention

March 6	Confederate Congress authorizes the raising of 100,000 troops
March 11	Permanent Confederate Constitution created in Montgomery, Alabama
March 19	Missouri votes against secession
March 26	Permanent Confederate Constitution officially adopted
April 3	Kentucky Legislature calls for Border Slave State Convention
April 12	Bombardment of Fort Sumter begins
April 15	Lincoln calls for 75,000 troops
May 6	Arkansas secedes
May 20	North Carolina convenes secession convention
May 20	North Carolina secedes
May 23	Virginia secedes
May 27	Border Slave State Convention convenes
June 8	Tennessee secedes

NOTES

Introduction

1. On August 2, 1858, only after years of physical and political battles, Kansas settlers overwhelmingly voted against the proslavery English Compromise (11,300 to 1,788) paving the way for Kansas statehood which became a reality on January 29, 1861. See Nicole Etcheson, *Bleeding Kansas: Contested Liberty in the Civil War Era* (Lawrence: University Press of Kansas, 2004).

2. See Michael F. Holt, *The Election of 1860: "A Campaign Fraught with Consequences"* (Lawrence: University Press of Kansas, 2017).

3. Bell's Unionist Party conscientiously occupied a middle ground between the anti-slavery extremists in the North and the proslavery secessionists in the South. The earlier Opposition Party (composed mostly of disaffected Democrats) had developed during the latter years of the Buchanan administration in response to the president's dishonesty and corruption. The American Party organized in 1854–1855 partly in response to the Kansas-Nebraska Act, but also as an anti-immigrant, anti-Catholic coalition originally known as the Know Nothings. See Holt, *The Election of 1860*, 5–6, 27, 48, 141, 184.

4. *Congressional Globe*, 36th Cong., 2nd Sess., December 3, 1860, Appendix, 1–7. See also Jean H. Baker, *James Buchanan* (New York: Times Books, 2004), 124–25.

5. See Thomas D. Morris, *Southern Slavery and the Law, 1619–1860* (Chapel Hill: University of North Carolina Press, 1996).

6. *Congressional Globe*, 36th Cong., 2nd Sess., December 6, 1860, 19.

7. *Congressional Globe*, 36th Cong., 2nd Sess., Senate Report No. 288 (Journal of the Committee of Thirteen).

8. Albert D. Kirwan, *John J. Crittenden: The Struggle for the Union* (Lexington: University of Kentucky Press, 1962), 160–61.

9. *Congressional Globe*, 36th Cong., 2nd Sess., December 18, 1860, 114. See also Kirwan, *John J. Crittenden*, 374–78.

10. Robert E. May, *The Southern Dream of a Caribbean Empire* (Gainesville: University Press of Florida, 2002; first published in 1973); Matthew Karp, *This Vast Southern Empire: Slaveholders at the Helm of American Foreign Policy* (Cambridge: Harvard University Press, 2016). See also William W. Freehling, *The Road to Disunion: Secessionists Triumphant*, II (New York: Oxford University Press, 2007), 471–75; David M. Potter, *Lincoln and His Party in the Secession Crisis* (Baton Rouge: Louisiana State University Press, 1995; first published in 1942), 222–24.

11. A sampling of these memorials and petitions has been reproduced in chapter 7.

12. *Journal and Proceedings of the Missouri State Convention, Held at Jefferson City and St. Louis, March, 1861* (St. Louis: Knapp & Co., Printers and Binders, 1861), 70–73.

13. *Congressional Globe*, 36th Cong., 2nd Sess., 677–80.

14. *Congressional Globe*, 36th Cong., 2nd Sess., Appendix, 261–63.

15. Ibid., 202–3.

16. Ibid., 276–80.

17. *Congressional Globe*, 36th Cong., 2nd Sess., February 12, 1861, 862–64.

18. Ibid., 1405.

19. *Congressional Globe*, 36th Cong., 2nd Sess., House of Representatives Report No. 31 (Journal of the Committee of Thirty-Three). For a detailed analysis of the Corwin amendment, see Daniel W. Crofts, *Lincoln and the Politics of Slavery: The Other Thirteenth Amendment and the Struggle to Save the Union* (Chapel Hill: University of North Carolina Press, 2016).

20. *Journal of the Called Session of the House of Representatives of the Commonwealth of Kentucky, Begun and Held in the Town of Frankfort, on Thursday the Seventeenth Day of January, in the Year of Our Lord 1861, and of the Commonwealth the Sixty-ninth* (Frankfort: Printed at the Kentucky Yeoman Office, John B. Major, State Printer, 1861), 13–15. For a short overview of Magoffin as governor, see Lowell H. Harrison, *Kentucky's Governors* (Lexington: University Press of Kentucky, 2004), 78–81.

21. *Journal of the Called Session*, 30–31.

22. Although the 119 runaway slaves in 1860 represented less than one percent of the state's 225,483 slaves, their loss had great symbolic value. See Joseph C. G. Kennedy, *Preliminary Report of the Eighth Census, 1860* (Washington: Government Printing Office, 1862), 11–12, 137.

23. Patrick A. Lewis, *For Slavery and Union: Benjamin Buckner and Kentucky Loyalties in the Civil War* (Lexington: University Press of Kentucky, 2015), 2–3.

24. Ibid., 19. For a concise history of Kentucky over Secession Winter, see Lowell H. Harrison, *The Civil War in Kentucky* (Lexington: University Press of Kentucky, 1975), 1–13.

25. *Journal of the Called Session*, 5.

26. Judith M. Jacob, *The Washington Monument: A Technical History and Catalog of the Commemorative Stones* (Washington, D.C.: National Park Service, 2005), 165. See also William T. McKinney, "The Defeat of the Secessionists in Kentucky in 1861," *Journal of Negro History* 1, no. 4 (October 1916), 377–91. For an excellent analysis of Border South moderation, see Michael D. Robinson, *A Union Indivisible: Secession and the Politics of Slavery in the Border South* (Chapel Hill: University of North Carolina Press, 2017), 92–99.

27. *Journal of the House of Delegates of the State of Virginia, for the Extra Session, 1861* (Richmond: William F. Ritchie, Public Printer, 1861), Doc. I, iii–xxvii.

28. Ibid., xx–xxi.

29. Ibid., 65–66.

30. Lucius E. Chittenden, *A Report of the Debates and Proceedings in the Secret Sessions of the Conference Convention, for Proposing Amendments to the Constitution of the United States, Held at Washington, D.C., in February, A.D. 1861* (New York: D. Appleton & Company, 1864), 465–66.

31. *New York Times*, September 28, 1861.

32. In 1860, five northern states allowed free blacks to vote without restrictions, and three permitted the franchise with restrictions. See James Oliver Horton and Lois E. Horton, *In Hope of Liberty: Culture, Community, and Protest Among Northern Free Blacks, 1700–1860* (New York: Oxford University Press, 1997), 169.

33. Chittenden, *A Report of the Debates*, 421–24.

34. For a recent study of the Peace Conference, see Mark Tooley, *The Peace That Almost Was: The Forgotten Story of the 1861 Washington Peace Conference and the Final Attempt to Avert the Civil War* (Nashville: Nelson Books, 2015).

35. *Congressional Globe*, 36th Cong., 2nd Sess., March 1, 1861, 1333; March 4, 1861, 1405.

36. *Report of the Kentucky Commissioners to the Late Peace Conference Held at Washington City, Made to the Legislature of Kentucky* (Frankfort: Printed at the Yeoman Office, Jno. B. Major, State Printer, 1861), 5–10.

37. Ibid., 11–17.

38. For a detailed analysis of these amendments, see Dwight T. Pitcaithley, *The U.S. Constitution and Secession: A Documentary Anthology of Slavery and White Supremacy* (Lawrence: University Press of Kansas, 2018).

39. *Journal of the Called Session*, 91.

40. Printed broadside in David M. Rubenstein Rare Book and Manuscript Library, Broadsides and Ephemera Collection, Folder KY2, Duke University. Original manuscript: "Office of the Governor, Beriah Magoffin, May 28, 1861: Governor's Official Correspondence File – Executive Journal, 1859–1862," Kentucky Department for Library and Archives, Frankfort, Kentucky.

41. *Acts of the General Assembly of the Commonwealth of Kentucky, Passed at the Called Session Which was Begun and Held in the City of Frankfort, on Monday, the 6th Day of May, 1861, and Ended on Friday, the 24th Day of May, 1861* (Frankfort: Jno. B. Major, State Printer, 1861), 4–6.

42. *New York Times*, May 22, 1861. Kentucky's neutrality lasted until September 3, 1861, when Confederate forces under the command of Leonidas Polk entered the state and occupied Columbus on the Mississippi River. A few days later, Ulysses S. Grant crossed the Ohio River and occupied Paducah. In response, the General Assembly passed a resolution ordering the withdrawal of Polk's army. Harrison, *Kentucky's Governors*, 79.

43. Tennessee's lone delegate was John Caldwell who represented McMinn and Sevier Counties. His participation was unusual because on May 6, Tennessee's General Assembly had approved an ordinance of secession. Tennessee was one of only three states (Texas and Virginia being the others) that required a statewide referendum on the issue of secession. On June 8, 1861, the voters approved the ordinance making Tennessee the last state to secede.

44. *Journal and Proceedings of the Convention of the Border Slave States, Begun and Held in the City of Frankfort, and State of Kentucky, on the 27th Day of May, 1861* (Frankfort: Printed at the Yeoman Office, Jno. B. Major, State Printer, 1861).

45. Ibid., 18–22. See also Kirwan, *John J. Crittenden*, 436–38; Robinson, *A Union Indivisible*, 180–82.

46. Robinson, *A Union Indivisible*, 215. Over the course of the war, Kentucky supplied 35,000 troops to the Confederacy and 74,000 to the United States. Of the latter number, 24,000 were black volunteers. One notable son of Kentucky who fought for the United States was John Marshall Harlan who later served on the US Supreme Court and distinguished himself as the lone dissenter in *Plessy v. Ferguson* (1896). See Peter S. Canellos, *The Great Dissenter: The Story of John Marshall Harlan, America's Judicial Hero* (New York: Simon & Schuster, 2021).

47. For a fascinating look at Kentucky after the war, see Anne E. Marshall, *Creating a Confederate Kentucky: The Lost Cause and Civil War Memory in a Border State* (Chapel Hill: University of North Carolina Press, 2010).

48. The Confederate Constitution retained verbatim all twelve amendments from the United States Constitution but embedded them in the body of the southern charter. Charles Robert Lee Jr., *The Confederate Constitution* (Chapel Hill: University of North Carolina Press, 1963), 184. For a more detailed explanation of the Confederate Constitution in this regard, see Pitcaithley, *The U.S. Constitution and Secession*, 54–55.

49. Crittenden proposed his amendment on December 18, 1860; Seward certified the ratification of the Thirteenth Amendment on December 18, 1865.

1. Governor Beriah Magoffin

1. The Southern wing of the Democratic Party nominated Kentucky native (and James Buchanan's vice president) John C. Breckinridge in Baltimore on June 23, 1860, upon a platform that affirmed the right of citizens to emigrate to the western territories with their slaves and have that form of property protected "when necessary" by the federal government throughout the territorial period; declared northern personal liberty laws "hostile in character, subversive of the Constitution, and revolutionary in their effect"; and proclaimed the party in favor of the acquisition of Cuba and the construction of a transcontinental railroad "at the earliest practicable moment."

2. For a detailed treatment of personal liberty laws, see Thomas D. Morris, *Free Men All: The Personal Liberty Laws of the North, 1780–1861* (Baltimore: Johns Hopkins University Press, 1974).

3. The 1860 census reported Kentucky's loss in fugitive slaves to be 119 or .0527 percent of total slaves in the state. Nationally, the census reported a total of 803 fugitive slaves or .0203 percent of total slaves. The 1850 census reported 1,011 fugitive slaves nationally. Kennedy, *Preliminary Report of the Eighth Census, 1860*, 11–12, 137.

4. In 1854, a Wisconsin district federal court convicted Sherman Booth (correct spelling) of assisting in the escape of a fugitive slave. The state's supreme court reversed the conviction declaring the 1850 Fugitive Slave Law not legally binding. After the case was appealed to the US Supreme Court, Chief Justice Roger B. Taney (in 1859) declared that the Fugitive Slave Law was constitutional and denied the right of the state judiciary to interfere in federal cases.

5. In 1859, Ohio governor William Dennison Jr. (1815–1882) refused to surrender a free black man accused of helping a slave escape from Kentucky declaring that the man had committed no crime under the laws of Ohio.

6. In his *Dred Scott* decision, Chief Justice Robert B. Taney pronounced that "the right of property in a slave is distinctly and expressly affirmed in the Constitution."

7. Although he won decisively in the Electoral College, Lincoln won but 39.9 percent of the popular vote.

8. Charles B. Dew, *Apostles of Disunion: Southern Secession Commissioners and the Causes of the Civil War* (Charlottesville: University Press of Virginia, 2001), 51–56.

9. A command.

10. During the especially hot and dry summer of 1860, fires broke out in numerous towns in north Texas. Although blamed on northern abolitionists attempting to incite slave rebellions, no evidence to support the claim was ever uncovered. Analysis of the various conflagrations indicates that the real culprit was the spontaneous combustion of new phosphorous matches. See Donald E. Reynolds, *Texas Terror: The Slave Insurrection Panic of 1860 and the Secession of the Lower South* (Baton Rouge: Louisiana State University Press, 2007). See also *Twenty-Eighth Annual Report of the American Anti-Slavery Society: By the Executive Committee for the Year Ending May 1, 1861* (New York: American Anti-Slavery Society, 1861), 200–209.

11. For a keen analysis of the political issue of slavery in the Kansas Territory, see Etcheson, *Bleeding Kansas*.

12. On March 11, 1850, during Senate debates over the disposition of the Mexican Cession, William H. Seward (a Whig at the time) delivered his controversial "Higher Law" speech. Speaking in opposition to the compromise which allowed the possibility of slavery in the newly acquired territory, Seward claimed, "there is a higher law than the Constitution, which regulates our authority over the domain, and devotes it to the same noble purposes. The territory is a part, no inconsiderable part, of the common heritage of mankind, bestowed upon them by the Creator of the universe." Seward's notion that God's law was higher than that of the Constitution became part of Democratic grievances against Lincoln and the Republican Party. Seward's "Irrepressible Conflict" speech was delivered on October 25, 1858, in Rochester, New York.

13. Beginning in 1791, a slave revolt on the Caribbean island of Saint-Domingue successfully overthrew French rule and established the new nation of Haiti in 1804. See Michel-Rolph Trouillot, *Silencing the Past: Power and the Production of History* (Boston: Beacon Press, 1995).

14. Great Britain abolished slavery in the West Indies in 1833 through an act that provided for gradual emancipation and financial compensation to the owners. See Karp, *This Vast Southern Empire*, 15–16, 26–28.

15. Alabama's resolution stated that the election of a Republican as president in the upcoming November 1860 election would trigger a call for a convention to determine the future of the state. On November 10, the Alabama legislature approved a bill calling for the convention.

16. A reference to the Republican platform of 1860.

17. On January 9, 1861, South Carolina artillery fired on the *Star of the West*, an unarmed merchant ship sent by President Buchanan to reinforce Fort Sumter.

18. The full text of Magoffin's letter of December 9, is included in chapter 6.

19. Winfield Scott Featherston (1820–1891) served as brigadier general in the Confederate States Army.

20. Mississippi's secession convention voted to secede on January 9, 1861, after declining a motion to have the decision ratified by a popular vote.

21. Florida's convention voted to secede on January 10; Alabama's on January 11, 1861.

22. On February 9, 1861, the white male electorate of Tennessee would decide against calling a secession convention and reject secession by a vote of 80 percent to 20 percent.

23. Virginia would officially secede on May 23, 1861, via a ratification vote of the white male population. Its convention had earlier approved disunion on April 17. North Carolina's secession convention specifically declined to approve a popular vote on the issue and voted unanimously to secede on May 20, 1861.

24. By a vote of 89 to 1 on March 19, 1861, Missouri's secession convention would elect to remain in the Union.

25. Of the first four states to approve disunion, the vote to secede was unanimous only in South Carolina. In Mississippi's convention, the vote was 85 percent to 15 percent, in Florida's, 90 percent to 10 percent and in Alabama's, 61 percent to 39 percent.

26. Simon Bolivar Buckner (1823–1914), later lieutenant general in the Confederate States Army and governor of Kentucky (1887–1891).

2. Constitutional Amendment Proposed by Senator John Jordan Crittenden

1. US Constitution, Article I, Section 2.

2. After the American Revolution, several states, including Virginia, ceded to the federal government their claims on land west of Pennsylvania, north of the Ohio River, and east of the Mississippi. In 1787, Congress organized this area into the Northwest Territory and prohibited slavery throughout. Thomas Jefferson's original 1784 plan for the organization for the territory, which served as the basis for the 1787 ordinance, also excluded slavery. Congress reaffirmed the ordinance under the new Constitution in 1789.

3. Democrat Benjamin Fitzpatrick (1802–1869) from Alabama.

4. Democrat James S. Green (1817–1870) from Missouri.

5. These paragraphs refer to the clauses that allow three-fifths of slaves (as "persons") to be counted toward southern representation in Congress, and that require the return of fugitive slaves.

3. Crittenden Debated: Pro-Crittenden

1. The Utah slave code required slave owners to provide "comfortable habitations, clothing, bedding, sufficient food, and recreation" for their slaves and a minimal education. Owners could "correct and punish" slaves, but not excessively. In addition, owners

had to file an agreement in the Probate Court attesting that the slaves would receive "reasonable compensation" for their services. Sexual or "carnal intercourse" between the races was specifically prohibited with punishment resulting in fines not to exceed $1,000 and imprisonment not exceeding three years. See *Acts, Resolutions and Memorials, Passed by the First Annual, and Special Sessions, of the Legislative Assembly, of the Territory of Utah, Begun and Held at Great Salt Lake City, on the 22nd Day of September, A. D., 1851 Also of the Constitution of the United States, and the Act Organizing the Territory of Utah* (G. S. L City, U. T.: Brigham H. Young, Printer, 1851), 80–82.

2. Crittenden's original Joint Resolution No. 50 became Joint Resolution No. 54 when he reintroduced it on January 3, with the added seventh article.

3. *Laws of the Territory of New Mexico Passed by the Legislative Assembly, Session of 1859–60* (Santa Fe, N. M.: O. P. Hovey, Public Printer, 1860), 64–80. See also John P. Hays, "The Curious Case of New Mexico's Pre-Civil War Slave Code," *New Mexico Historical Review* 92, No. 3 (Summer 2017), 251–83. Republicans in the US House of Representatives debated the constitutionality of the New Mexico slave bill in an unsuccessful attempt to nullify it. The essence of that debate can be found in *Slavery in the Territory of New Mexico*, 36th Cong., 1st Sess., Report No. 508, May 10, 1860.

4 Senator Judah P. Benjamin (1811–1884) later served as Confederate attorney general, secretary of war, and secretary of state.

5. James Madison (1751–1836); Daniel Webster (1782–1852).

6. Article IV, Section 3: "The Congress shall have Power to dispose of and make all needful Rules and Regulations respecting the Territory or other Property belonging to the United States; and nothing in this Constitution shall be construed as to Prejudice any Claims of the United States, or of any particular State."

7. On August 8, 1846, Pennsylvania Democratic representative David Wilmot (1814–1868) proposed that if any land be acquired from Mexico as a result of the impending war, slavery would not be permitted therein. The Wilmot Proviso was not intended to affect slavery in territory previously acquired, and it never became law.

8. This 1855 case involved a saloon keeper, Roderick Beebe, who was arrested for brewing and selling beer in contradiction to the Indiana State Constitution. As it debated the regulation versus the prohibition of the manufacture and sale of alcoholic beverages, the state supreme court ended with a divided decision, leaving the issue "unsettled."

9. A full acknowledgment of error with apology.

10. On January 25, 1861, just days before Niblack spoke, Rhode Island's legislature repealed the state's 1854 personal liberty law which had discouraged the capture of fugitive slaves. *New York Times*, January 26, 1861.

11. By that very fact or act.

12. Genesis 13:8.

13. George W. Summers (1804–1868) represented Kanawha County, Virginia (presently West Virginia).

14. As such, or by that name.

15. Detinue, trover, and case were actions at common law to recover property

wrongfully taken, or to recover damages for the loss of personal property. Derived from English law, they were familiar features of American legal practice in the nineteenth century.

16. The text of Brockenbrough's report includes a citation here: "2 Seward's Works, vol. II, p. 453–4." In *Somerset v. Stewart* (1772) the English court ruled that because British common law did not recognize slavery, a slave brought to England could not be compelled to leave the country. In *Anderson v. Poindexter* (1856) the Ohio Supreme Court held that Henry Poindexter, a Kentucky slave, was free the moment he crossed over the Ohio River.

17. Both southern and northern Democratic platforms in the election of 1860 supported the acquisition of Cuba.

18. Literally, "in series." In this case, each section of the amendment was voted on separately.

19. Moss's political affiliation is undetermined.

20. Many of these are reproduced in chapter 7.

21. The original has no closing parenthesis.

22. By March 11, twenty-four amendments had been proposed that would have prohibited Congress from interfering with slavery in the states. Benjamin Cissell in the Kentucky Legislature and James B. Clay in the Washington Peace Conference introduced amendments containing this provision. See chapter 6 for the full text of Cissell's and Clay's amendments.

23. James Harvey Birch (1804–1878), a lawyer from Plattsburg, Clinton County, Missouri.

24. Millard Fillmore (1800–1874) from Buffalo, New York; president from 1850 to 1853.

25. In the 1856 election against John C. Fremont (Republican) and Millard Fillmore (Know Nothing), James Buchanan won 45.3 percent of the popular vote. The results in the Electoral College, however, were Buchanan, 174; Fremont, 11; and Fillmore, 8.

4. Crittenden Debated: Anti-Crittenden

1. Opposition Party member Alexander Robinson Boteler (1815–1892) from Shepherdstown, Virginia (presently West Virginia).

2. Wilson here quoted directly from President James Buchanan's address to Congress on December 3, 1860; *Congressional Globe*, 36th Cong., 2nd Sess., Appendix, 1–4.

3. US Constitution, Article V.

4. Thomas Carlyle (1795–1881) was a British historian, satirical writer, essayist, philosopher, and mathematician.

5. John Milton (1608–1674), British poet and intellectual; from *Areopagitica*, a speech to the Parliament of England in favor of freedom of the press, published in 1644.

6. Democratic representative Samuel Sullivan Cox (1824–1889).

7. Despite the political tension evident throughout the Thirty-Sixth Congress, there was a fair amount of humor displayed in speeches and comments. Many of the congressmen had known each other for years and socialized regularly across party lines.

An insightful look into Washington's vibrant social culture can be found in Rachel A. Shelden, *Washington Brotherhood: Politics, Social Life, and the Coming of the Civil War* (Chapel Hill: University of North Carolina Press, 2013).

8. For the complete text of Representative Cox's speech, see *Congressional Globe*, 36th Cong., 2nd Sess., January 14, 1861, 372–77.

9. During a Jefferson Day dinner on April 13, 1830, President Andrew Jackson toasted "Our Federal Union—It must be preserved." Jackson was in the midst of facing down the state of South Carolina as it threatened to nullify the tariff bill of 1828. See William W. Freehling, *Prelude to Civil War: The Nullification Controversy in South Carolina, 1816–1836* (New York: Harper & Row, Publishers, 1968).

10. Unitarian minister William Ellery Channing (1780–1842), "An Address Introductory to the Franklin Lectures" (1838).

11. Historian William W. Freehling estimates that no more than two percent of the northern electorate self-identified as abolitionists. See *The Road to Disunion*, 12.

12. American Party representative James Morrison Harris (1817–1898). The Border State Plan which Representative Harris helped devise was presented to the House on January 7, 1861, by Tennessee representative Emerson Etheridge. The propositions attempted to alter the Crittenden amendment to make it more palatable to Republicans. See Daniel W. Crofts, *Reluctant Confederates: Upper South Unionists in the Secession Crisis* (Chapel Hill: University of North Carolina Press, 1989), 201.

13. Crittenden's first article was footnoted here.

14. The Lecompton Constitution; see Etcheson, *Bleeding Kansas*, 139–67.

15. Opposition Party member Emerson Etheridge (1819–1902).

16. American Party member James Morrison Harris (1817–1898).

5. Exchange between Senators Charles Sumner and John J. Crittenden

1. Examples of petitions submitted to Congress are reproduced in chapter 7.

2. Henry Wilson (1812–1875), later became President Ulysses S. Grant's vice president in 1873.

3. Republican senator Lafayette Sabine Foster (1806–1880) from Connecticut.

4. Marquis de Lafayette (1757–1834), French supporter of the American Revolution.

5. Republican Daniel Clark (1809–1891).

6. *Congressional Globe*, 36th Cong., 2nd Sess., January 9, 1861, 283.

6. Constitutional Amendments Proposed by Kentuckians

1. Because Magoffin's letter was proposed to be sent to the governors of multiple states, no specific state was included in the salutation line.

2. The thirty-seventh parallel marked the boundary line between the New Mexico and Utah Territories.

3. Cissell's political affiliation is undetermined.

7. Selected Memorials, Petitions, and Resolutions

1. Republican senator John Conover Ten Eyck (1814–1879) from New Jersey.

2. Democratic senator William Bigler (1814–1880) from Pennsylvania.

3. Republican senator Charles Sumner (1811–1874) from Massachusetts.

4. Opposition Party representative James Madison Leach (1815–1891).

5. Republican senator Henry Wilson (1812–1875) from Massachusetts.

6. Opposition Party representative Alexander Robinson Boteler (1815–1892) from Virginia.

7. Democratic representative John William Noell (1816–1863) from Missouri.

8. Democratic senator John Renshaw Thomson (1800–1862) from New Jersey.

9. Republican senator Preston King (1806–1865) from New York.

10. Democratic senator William Bigler (1814–1880) from Pennsylvania.

11. Republican representative William Pennington (1796–1862) from New Jersey; former governor of New Jersey (1837–1843).

12. Democratic senator Henry Mower Rice (1816–1894) from Minnesota. A member of the Senate's Committee of Thirteen, Rice submitted a resolution on December 28, 1860, that would have created the "State of Washington" in all the territory lying north of 36°30', and the "State of Jefferson" in all territory lying south of that line. While designed to cease all "the agitation of the question of slavery," Rice's proposal did not suggest how slavery should be treated in his two new states. See 36th Cong., 2nd Sess., Senate Report No. 288 (Journal of the Committee of Thirteen), 17–18.

13. Democratic senator Robert Ward Johnson (1814–1879); member of the Confederate Senate (1862–1865).

14. Democrat John Cabell Breckinridge (1821–1875) from Kentucky.

15. William Henry Seward (1801–1872), governor of New York (1838–1842) and US senator (1849–1861), served as secretary of state under Abraham Lincoln and Andrew Johnson (1861–1869).

16. Republican senator James Rood Doolittle (1815–1897) from Wisconsin.

17. Democratic senator Lazarus Whitehead Powell (1812–1867) from Kentucky; former governor of Kentucky (1851–1855).

18. Republican senator Henry Bowen Anthony (1815–1884) from Rhode Island; former governor of Rhode Island (1849–1851).

19. Republican senator William Pitt Fessenden (1839–1906) from Maine; later secretary of the treasury (1864–1865).

20. Democratic senator John Renshaw Thomson (1800–1862) from New Jersey.

21. Theodore Frelinghuysen (1787–1862) had a long career as a public servant serving as attorney general of New Jersey (1817–1829), US senator (1829–1835), mayor of Newark (1837–1838), Henry Clay's running mate in the election of 1844, and president of both New York University (1839–1850) and Rutgers University (1850–1862).

22. Republican senator Lyman Trumbull (1813–1896) from Illinois; former justice of the supreme court of Illinois (1848–1853).

23. Republican senator Benjamin Franklin Wade (1800–1878) from Ohio.

24. Democratic senator James Stephen Green (1817–1870) from Missouri.

25. David Wilmot, a congressional representative from Pennsylvania, introduced the Wilmot Proviso on August 6, 1846, as the US House of Representatives was debating a bill to fund the upcoming war with Mexico. The proviso would have banned slavery from any land subsequently acquired as a result of the war. The House approved his proposal, but it failed in the Senate. In any event, the Wilmot Proviso applied only to land possibly acquired from Mexico; the Dakota Territory had been acquired from France as part of the Louisiana Purchase.

26. Democratic senator Stephen Arnold Douglas (1813–1861) from Illinois; on Christmas Eve, 1860, Douglas proposed an amendment similar to Crittenden's that elaborated on the territorial issue and contained an article prohibiting "persons of the African race" from voting or holding office. See 36th Cong., 2nd Sess., Senate Report 288, 8–10.

27. Republican senator Morton Smith Wilkinson (1819–1894) from Minnesota.

28. On January 9, 1861, South Carolinian batteries prevented the *Star of the West*, dispatched by President Buchanan to reinforce Fort Sumter, from entering Charleston Harbor.

8. Washington Peace Conference

1. In 1852, Jonathan and Juliet Lemon traveled from Virginia to New York City with seven children and eight slaves. Upon arrival, the Lemons were arraigned in a local court and their slaves freed in compliance with New York state law. Virginia appealed the case which was decided in New York's favor in 1860. The New York press and courts changed "Lemon" to "Lemmon." See Marie Tyler-McGraw and Dwight T. Pitcaithley, "The Lemmon Slave Case: Courtroom Drama, Constitutional Crisis, and the Southern Quest to Nationalize Slavery," *Common Place* 14, no. 1 (Fall 2013): http://commonplace.online/article/lemmon-slave-case/.

2. The senate added Charles A. Wickliffe as a commissioner by a procedural vote immediately following approval of the committee's report.

3. Kentucky delegate Charles A. Wickliffe suggested the addition of "coolies," remarking on February 25, "I refer to the importation of coolies and other persons from China and the East. In my judgment, this is the slave-trade in one of its worst forms." Chittenden, *A Report of the Debates*, 379. The northern state opposition to this article may have simply been based on the belief, as evidenced in several of the memorials in the previous chapter, that Republicans should "stand firm for the Union of the States, and the Constitution as it is."

4. According to the terms of the Compromise of 1850, Congress gave the Utah and New Mexico Territories the option of protecting or abolishing slavery. On February 3, 1859, the New Mexico territorial legislature enacted a law "to provide for the protection of property in slaves."

5. In *Prigg v. Pennsylvania* (1842).

6. Article IV, Section 2.

7. Formed in 1816 in Washington, DC, the American Colonization Society encouraged the migration of free African Americans to Africa.

8. Without setting a date to resume proceedings.

9. Kentucky's representative was James Guthrie.

10. The committee's draft amendment was reported out on February 15. Chittenden, *A Report of the Debates*, 43–45. See also Pitcaithley, *The U.S. Constitution and Secession*, 232–34.

11. David Settle Reid (1813–1891), governor of North Carolina (1851–1854), US senator (1854–1859).

12. James Alexander Seddon (1815–1880), future Confederate secretary of war (1862–1865), former owner of the White House of the Confederacy in Richmond.

13. Thomas Emlen Franklin (1810–1884).

14. A passing or incidental remark.

15. William Henry Seward.

16. Both the southern and northern Democratic platforms in 1860 called for the acquisition of Cuba.

9. Neutrality Proclaimed

1. In fact, the US Congress had adjourned on March 4 and was not scheduled to reconvene until July 4, 1861, but was called into special secession by President Lincoln in his April 15 proclamation.

2. Virginia's secession convention voted to secede on April 17 but provided for a plebiscite to confirm its action. A statewide referendum ratified the decision on May 23.

3. Lincoln's call on April 15 was for militia "to the aggregate of seventy-five thousand" to suppress the rebellion. The April 15 proclamation also noted that "the utmost care will be observed, consistently with the objects aforesaid, to avoid any devastation, any destruction of, or interference with, property, or any disturbance of peaceful citizens in any part of the country." Roy P. Basler, *The Collected Works of Abraham Lincoln*, 9 vols. (New Brunswick: Rutgers University Press, 1953), 4:331–32.

4. George Baird Hodge (1828–1892), Curtis Field Burnam (1820–1909), Nathaniel Wolfe (1810–1865), John Griffin Carlisle (1834–1910), James B. Lyne (?), Alfred Franklin Gowdy (1815–1876), Richard T. Jacob [not Jacobs] (1825–1903), and Richard Aylett Buckner, Jr. (1813–1900).

5. Samuel Gill (1824–1876) graduated from the US Military Academy at West Point in 1844, and served as superintendent of various railroads in Kentucky; George Twyman Wood (1796–1876) served as a land agent and attorney in Munfordville, Hart County, and as the county's clerk from 1819–1861; Peter Dudley (1787–1869) served in several Kentucky militia units (1813–1815), and as Kentucky adjutant general from 1829 to 1851; Dr. John B. Peyton (1811–1870) was a physician and bank clerk in Russellville, Logan County.

10. Border Slave State Convention

1. Missouri's delegates were H. R. Gamble, J. B. Henderson, William A. Hall, J. B. Henderson, and William G. Pomeroy.

2. John Caldwell.

3. A reference to the War of 1812 with Great Britain.

4. A reference to the war with Mexico, 1846–1848.

BIBLIOGRAPHY

Primary Sources

Chittenden, Lucius E. *A Report of the Debates and Proceedings in the Secret Sessions of the Conference Convention, for Proposing Amendments to the Constitution of the United States, Held at Washington, D.C., in February, A.D. 1861.* New York: D. Appleton & Company, 1864.

Journal and Proceedings of the Convention of the Border Slave States, Begun and Held in the City of Frankfort, and State of Kentucky, on the 27th Day of May, 1861. Frankfort: Printed at the Kentucky Yeoman Office, Jno. B. Major, State Printer, 1861.

Journal of the Called Session of the House of Representatives of the Commonwealth of Kentucky, Begun and Held in the Town of Frankfort, on Monday, the Sixth Day of May, in the Year of Our Lord 1861, and of the Commonwealth the Sixty-Ninth. Frankfort: Printed at the Kentucky Yeoman Office, John B. Major, State Printer, 1861.

Journal of the Called Session of the House of Representatives of the Commonwealth of Kentucky, Begun and Held in the Town of Frankfort, on Thursday the Seventeenth Day of January, in the Year of Our Lord 1861, and of the Commonwealth the Sixty-Ninth. Frankfort: Printed at the Kentucky Yeoman Office, John B. Major, State Printer, 1861.

Journal of the Called Session of the Senate of the Commonwealth of Kentucky, Begun and Held in the Town of Frankfort, on Monday, the Sixth Day of May, in the Year of Our Lord 1861, and of the Commonwealth the Sixty-Ninth. Frankfort: Printed at the Kentucky Yeoman Office, Jno. B. Major, State Printer, 1861.

Journal of the Called Session of the Senate of the Commonwealth of Kentucky, Begun and Held in the Town of Frankfort, on Thursday the Seventeenth Day of January, in the Year of Our Lord 1861, and of the Commonwealth the Sixty-Ninth. Frankfort: Printed at the Kentucky Yeoman Office, John B. Major, State Printer, 1861.

Report of the Commissioners to the Late Peace Conference Held at Washington City, Made to the Legislature of Kentucky. Frankfort: Printed at the Yeoman Office, J. B. Major, State Printer, 1861.

United States Congress. Congressional Globe, 36th Cong., 2nd Sess., December 1860–March 1861. http://memory.loc.gov/ammem/amlaw/lwcglink.html#anchor36.

Suggestions for Further Reading

Ayers, Edward L. *What Caused the Civil War?: Reflections on the South and Southern History.* New York: W. W. Norton & Company, 2005.

Bestor, Arthur. "The American Civil War as a Constitutional Crisis." *American Historical Review* 69, no. 2 (January 1964), 327–52.

——. "State Sovereignty and Slavery: A Reinterpretation of Proslavery Constitutional Doctrine, 1846–1860." *Journal of the Illinois State Historical Society* 54, no. 2 (Summer 1961), 117–80.

Bowman, Shearer Davis. *At the Precipice: Americans North and South During the Secession Crisis.* Chapel Hill: University of North Carolina Press, 2010.

Cook, Robert J., William L. Barney, and Elizabeth R. Varon. *Secession Winter: When the Union Fell Apart.* Baltimore: Johns Hopkins University Press, 2013.

Crofts, Daniel W. *Lincoln and the Politics of Slavery: The Other Thirteenth Amendment and the Struggle to Save the Union.* Chapel Hill: University of North Carolina Press, 2016.

——. *Reluctant Confederates: Upper South Unionists in the Secession Crisis.* Chapel Hill: University of North Carolina Press, 1989.

Dew, Charles B. *Apostles of Disunion: Southern Secession Commissioners and the Causes of the Civil War.* Charlottesville: University Press of Virginia, 2001.

Fehrenbacher, Don E. *The Slaveholding Republic: An Account of the United States Government's Relations to Slavery.* New York: Oxford University Press, 2001.

Freehling, William W. *The Road to Disunion: Secessionists Triumphant, II.* New York: Oxford University Press, 2007.

Gunderson, Robert G. *Old Gentleman's Convention: The Washington Peace Conference of 1861.* Madison: University of Wisconsin Press, 1961.

Harrison, Lowell H. *The Civil War in Kentucky.* Louisville: University Press of Kentucky, 1975.

——, ed. *Kentucky's Governors.* Louisville: University Press of Kentucky, 1985.

Heck, Frank H. *Proud Kentuckian: John C. Breckinridge, 1821–1875.* Lexington: University Press of Kentucky, 1976.

Kirwan, Albert D. *John J. Crittenden: The Struggle for the Union.* Lexington: University of Kentucky Press, 1962.

Lee, Charles Robert, Jr. *The Confederate Constitutions.* Chapel Hill: University of North Carolina.

QUESTIONS FOR DISCUSSION

1. Given Governor Magoffin's several speeches and letters, would you describe him as a Unionist, a secessionist, or somewhere in between? Why?
2. In what ways does Stephen F. Hale characterize the election of Lincoln as a threat to white supremacy in the slave states?
3. In what ways would John J. Crittenden's compromise amendment have affected Kentucky?
4. Compare and contrast Kentucky's six proposed constitutional amendments. How are they similar? Different? If they represent Kentucky's solution to the secession crisis, how would you define the problem?
5. What would Republicans have given up (if anything) had they been willing to agree to any of Kentucky's amendments? What would they have gained?
6. Compare and contrast the majority and minority reports from Kentucky's delegation to the Washington Peace Conference. Which side seems more reasonable? Why?
7. Considering the debate between John J. Crittenden and Charles Sumner, with whom do you most agree? Most disagree? Why?
8. Given that the election of 1860 was a fair and honest contest, were the numerous demands that the Constitution be amended reasonable? Were the southern states justified in demanding constitutional protections for slavery merely on the grounds that a Republican had been elected president?
9. In 1860/1861, how could slavery have been constitutionally abolished? What constitutional checks would have been placed on Republicans if they had taken steps to abolish slavery?
10. Discuss the popular notion today that the South seceded to protect states' rights when Kentucky's six constitutional amendments—if passed by Congress and ratified—would have greatly expanded federal authority at the expense of state authority.
11. Place yourself in the political discussion over Secession Winter. What constitutional amendment would you have proposed? Would you have proposed a constitutional amendment at all?
12. Consider Kentucky's position of neutrality in 1861. Was it politically the correct decision? Was the decision realistic? What did the state gain?
13. Imagine that the Crittenden amendment, not the Seward/Corwin amendment, had passed both houses of Congress and war had been averted. With the institution of slavery thus strengthened through federal protection, would it have eventually died out as Republicans had hoped? Or might it have continued into the twentieth century in some modified form? Could the end of slavery have been brought about by any means short of war?

INDEX